Elevating the Teaching Profession

Elevating the Teaching Profession

Cultivating Progressive Agency

Matthew Weber

ROWMAN & LITTLEFIELD
Lanham • Boulder • New York • London

Published by Rowman & Littlefield
An imprint of The Rowman & Littlefield Publishing Group, Inc.
4501 Forbes Boulevard, Suite 200, Lanham, Maryland 20706
www.rowman.com

86-90 Paul Street, London EC2A 4NE

Copyright © 2023 by Matthew Weber

All rights reserved. No part of this book may be reproduced in any form or by any electronic or mechanical means, including information storage and retrieval systems, without written permission from the publisher, except by a reviewer who may quote passages in a review.

British Library Cataloguing in Publication Information Available

Library of Congress Cataloging-in-Publication Data

Names: Weber, Matt (Matthew C.), author.
Title: Elevating the teaching profession : cultivating progressive agency / by Matthew Weber.
Description: Lanham, Maryland : Rowman & Littlefield, [2023] | Includes bibliographical references and index. | Summary: "Matthew Weber, PhD, has served as a teacher, principal, department director, district program evaluator, and deputy superintendent. After 41 years as a public-school educator, he retired as an idealist, believing in incorporating the most current knowledge from research and practice"— Provided by publisher.
Identifiers: LCCN 2022054463 (print) | LCCN 2022054464 (ebook) | ISBN 9781475870497 (Cloth) | ISBN 9781475870503 (Paperback) | ISBN 9781475870510 (epub)
Subjects: LCSH: Teaching—Vocational guidance.
Classification: LCC LB1775 .W398 2023 (print) | LCC LB1775 (ebook) | DDC 371.102—dc23/eng/20221207
LC record available at https://lccn.loc.gov/2022054463
LC ebook record available at https://lccn.loc.gov/2022054464

Contents

Preface		vii
Acknowledgments		xiii
1	Why Start with Teachers?	1
2	Teachers as Professionals	19
3	Authenticating Teacher Agency	33
4	Embracing Research	43
5	Meaningful Teacher Evaluations	57
6	Teacher Pathways	69
7	Master Teachers in Distinctive Roles	83
8	Recasting Teacher Unions	95
9	Reimagining Professional Learning	109
10	Critical-Need Educators: Substitute Teachers and Instructional Assistants	119
11	Critical-Need Teachers: Early Childhood, Special Education, and Bilingual	131
12	Critical-Need Teachers: Math, Science, and Computer Science	143
13	Executing the Teacher Plan	155
14	Financing for Stability	169

Postlude: One Viewpoint in an Idea World	183
Appendix: Acronyms	187
Bibliography	189
Index	207
About the Author	211

Preface

> From the ashes, a fire shall be woken, A light from the shadows shall spring . . .
>
> —J.R.R. Tolkien, *The Fellowship of the Ring*

An unconventional forty-one-year career as an educator has given me a unique perspective on teaching from distinct vantage points. Alternating work with research and classroom practice, my progression in education was atypical:

- Sixteen years of teaching at ten different grade levels;
- Twenty-five subsequent years providing administrative support in multiple roles;
- Serving as a principal, department director, and district program evaluator;
- Starting as an elementary instrumental music teacher;
- Ending as a deputy superintendent in a large urban district for five years; and
- Earning three degrees and four certificates at five different universities.

My entire public-school service experience was in Title I districts with high poverty rates (65 percent to 91 percent). After retiring as both an idealist and pragmatist, the past three years have been a time of reflection on both the past and present.

We live in a turbulent time for education; health issues have upended traditional routines, and divisiveness lingers over school safety. The Covid-19 pandemic has been disruptive to students' education, ushering in a formidable shift in how teachers deliver instruction. Evaluating the impact on learning, particularly on economically disadvantaged students, will take time. One early large-scale study by Engzell et al. examined primary school performance in the Netherlands ($n \approx 350{,}000$), where campuses administered national examinations before and after the safety lockdown. The authors compared progress during the infectious period and in the same time frame during the three previous years:

> Our results reveal a learning loss of about 3 percentile points or 0.08 standard deviations. The effect is equivalent to one-fifth of a school year, the same period that schools remained closed. Losses are up to 60% larger among students from less-educated homes, confirming worries about the uneven toll of the pandemic on children and families.[1]

Other early assessment results and anecdotal feedback on student achievement have been discouraging. The pandemic's academic setback to students worldwide is an accepted assumption. Moreover, as the Dutch study suggests, the harm is disproportionate regarding socioeconomic status. However, the adversity should also be viewed as an opportunity to reflect, assess, and reimagine teaching. The longer-term impact may be constructive if the disruption derails education complacency and inspires reinvestment and innovation. The US vision from fifty-six years ago of a "great society" and its "war on poverty" is ripe for the next level of foresight and action.

In 1965, Lyndon Johnson persuaded Congress to approve the Elementary and Secondary Education Act, the most extensive and system-altering educational bill ever legislated by the US federal government. That same year, at a Howard University commencement ceremony, the president delivered a speech titled *To Fulfill These Rights*, which included the following egalitarian words:

> Men and women of all races are born with the same range of abilities. But ability is not just the product of birth. Ability is stretched or stunted by the family that you live with, and the neighborhood you live in—by the school you go to and the poverty or the richness of your surroundings. It is the product of a hundred unseen forces playing upon the little infant, the child, and finally the man.[2]

In subsequent years, educators have become more cognizant of the profound influence of those unseen forces. Studies in psychology and human development have raised awareness of the distinct needs of students born in poverty and the lasting effects of a deprived home environment. Still, progress has been slow and uneven with student achievement across developmental domains (i.e., physical, cognitive, social, and emotional). Since that historic legislation, other countries' education systems have also begun outperforming the United States on the global stage.

While some students performed well during the pandemic, educators report that those without a reliable internet connection, time management skills, or family support suffered disproportionally during virtual learning. In addition to a learning loss in core subjects, depression and anxiety magnified students' distress.[3] Moreover, many of these problems were exacerbated due to significant declines in student school enrollment, attendance, and general engagement.

Consequently, educators were forced to adapt during the Covid-19 period and implemented nascent approaches in their pedagogy, given the various emergency measures. Congruent with the learning setbacks, some resultant upsides emerged from necessity. Many schools and districts were forced to upgrade their technology infrastructure, adaptive learning software, and virtual learning capability. Teachers' general capacity to creatively use and apply technology increased dramatically. Many students had to become more independent and improve their time management skills. In coordinating remote learning, household communication improved as parents became aware of expanded learning options for their children.

The crisis spurred government leaders to acknowledge that access to universal Wi-Fi and instructional devices is no longer a luxury but a necessity for educational parity. Deep losses in state revenue for education were countered with an infusion of $269.2 billion in federal dollars, with $193.2 billion earmarked for K-12 schools (see table P.1). The spotlight on students' educational struggles has provided the Biden administration with the political justification to provide more amenable federal funding. States were granted the flexibility to infuse the new funds to mitigate pandemic learning gaps. Beyond the CARES Act, Covid Relief Package, and American Rescue Plan, President Biden has proposed a 41 percent spending increase for education in 2022.

Perhaps the most salient lesson learned from the pandemic was *how much we still need teachers*. Technology will never usurp the fundamental auspices of principals, master teachers, counselors, and other support staff. As social learners, students require guidance, structure, and reassurance from adults. Empirical evidence suggests that economically disadvantaged students suffer the most from the restricted personal connection of over-reliance on

Table P.1 Congressional Support for Education during Covid-19

New Revenue	CARES Act March 2020	Covid Relief Package December 2020	American Rescue Plan March 2021
K-12	13.2 billion	54 billion	126 billion
Higher Education	14 billion	22 billion	40 billion
Total	27.2 billion	76 billion	166 billion

technology. Students' relationships with teachers promote psychological well-being, and this alliance is necessary for cognitive, social, and emotional development. Digital tools such as dashboards and teaching alerts serve as increasingly powerful instructional assistants for learning reinforcement and enrichment. Astute educators will reflect on the real-life pandemic experiment as an opportune juncture to assess and refine technology integration for instructional efficiency.

Accepting the premise that teachers (1) cannot be replaced in the foreseeable future and (2) are the most critical component of student realization of future readiness,[4] how do education and government leaders transform and enhance the profession? The status quo is antiquated: it falters with crisis talent shortages, and the situation is only projected to intensify further. Preserving the United States' global standing and the country's expanding democratic principles for equality are inseparably coupled with the plight of teachers. Reinvigorating the teaching profession requires decisive and calculated action to reorganize the culture and education ecosystem.

Enticing growing pools of talent into the teaching profession involves establishing a vibrant academic culture and altering the perception of a teacher's value. Attracting and retaining effective teachers require flexibility, investing in development, advancing career opportunities, earning classroom autonomy, promoting leadership responsibilities, and offering higher compensation for outstanding performance.

As educators move on from the distress of online schooling, a unique opportunity has arrived for molding efficacious teaching systems and shaping a teaching profession of the highest caliber. Returning to "business as usual" without adjusting from reflection and objective analysis is willful blindness. Learning from our current setbacks, educators can view returning to the classroom as an invitation to emerge, evolve, and reach a higher level. By redefining the role of the teacher as a progressively flourishing leader and researcher, school districts move closer to a culture that will ensure student agency for life. Like the desired graduating student's profile, the teaching structure should promote lifelong learners.

What research has confirmed has long been instinctively surmised by parents. Across all types of schools, parents' first consideration when selecting where to enroll their children is the staff, teachers in particular. Figure P.1[5] from the National Center for Education Statistics illustrates that staff quality exceeds curriculum or safety as "very important" criteria in school preference.

Thus, progress begins with honestly acknowledging the present status of the teaching workforce and forecasting the profession's efficacy for the coming decades if nothing changes. The blueprint includes studying external exemplar models, designing systems to stimulate the enhancement of

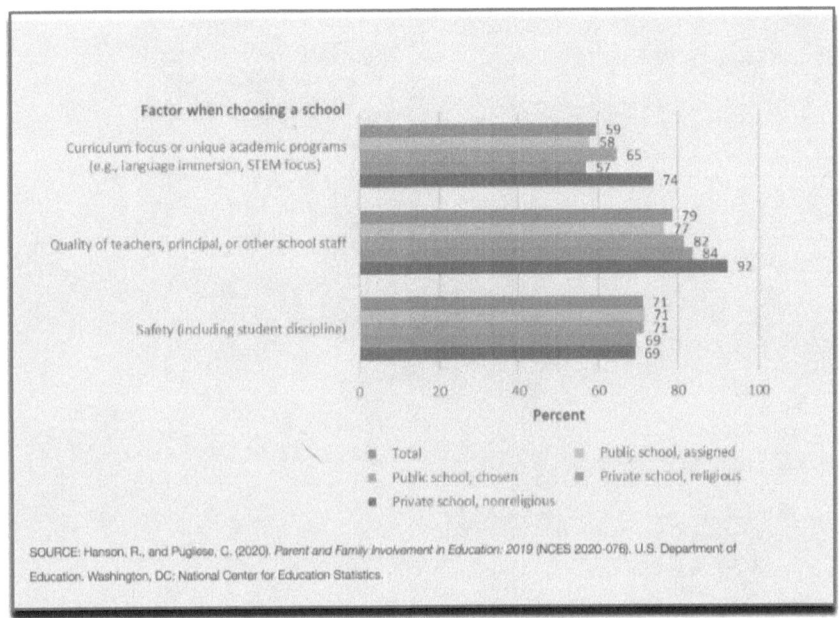

Figure P.1 Factors Parents Consider in Selecting Their Child's School. *Source*: National Center for Education Statistics (2020). Why do parents choose schools for their children? Retrieved from https://nces.ed.gov/blogs/nces/post/why-do-parents-choose- schools-for-their-children

teachers, and committing to the plan. Our tools for a renaissance are mirrors for reflection, windows to observe, a collective conscience to guide, and the persistence to transform.

Incidental remark: The prevalence of examples from Texas, the third-largest school system after California and New York, merely reflects the author's long tenure in the state. Nevertheless, models and studies from many other states are frequently cited as examples. State references serve to illustrate practices or programs for examination and understanding. This author has no intention of promoting any state's education system above another. Instead, relating ideas and prototypes from multiple sources contribute to this book's proposals.

NOTES

1. Engzell, Frey & Verhagen, 2021, 1.
2. Johnson, 1965 speech at Howard University.
3. Dorn et al., 2021.
4. Opper, 2019.
5. "Why Do Parents Choose Schools for Their Children?," 2020.

Acknowledgments

In writing an education book, I am fortunate to live in a society with the freedom to express beliefs and personal opinions. By taking a position(s) on salient topics, an author becomes vulnerable. With respect to opposing viewpoints on any particular issue, my ideas are articulated for reflection, consideration, and choice. What is critical for educational progress is the commitment, conversation, and democratic process.

We are all individuals molded by our interactions with others. I have been most fortunate to have family, friends, and coworkers who provided me with support and opportunity. A sincere thanks to my parents Gene and Mary Lou, my four siblings, son Josh and his wife Tina, teacher-son Zachary, and Joan, my wife and confidant of forty-two years.

Having the good fortune to procure degrees, certificates, and coursework at several universities, I experienced many inspiring professors. I am indebted to my numerous mentors at Mansfield University, the University of Rochester Eastman School, and the University of North Texas. They guided my research and critical thinking in approaching the challenging work in education.

Thank you to all my public-school educational coworkers. Thirty-two years in the McAllen Independent School District offered learning experiences from numerous dedicated educators. I was privileged to serve with some amazing leaders for five years in the San Antonio Independent School District. My earnest appreciation is also extended to colleagues at Texas A&M University–San Antonio, University of Texas at San Antonio, and Our Lady of the Lake University.

Finally, thank you to Rowman & Littlefield, Carlie Wall, my managing editor, and Monica Sukumar, Senior Project Manager with Deanta for their support and confidence in the manuscript.

Chapter 1

Why Start with Teachers?

> Why does the eye see a thing more clearly in dreams than the imagination when awake?
>
> —Leonardo da Vinci

My 2021 book, *Confronting the Education Complex: Catalysts for Advancing Pre-K–12 Systems* proposed that the most robust catalysts for a prosperous education structure should encompass three areas: early childhood programs, leadership talent, and master teachers. Numerous other factors (e.g., socioeconomic level, parenting) contribute to a child's preparation in our incredibly fast-changing world. In the contemporary school, these three components are transcendent in scope and permanence. Each element warrants extensive study, reflection, and investment, considering its capacity for preparing students. This book exclusively examines the status and potentialities of the teaching profession. Teaching is a career at a crossroads, and this narrative presents models for an auspicious transition in the information age.

Envision a nation where teachers are among society's most appreciated, respected, and requisite professionals. Over time, the prestige of the pre-K-12 classroom teacher further escalates thanks to their profound influence in molding future scholars and ethical leaders. This scenario represents a substantive attitudinal and cultural shift. A world where teachers are more admired than movie stars, gifted athletes, or even rap artists may be an unrealistic scenario to imagine. However, while the arts, entertainment, and sports impart enjoyment and diversion, education is the bedrock for innovation, advancement, and sustaining world leadership. Perception is not necessarily reality, but an upgraded image of teachers and a new stature level for their vocation might give rise to an emerging profession.

History reminds us that sovereign nations' relative prominence is never static. Countries are progressing and leading or declining depending on disruptions in global competition. A robust and burgeoning economy has been one consistent barometer of incipient national power throughout history. James Heckman, University of Chicago professor and Nobel Memorial Prize winner in economics, maintains that education is the foremost dynamic driver of a country's economic health. Early childhood learning is the significant sub-factor in the equation (see figure 1.1).[1]

While early childhood education suggests an appreciable long-term impact, education efficacy at all levels feeds a vibrant economy. Once a global leader in universal education, the United States' relative ranking has declined in several international measures. The Organization for Economic Cooperation and Development released a list of the world's most educated countries in 2021. Compiled data identify the number of adults aged twenty-five to sixty-four who completed a two- or four-year degree or a vocational program. The percentages of the top nations listed are (1) Canada at 56.71 percent, (2) Japan at 51.44 percent, (3) Israel at 50.92 percent, (4) South Korea at 47.74 percent, and (5) the United States at 46.36 percent.[2] Complacency and indifference to educational systems lead to economic disruption in a rapidly fluctuating world economy.

In amassing economic power, the United States has historically promoted innovation and leadership. Encouragement for entrepreneurship remains

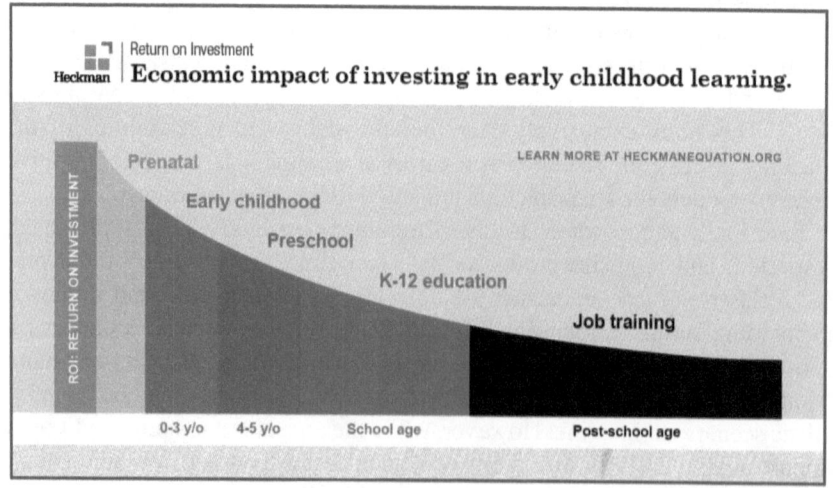

Figure 1.1 The Economic Impact of Early Childhood Education. *Source*: Reproduced with permission, from Heckman, J. J. (2012). *Invest in early childhood development: Reduce deficits, strengthen the economy.* Retrieved from https://heckmanequation.org/www/assets/2013/07/F_HeckmanDeficitPieceCUSTOM-Generic_052714-3-1.pdf.

a part of that legacy. Fostering a culture of individualized learning nurtures impresarios in all disciplines by enabling valued risk-taking. Pundit proclamations for global pre-eminence ring hollow if they lose sight of the correlation with mainstay teacher quality within educational institutions. Uninterrupted communal progress is never a certainty, particularly if the foundation is crumbling.

Kemp identified the danger indicators for the collapse of previous societies, including climate change, *inequality*, environmental control, complexity, and bureaucracy.[3] In recent decades, the barometer for equality based on income growth has skewed toward the upper-income class. During the same period, middle- and lower-income household wealth has diminished (see figure 1.2). "The wealth gap between America's richest and poorer families more than doubled from 1989 to 2016."[4] Pickett and Wilkinson have documented recent data showing that low-income individuals have higher rates of obesity, mental illness, homicides, teenage births, incarceration, drug use, and lower life expectancy.[5] Through bipartisanship and commitment to education, solutions are achievable for mitigating disparity, complacency, and decline.

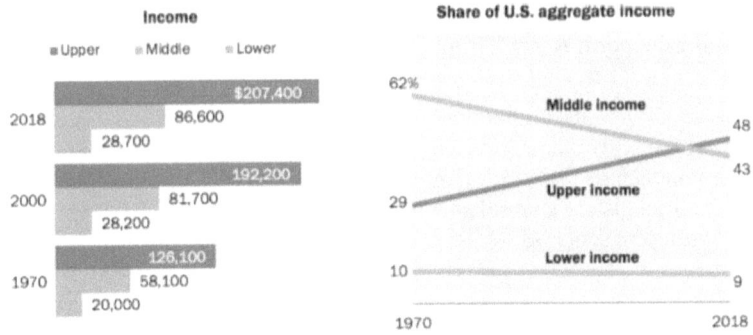

Figure 1.2 **Trends in Income and Wealth Inequality.** Reproduced from Pew Research Center. *Source*: Horowitz, J., Igielnik, R. & Kochhar, R. (2020). Trends in income and wealth inequality, p. 19. Retrieved from https://www.pewresearch.org/social-trends/2020/01/09/trends-in-income-and-wealth-inequality/.

EDUCATIONAL EQUITY AND ECONOMICS

Vinelli and Weller from the Center for American Progress propose an economic model demanding an increasingly educated workforce. They write that "high inequality and widespread income uncertainty beget low investments and slow productivity growth." Support for public investments such as infrastructure, education, and innovation is sadly inadequate and inhibits private sector expansion.[6]

Equity in education is a goal few would dispute. Decision-makers committed to fairness in education serve to propagate social equity in life. The purpose of pre-K-12 education has become more comprehensive, and high school graduation is no longer a terminal goal. Instead, those walking the stage for diplomas must be "college-ready graduates, confident with academic knowledge, workplace proficiencies, relationship skills, and motivation to continue learning."[7] In *Rethinking Society for the 21st Century*, Spiel et al. expanded on this premise:

> Overall, education is about the unleashing of human capabilities: economic, civic, and humanistic. When education is successful, it enables individuals not merely to exercise their agency in participating in economic, civic, and humanistic activity but also to shape or re-shape economic, civic, and humanistic life.[8]

President Biden made education a pillar of his domestic platform. Along with promoting universal pre-K for all three- and four-year-old children, he made the following resounding affirmation of teachers to the members of the National Education Association:

> You are . . . the most important profession in the United States. You are the ones that . . . give these kids wings. You give them confidence. You let them believe in themselves. You equip them. And I promise you, you will never find in American history a president who is more teacher-centric and more supportive of teachers than me.[9]

In 2021, the proposed federal budget increases in education confirmed the president's rhetoric, but legislation passing through the shoals of Congress is uncertain. Moreover, if the infusions of desired resources are approved, will funding alone strategically move toward better systems? Mandatory and discretionary spending on the 2001 No Child Left Behind (NCLB) initiative for elementary and secondary schools increased federal investment by $9.5 billion, or 64 percent.[10] This broad national initiative was implemented differently in every state, failed to reach targeted goals, and was unceremoniously abandoned after more than a decade.

Why Start with Teachers?

Prudent educational investments should funnel into research-based strategies, not lofty performance targets connected to punitive sanctions such as with the NCLB. A well-reasoned argument to consider for achieving headway in school systems is elevating the role of teachers. When educational outcomes are upgraded, teachers are the most consequential change agents for advancement.[11] But simply raising salaries for *all* teachers is not an adequate solution for addressing (1) the supply of applicants or (2) moving toward professional excellence. Redesigning the roadmap for emerging school systems requires *transforming* the teaching profession. Designing a reliable structure involves addressing the perception and expectations of teachers both internally and externally. Establishing a respected hierarchy must transcend the current salary step schedule of guaranteed monetary rewards for years of service.

The influence of an esteemed profession of teachers has bolstered the trajectory of academic success in Singapore, Finland, and parts of Australia, Canada, and China.[12] Through national systems and cultural adaptation, all US students deserve a parallel legacy. Elevating teachers' status in the United States would have extensive ramifications for social equity and economic progress. In order to make this vision a reality, farsighted leaders must address the basic societal tenets of supply, demand, and personal motivation. Teacher shortages (severe in some areas) and inconsistent instructional quality constitute perilous roadblocks to advancement. The root causes for this persistent condition are both cultural and systemic. Understanding the progression of the teacher's role within an evolving context leads to improved planning for modern efficacy.

EVOLVING CLASSROOMS AND EXPECTATIONS

The purpose of pre-K-12 education and its standards for graduation has changed appreciably over the past 150 years. Teaching and learning must keep pace with new advancements in technology, science, and the humanities. The undertaking is imposing when the rate of acceleration for new knowledge is exponential.

> They always say that time changes things, but you actually have to change them yourself.—Andy Warhol[13]

Literacy. Early seventeenth-century education pioneers in Massachusetts fostered student literacy to prepare young adults for reading the Bible and learning Puritan principles. The movement from private religious schools to state-sponsored secular education gradually shifted the rationale for education and expanded access. Still, the bar was low and illiteracy high. Adult literacy was commonly defined as individuals fifteen or older with the ability to read and write.

Measuring competency levels in reading and writing remained imprecise through most of the twentieth century. There were considerable disparities in literacy among race and gender groups. Gradually, as classrooms became more inclusive, the meaning of literacy evolved. Its present-day connotation has expanded to include interpreting and understanding content from various sources. The broader view of literacy has increased expectations for teaching appreciably more skillsets that contribute to college and career readiness.

Enrollment and Attendance. In the second half of the nineteenth century, membership rates fluctuated regionally, with an estimated 50 percent of all five- to nineteen-year-olds enrolled in school.[14] In 1852, Massachusetts enacted the first mandatory school attendance law, with all states replicating the compulsory statute by 1918. Attendance dramatically improved from 1900 through 1990 (see figure 1.3). Inconsistent attendance laws, racial discrimination, and economic disparities favored education for upper-income male students. The philosophy of implicitly prioritizing education for the privileged unequivocally hindered the progression of universal education. Mandating integration and inclusion has had far-reaching effects on revamping education for all students, while redefining teachers' roles.

Figure 1.3 Percent of Five- to Nineteen-Year-Olds Enrolled in School by Race: 1850 to 1991. *Source*: Snyder, Thomas D. (1993). *120 years of American education: A Statistical Portrait*. District of Columbia: US Dept. of Education, Office of Educational Research and Improvement, National Center for Education Statistics.

Since 1900, the predominant school calendar in the United States has included an academic year comprising 180 days spread over 9 to 10 months, with 6.5 hours per day of instruction. States have some latitude regarding the requirements of minimum instructional time for a typical day and total time for the school year. The summer break, including some parts of June, July, and August, can be traced back to when many students were expected to harvest crops. The agrarian need for student workers has dissipated, but the tradition of having the academic recess span the summer months remains fixed in national culture. Researchers differ on the extent of summer learning loss, predominantly regarding low-income students. However, scholars agree that instructional days and daily hours should correlate with learning theory and teaching effectiveness.

Accountability. Perhaps the most significant change for the teaching profession has been classroom accountability. The rules listed below, attached to a (female) Sacramento teacher's contract in 1915, illustrate profound differences in the role and expectations of teachers from a century ago; standards for student learning were nonexistent, and the repressive social norms would be considered misogynistic today.

1. You will not marry during the term of your contract.
2. You are not to keep company with men.
3. You must be home between the hours of 8:00 p.m. and 6:00 a.m. unless attending a school function.
4. You may not loiter downtown in ice cream stores.
5. You may not travel beyond the city limits unless you have the permission of the chairman of the board.
6. You may not ride in a carriage or automobile with any man except your father or brother.
7. You may not smoke cigarettes.
8. You may not dress in bright colors.
9. You may under no circumstances dye your hair.
10. You must wear at least two petticoats.
11. Your dresses may not be any shorter than two inches above the ankles.
12. To keep the classroom neat and clean you must sweep the floor at least once a day, scrub the floor at least once a week with hot, soapy water, clean the blackboards at least once a day, and start the fire at 7:00 a.m. to have the school warm by 8:00 a.m.[15]

Nowadays, a current teacher's job description includes required degrees and certifications, specialized knowledge and skills, detailed teaching responsibilities, and evaluation requirements. A primary purpose is common to most teacher job descriptions. Emphasis is on providing students with the appropriate learning activities in specific subject areas. Instructional goals aim to realize the maximum potential for a student's intellectual, emotional, physical, and social growth. Ultimately, the objective is to develop competencies and skills to prepare students for higher education and society.

The accountability movement in education has substantially altered expectations for teacher performance. As recently as fifty years ago, teacher accountability for student learning was minimal. Few valid metrics for student progress were available, and learning standards were local. Fearing the loss of global prominence after Sputnik's launch in 1957, the country's level of concern for the quality of educational systems escalated nationally. Senator Robert Kennedy anticipated the drive toward accountability during a senate debate before ratifying the historic Elementary and Secondary Education Act of 1965. He declared:

> I wonder if we couldn't have some system of reporting . . . through some testing system that would be established (by) which the people at the local community would know periodically . . . what progress had been made.[16]

The National Assessment of Education Progress was established in 1969. Bipartisan support for testing and accountability gained momentum in the 1970s and 1980s, leading eventually to the NCLB legislation in 2001. Teachers became more accountable for student learning and growth in multiple subjects.

Diversity and Behavior Management. Classroom culture and dynamics continue to evolve in tandem with student demographics and behavior management. The school-age population in the United States continues to become more racially and ethnically diverse. An NCES report released in 2019 highlighted the shifts in only the past two decades:

> Between 2000 and 2017, the percentage of U.S. school-age children who were White decreased from 62 to 51 percent and the percentage who were Black decreased from 15 to 14 percent. In contrast, the percentages of school-age children from other racial/ethnic groups increased: Hispanic children, from 16 to 25 percent; Asian children, from 3 to 5 percent; and children of two or more races, from 2 to 4 percent.[17]

The challenges for teachers to meet academic benchmarks in a more diverse classroom are significant. During the first half of the twentieth century, resistance to non-English-speaking immigrants was pervasive. Efforts to "Americanize" students and a dominant "English only" language ideology prevailed and exonerated teachers from meeting students' developmental language needs. Students were generally retained "in the same grade level until enough English was mastered to advance in subject matter."[18] Fortunately, that dogma has given way to increased tolerance and inclusion. English as a second language (ESL) and bilingual classes have expanded exponentially since the Bilingual Education Act of 1968.

Recent estimates of languages other than English spoken in metropolitan areas highlight the diversity represented in their public schools. Spanish is the most prevalent second language in classrooms (37.5 million),[19] but the expansion of multiple languages in some districts can be overwhelming. The three highest multi-language cities were New York (192), Los Angeles (185), and Houston (145).[20]

Teaching students with multiple language backgrounds is only one of the dilemmas in the contemporary classroom. The heterogeneous class often includes sizeable differences in culture, academic skills, physical health, and social-emotional readiness. In years past, student retention was an extensively prescribed practice. University educational leaders and campus administrators increasingly promote humanistic and individualized instruction addressing every student. The detrimental effects of student retention are well documented.[21] This evolving standard, in effect, raises teacher expectations.

Pupil/teacher ratios have declined considerably over the past eighty years (see figure 1.4). Behavior management with larger classes operated with little tolerance for inappropriate conduct. Students were easily suspended, expelled, or received corporal punishment for failure to conform to rules through the 1970s. Few accountability guardrails were in place to issue punitive discipline, particularly in terms of race, ethnicity, or gender. As late as 1977, the US Supreme

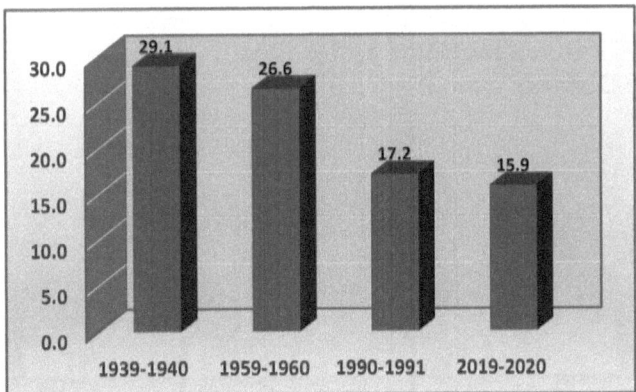

Figure 1.4 Classroom Pupil/Teacher Ratios. *Source*: Data from Ravitch, D. (2003). A brief history of teacher professionalism. U.S. Department of Education. Retrieved from https://www2.ed.gov/admins/tchrqual/learn/preparingteachersconference/ravitch.html; National Center for Education Statistics. (2017). Staff, teachers, and teachers as a percentage of staff in public elementary and secondary school systems, by state or jurisdiction. Retrieved from https://nces.ed.gov/programs/digest/d17/tables/dt17_213.40.asp.

Court ruled (five to four) that corporal punishment did not violate the "cruel and unusual punishment" clause of the Constitution's Eighth Amendment.

The research on corporal punishment is extensive and consistent in its conclusions; schools, families, and students receive *no* benefits from paddling. Moreover, the enduring harm can be physical, social-emotional, and academic.[22] The practices of retention, suspension, corporal punishment, and expulsion have proved to be obsolete. Restorative discipline practices are increasingly implemented in schools. Teachers can approach behavior management with culturally sensitive, age-appropriate, and individualized education systems when abandoning punitive control. Shifting to more humanistic practices augments a teacher's responsibility and accountability.

TEACHERS AND EQUITY

The argument for educational equity is supported by a sound rationale from economic and ethical platforms. The legal foundations for equity exist in federal and state constitutions and court rulings (e.g., *Brown v. Board of Education*, 1954). Analogous to civil rights efforts, practice lags behind theory and law. Equitable performance results in education require rethinking the connotation of equity (see figure 1.5). Education has yet to make adequate progress in the class divide based on socioeconomic conditions. There is a negligible correlation between receiving a public education and societal readiness. Realizing a national vision of fairness and opportunity for students is contingent on the ascendancy of teachers.

Everyone Is Given the Same Ball . . . Not the Same Distance from the Goal . . .

Figure 1.5 **Equality versus Equity.** *Source*: Chen, S. (2022). Illustrations on classroom equity. Reproduced with permission.

Providing all children with the *same* services in the classroom falls woefully short of achieving equity. Every individual must be considered in the context of their preschool history and their baseline of knowledge and skills in multiple domains. Holistically, that baseline includes physical health, social-emotional skills, self-regulation, and academic threshold. Planning for each child involves preparing the resources and strategies necessary to reach set standards.

A differentiated needs and support model are customary with special education, dyslexic, and English language learners. Weighted student funding targets fairness and better outcomes for at-risk students. Students are better positioned for success with modifications (see figure 1.6). Individualized plans and tailored instruction are basal for closing significant learning gaps and approaching equity. The practice should expand in keeping with student data at the local level. Not every student requiring additional guidance fits a funded category, and flexibility with local and state funds provides viable options. The differential instructional model's execution depends on the judicious deployment of select teachers.

The Same Ball . . . Modifying the Odds . . .

Figure 1.6 Accommodating for Equity. *Source*: Chen, S. (2022). Illustrations on classroom equity. Reproduced with permission.

An at-risk student spending one year with a weak teacher is potentially academically irreparable. In addition to lowering the student's academic standards, the teacher may also damage that student's confidence, self-perception, and interest in learning. Conversely, continuity with proven teachers is a dynamic approach toward equity. Strategies such as selective looping (student remains for two years with the same teacher) can considerably close learning gaps, especially for younger children.[23] Decisions for looping should occur after reviewing the student's academic progress and social-emotional connection with a teacher and be made case by case. Student looping is one small approach to addressing a latent problem. Support for identified students should be examined broadly across systems to match teacher profile strengths with the student's specific needs. Teacher-student alignment may yield the highest pay-off in approaching educational equity.

INDIVIDUAL STUDENT AGENCY

"Agency is a concept that is generally understood as a capacity to act or cause change."[24] A wide-ranging goal for student agency is for the individual graduate to make knowledge-based, ethical decisions in his or her own and the community's interest. Teachers inextricably guide the students' journey toward realizing agency for themselves and shaping others. If we aspire to social equity and economic progress, the role of teachers cannot be undervalued. The fulfilled agency must exude self-sufficiency and student ownership of learning.

Quality of life comprises more than the financial advantages of an education. The benefits include countless physical and emotional rewards throughout a person's lifetime. The United Nations specified those advantages for college graduates compared to someone with only a high school diploma. The residual byproducts identified include the following:

- longer life spans, better access to health care, better dietary and health practices;
- greater economic stability and security;
- more stable employment and greater job satisfaction;
- less dependency on government assistance, greater understanding of government;
- increased community service and leadership;
- more self-confidence, and less criminal activity and incarceration.[25]

Teachers are the critical architects of student success, particularly for students most at risk. Students can still thrive if they lose funding, use fifteen-year-old textbooks, and have no technology—but they cannot do so without a talented teacher. A RAND Corporation study reporting on the effect of teachers states the following:

> Research suggests that, among school-related factors, teachers matter most. When it comes to student performance on reading and math tests, a teacher is estimated to have two to three times the impact of any other school factor, including services, facilities, and even leadership.[26]

Harvard University economists Chetty and Friedman and Columbia University economist Jonah Rockoff corroborated the RAND report. The authors tracked one million students from elementary school to adulthood. They found that the influence of skilled teachers is significant, with long-term academic and clear economic benefits for students assigned to high-VA (value-added) teachers. These students are more likely to

- attend college and attend higher-ranked colleges;
- earn higher salaries;
- live in higher socioeconomic status neighborhoods;
- save more for retirement; and
- are less likely to have children as teenagers.

Identifying a teacher in the bottom 5 percent and replacing them with even an average teacher increases a student's lifetime income by more than $250,000. The RAND study concluded that good teachers generate substantial economic value and that test score impacts are one helpful tool in locating such teachers.[27]

While public approval surveys of teachers and public education in the United States remain supportive, citizens are divided on increasing funding for public schools. Raising teacher salaries is a necessary reform, but the current system of uniform salary scales is not favorable for elevating professional status. Elected representatives and the public are inclined to support investments linked to performance results. Surviving another academic year is an inadequate bar for an automatic step raise in salary. Each teacher is viewed as an identical spoke on a collective wheel.

Teachers must secure credibility, trust, and status by demonstrating tangible learning, for example, closing learning gaps, exceeding proficiency standards, and graduating college-ready students. Buy-in from the community will grow as goals are met. A shift in public perception would accelerate the political resolve to transform teaching and help revitalize public education. A restructured, higher-performing system enhances respect for teachers, which in turn leads to retention and stability.

> Compared to high-achieving jurisdictions like Finland, Singapore, and Ontario, Canada—where only about 3 to 4% of teachers leave in a given year—U.S. attrition rates are quite high, hovering near 8% over the last decade, and are much higher for beginners and teachers in high-poverty schools and districts. If attrition rates were reduced to the levels of those nations, the United States would eliminate overall teacher shortages.[28]

The countries listed above have prominent innovative commonalities that deserve to be emulated at home. Educational leaders in the United States should humbly learn from exemplar models. Insightful ventures by progressive countries have raised teachers' status, thus enriching student learning. Hierarchal pathways expand teacher agency and hence that of students.

PURPOSEFUL DEPLOYMENT OF TEACHERS

Skilled teaching generalists, most prevalent in elementary grades, remain crucial to meeting the educational standards for the mainstream of children. However, the most exceptional teachers offer the best prospects for engaging underprivileged students. At-risk students at all levels most effectively close learning gaps when assigned to skilled teaching specialists. A robust pool of master teachers allows for the flexible management of campus needs. Teachers with specific expert skillsets play a pivotal role in altering the trajectory of failure, retention, and disengagement.

Breaking the cycle of high-poverty schools having the most inexperienced and transient teachers is a fundamental step toward closing learning gaps between demographic groups. Teacher pathways linked to performance, reward, and career prestige offer a realistic solution to this deficit. Correctly identifying, positioning, supporting, and rewarding teachers requires valid and transparent processes. Teachers progressively becoming leaders within a hierarchy of categorical roles expand career flexibility, intrinsic motivation, and subsequent student achievement. A future generation of teachers and students will thrive in an analytics-based talent alignment with individualized learning.

WHAT COMES FIRST?

High-quality, universal early childhood education (ECE) programs promise students the most profound long-term benefits. However, preparing a deep pool of ECE teachers is a necessary prelude to this vital endeavor. The US Bureau of Labor Statistics reported that in 2019, the median annual salary for pre-K teachers was $30,520, compared to $59,420 for kindergarten teachers—not an enticing career prospect for the former.[29] Consequently, teacher shortages in early childhood are more extensive than in general K-12 teaching positions.

According to the Bureau of Labor, the demand for preschool teachers is projected to grow by 10 percent in the decade up to 2026, faster than the average for all occupations. During the same time frame, fewer early childhood teachers are entering the workforce. The reasons for this are complex, but the implications are concerning: a shortage of early childhood teachers that is rising to a crisis level for early childhood centers.[30]

The ECE teacher shortage is considerable and even more severe for early childhood special education. Initiating universal pre-K without a corresponding cadre of prepared ECE teachers will not satisfy students' developmental needs. The preliminary task at hand is to cultivate qualified teachers. The design for a cohesive teaching framework should include all critical need teaching areas: ECE, bilingual/ESL, career and technical education, computer science/technology applications, mathematics, science, and special education.

High school programs do not offer the optimum number of career-enhancing dual credit (DC) courses because of the shortage of certified DC teachers. Talented technology prospects do not gravitate to teaching introductory computer science courses when the business world is more lucrative. Math and science majors have more career options than certified elementary teachers. The supply-demand-quality issues prevailing in the teaching profession cannot be solved by patchwork or one-size-fits-all approaches. To build an appealing and sustainable ecosystem to entice and retain teachers, one must first examine the global perception and the specialized individuals.

The learning culture essential to academic progress is created by teachers and principals. The caliber of campus leadership is a substantial determinant of student learning. Successful principals attract and retain teachers at rates exceeding their less successful counterparts.[31] The rationale for and urgency in prioritizing teachers derive from the difference in the applicant pools. The number of certified principal applicants is sufficient in most districts. Assistant principals provide an additional contingency for vacancies. Much work remains in building resilient pathways for principals. However, the teacher shortage is ominous and demands an immediate response.

CONCLUSION

Leadership, technology, curriculum, policy, and parental engagement are educational factors for continued investment and study. However, *all* contributing elements support *one* rudimentary interaction: *teachers* ⇔ *students*. Parents should expect their children to advance and grow regardless of their residential zip code. Society could make remarkably swift progress across all content standards if entrusted with highly skilled teachers. Simultaneously, teachers could lead such ethical educational efforts as protecting the environment and reducing bias for a more tolerant society. Teachers are the fulcrum of universal education: the system's balance and utility depend on their prosperity.

New educational priorities must usurp ideals of the industrial age. Society, students, and expectations continuously change, and success depends on internal perseverance for concurrent adaptation. Progress in a period of exponentially compounding information is still beholden to teachers. Visionary leaders recognize that school ecosystems of assembly-line classrooms are obsolete in meeting desired present-day outcomes. A transformation is warranted whereby teachers flourish and align their instructional talent to progressive student outcomes.

Why start with teachers? Because teachers are the conduit for equity, for economic prosperity, and for civil society. As the instructional frontline, they possess underutilized and robust potential as certified crusaders for future-ready graduates. Research and logic dictate the wisdom of investing in a stock yielding the highest annual return, and with education, that stock is teachers. As the current pandemic has affirmed, teachers are indispensable now and in the coming decades. The salient priority of upgrading the national school structure for teachers involves designing a hierarchical system and pathways for a progressive institutional agency.

NOTES

1. Heckman, 2012.
2. "Most Educated Countries 2021," 2021.
3. Kemp, 2019.
4. Horowitz, Igielnik, & Kochhar, 2020, 20.
5. Pickett & Wilkinson, 2015.
6. Vinelli & Weller, 2021, 5.
7. Weber, 2021, 302.
8. Spiel et al., 2018, 745.
9. Biden, 2020.
10. Harrington, 2011.
11. Opper, 2019.
12. Darling-Hammond et al., 2017.
13. Warhol, 1976, 39.
14. Snyder, 1993.
15. "Rules for Teachers in 1872 & 1915," 2013.
16. McKenzie & Kress, 2015.
17. "Status and Trends in the Education of Racial and Ethnic Groups 2018," 2019.
18. Bybee, Henderson & Hinojosa, 2014, 139.
19. "Census Bureau Reports at Least 350 Languages," 2015.
20. Visit Houston, 2021.
21. "Position Statement on Student Grade Retention," 2011.
22. Caron, 2018.

23. Hill & Jones, 2018.
24. Littlejohn & Foss, 2009, 27.
25. "Higher Education," 2021.
26. Opper, 2019, 1.
27. Chetty, Friedman & Rockoff, 2011.
28. Sutcher, Darling-Hammond & Carver-Thomas, 2015, 4.
29. "Kindergarten and Elementary School Teachers: Occupational Outlook Handbook," 2019.
30. "Occupational Outlook Handbook: Preschool Teachers," 2022.
31. The New Teacher Project, 2012, 15.

Chapter 2

Teachers as Professionals

> There was a moment when I changed from an amateur to a professional. I assumed the burden of a profession, which is to write even when you don't want to, don't much like what you're writing, and aren't writing particularly well.
>
> —Agatha Christie

Hiring personnel occupied a substantial portion of my time in my multiple roles as an educator. In attempting to raise the efficacy of school systems, I considered teacher talent the most substantial determinant of student success. Finding the best staff always took precedence if I had to choose between planning, scheduling, professional development, or other responsibilities. Talent management (TM) is a year-round endeavor in today's educational environment.

Using every tool available—advertising, job fairs, social media, and college visits—it was evident that recruiting and retaining capable teachers was becoming progressively more difficult. Colleagues in neighboring school districts echoed similar sentiments: the teacher pool was steadily shrinking. The problem goes beyond out-finessing the surrounding human resource competition. Outstanding teacher recruitment by Harlem at the expense of Brooklyn perpetuates temporary winners and losers. Understanding the psychology and culture of the teaching profession is foundational to designing long-term solutions.

STATE OF THE TEACHING FRATERNITY

The National Center for Education Statistics (NCES) reported that in 2018, the characteristics of US public school teachers included 75 percent female (88 percent in elementary), 79 percent white, 58 percent with a postbaccalaureate degree, 90 percent with state certification, and 63 percent with ten or more years of teaching experience.[1] If requested to design the "ideal" demographic and educational composition for teachers, few would propose those 2018 percentages as a model. Educators and researchers in the social sciences would advocate for race, ethnicity, and gender numbers that better align with students' backgrounds. The desired targets for educational level, certification, and experience would represent higher percentages with standards for the workforce. Regrettably, when one examines the projected pool of applicants, it is clear that schools cannot improve on these statistics.

Supply and Demand. The United States has been experiencing an increasingly severe teacher shortage. The number of vacancies is alarming, and the trend is not projected to improve soon. NCES reported that the number of bachelor's degrees awarded in education from 1970–1971 to 2017–2018 decreased from 176,307 to 83,621 nationally, a 52.6 percent reduction. During a corresponding period, the K-12 student enrollment in all schools increased from 45 million in 1974 to 56.4 million in fall 2016, with an NCES projected enrollment of 57.4 million by 2028.[2]

Vacancies in critical endorsement positions are especially alarming. The Frontline Research and Learning Institute surveyed almost 1,200 school and district leaders across the country in 2020 to gauge the extent of specific teacher shortages. They reported the percentages of districts with unfilled vacancies by role. The six highest areas included the following:

- Special Education (71 percent)
- Substitute Teachers (67 percent)
- Secondary Math (46 percent)
- Paraprofessionals (35 percent)
- Secondary Physical Sciences (26 percent)
- Bilingual Education (25 percent)[3]

These critical shortage areas are not due to insufficient efforts by talent management (TM) departments. Salary, outside competition, and work environments contribute to the ongoing conditions. The teacher shortage scenario, a concern for decades, will continue to worsen unless we explicitly address the causes and formulate pragmatic and equitable solutions. As part of a comprehensive blueprint, solutions necessitate unique systems to address barriers, build viable pools of teachers, and meet student needs in "hard to fill" positions.

While some roles (e.g., K-5 elementary education) may have an adequate pool of certified candidates, elevating personnel quality in teaching is an analogous challenge. Talent in every classroom can be upgraded by attracting high scholastic achievers early in the process. Failure to entice more of the most academically talented students into the teaching profession runs counter to national progress. Our schools desperately need an infusion of high-achieving talent. The US dilemma contrasts markedly with the success of other high-performing countries. The goals for reframing the teaching profession include the quest for more applicants, heightened quality, and specialized teacher expertise.

Compounding these supply and quality issues are bachelor's degree programs eliminated in education and the closure of college programs. The University of South Florida recently closed the undergraduate program in its College of Education. Other universities are contemplating similar moves due to declining enrollment. This trend reflects the shifting job market and employment preferences. Districts are compelled to hire an increasing number of applicants from alternative teacher certification institutions instead of the traditional baccalaureate degree universities.[4]

Quality. The Programme for International Student Assessment (PISA) test is a respected measure of international academic performance. The highest-performing countries include Finland, Singapore, South Korea, and Canada. These countries report that the top 30 percent of their university graduates enter the teaching field. By comparison, the United States' and Great Britain's PISA performance scores are in the low teens, with teachers recruited from the bottom 40 percent of university graduates.[5] Applicants' academic abilities are considered essential indicators of (1) the capacity of employees in the occupations, and (2) the desirability of a profession.[6] Erosion of talent can lead to lower confidence in schools and the efficacy of the educational system, with the potential for a country to fall further in the global ranking. The United States should learn from high-performing nations in creating a culture to attract their best students to become teachers.

Another indicator of teacher quality is data from state licensing exams. A National Council on Teacher Quality (NCTQ) review of fifteen research studies found that eleven positively correlated states' licensure tests and student outcomes; the higher the teacher's scores, the better their students performed on state assessments.[7] Many prospective teachers failed these exams on their first attempt. Even within the same state, notable variation exists between licensure passing rates, with NCTQ identifying a 56 percent-point gap between the highest and lowest. Over 25 percent failed their first attempt at Praxis, the most widely used national licensing exam, between 2014 and 2016.[8]

Passing standards are inconsistent, with some states using comparatively easy tests or setting reduced thresholds, thereby reporting higher pass rates.[9]

Reliability in teacher certification standards promotes public confidence in teacher competence and safeguards student achievement. States need some flexibility to accommodate shortages and unique regional hiring concerns. At the same time, a minimum baseline of competence is vital to protecting students from negligent pedagogy.

Additional research is needed on (1) teacher preparation programs and (2) authorizing exams. Longitudinal teacher comparisons with measures of student achievement can strengthen decision-making processes to refine quality. This information can lead to stricter standards for these two state teaching requirements. Incorporating federal reports that compare states' success in teacher preparation also promotes improvement and exchanging strategies.

Why aren't students interested in teaching?

Students listing teaching as one of their top career aspirations is a desirable and attainable goal. The high-performing nations listed above intentionally upgraded and transformed their education systems. They revitalized the status and heightened the desirability of becoming a teacher. Their systemic actions in redefining teaching roles changed the culture, attracting the top 30 percent of their university graduates to become educators. These nations have demonstrated substantial revitalization approaches by creating coherent policies, systems, standards, and supports.

Barriers. In the United States, obstacles inhibiting innovation and change persist, negatively affecting teaching's public image and appeal. Substandard salaries and inadequate opportunities for career advancement (see figure 2.1) are two prominent reasons students cite as impediments to a career in the classroom. American College Testing (ACT) collected pre-test student responses on a questionnaire from 2007 to 2017. Nearly all assessed students (1.67 million in 2020) completed the questionnaire, providing a robust sample. The findings are informative for designing an incentive-based teaching ecosystem.

The honesty of survey respondents who stated, "I don't like working with children or young people" is constructive and pertinent. Some individuals are simply not suited for working with students and should pursue other career options. Students answering, "I wouldn't be good at it" or "Teachers do not get enough respect" are influenced by negative opinions or reports. "It doesn't initially pay very well" and "Not much opportunity for career development" are the two most prevalent survey responses and merit close scrutiny. Some of these candid perspectives arise from community and teacher feedback. For the teaching profession, perception too closely mirrors reality. However, with calculated planning and systems, attitudes toward careers can adapt to emerging new work cultures.

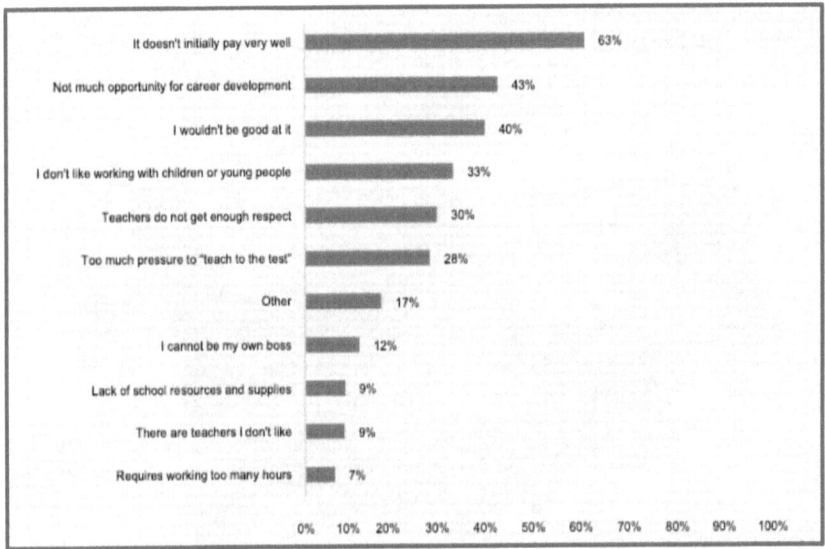

Figure 2.1 **Why Aren't Students Interested in Teaching?** ACT Research & Policy Survey, 2018, reproduced with permission. *Source*: Croft, M., Guffy, G. & Vitale, D. (2018). Encouraging More High School Students to Consider Teaching. Retrieved from https://www.act.org/content/dam/act/unsecured/documents/pdfs/Encouraging-More-HS-Students-to-Consider-Teaching.pdf.

The most significant concern for those considering a future teaching career is salary. With studies purporting the relative importance of teachers, particularly for the future of the US economy, neglected compensation places the nation in jeopardy. Tech-savvy students quickly access salary data when exploring careers (see figure 2.2). The realization that teachers earn appreciably less than other college-educated professions is an obvious impediment. Coupled with inadequate growth and career opportunities, the appeal of becoming a teacher is fast diminishing.

In a multifaceted educational system involving diverse constituents, leveraging teacher income to augment the applicant pool, ensure competence, and raise student attainment is also complex. Any new system must be perceived as fair and transparent. While increasing the initial wages for teachers is considered necessary for recruitment, automatic salary increases based on education level and years of service are outdated. The current step system for low-performing or minimum-effort employees offers financial security at the expense of students. The traditional framework limits incentives for the most dedicated, passionate, and capable teachers. Funding is finite, and the public rightfully expects results from investments. As personnel salaries and benefits already comprise approximately 80 percent

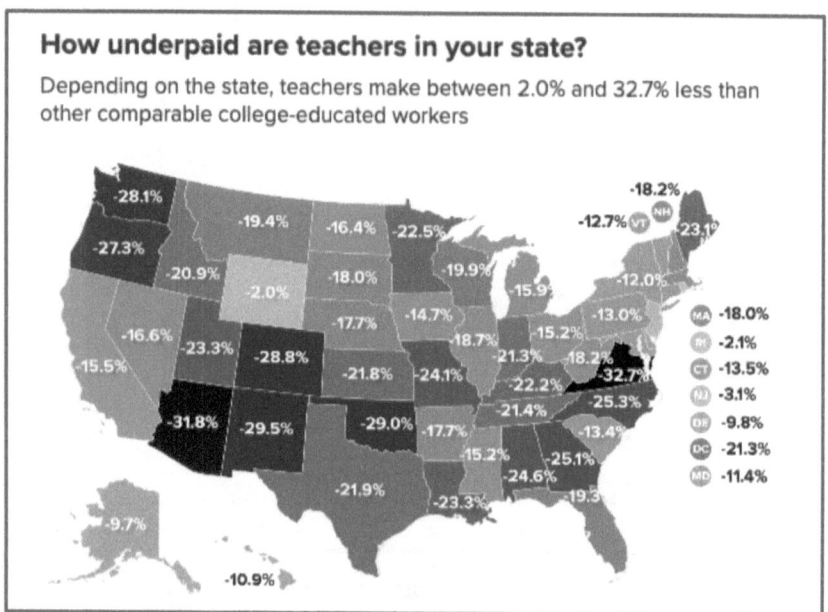

Figure 2.2 Teacher Pay versus Comparable College-Educated Workers. Reproduced with permission by the Economic Policy Institute and the University of California at Berkley's Center on Wage & Employment Dynamics. *Source*: Allegretto, S., & Mishel, L. (2020). Teacher pay penalty dips but persists in 2019. Retrieved from https://www.epi.org/publication/teacher-pay-penalty-dips-but-persists-in-2019-public-school-teachers-earn-about-20-less-in-weekly-wages-than-nonteacher-college-graduates/.

of expenditures in most school districts, the budgetary implications are substantial.

The second-highest survey response cited apprehension due to the scarce opportunities for career progression. This long-standing frustration requires a structural disruption of teaching roles. Along with salary considerations, high-achieving students contemplating college and careers assess the potential for challenges, recognition, and advancement, as indicated in the survey. The possibilities on most campuses for career alteration are negligible and usually require an additional degree and certification (e.g., administration, counseling). A passionate teacher may desire expanded leadership responsibility without relinquishing their teaching duties.

Phi Delta Kappa International (PDK) is a professional nonprofit organization for educators. The organization aims to support teachers and school leaders throughout their careers. In 2019, PDK conducted a public scientific survey with a random sample subgroup of 556 public school teachers. The results corroborate the ACT survey. The poll results are foreboding for a profession currently suffering from severe staffing shortages projected to worsen in the future. The teaching profession may have reached a tipping point, and parents in a wide range of communities sympathize with teachers' frustrations. Here are some notable findings:

- Teachers considered quitting, blaming pay, stress, and lack of respect = 50 percent;
- Teachers feel they are unfairly paid = 60 percent;
- Teachers say their schools are underfunded = 75 percent.[10]

First-year K-5 elementary teachers will soon realize their limited career options. They can anticipate teaching elementary classes for the next thirty years and beyond without an additional degree and certification. The only prospect for career advancement may be to abandon the direct instruction of children—the primary reason many entered the field. The outlook for career progression in most school districts can be disheartening. Realistic opportunities for personal growth, advancement, and economic security could revitalize the teaching profession.

For prospective and current teachers, priorities have shifted toward career-life balance and job satisfaction. With the prospects of investing so much time in earning a living, employees in general increasingly value workplace gratification. A 2021 Prudential Financial Company job survey of American workers found that almost 50 percent have seriously reevaluated their career goals since the pandemic. Nationally, 53 percent of workers, if given the opportunity, would retrain for a different career.[11]

Teacher Burnout. With extended hours, accountability expectations, and a heavy workload of continuous planning, the conscientious teacher is often overwhelmed, and this can lead to burnout. The above attrition figures support this reality. The World Health Organization describes burnout as a syndrome that results from persistent and unmanaged workplace stress. Three factors identify burnout occurrence:

- feelings of energy depletion or exhaustion;
- increased mental distance from one's job, or feelings of negativism or cynicism related to one's job; and
- reduced professional efficacy.[12]

I have witnessed burnout in many dedicated teachers. Both teachers and students could have avoided the adverse effects with altered circumstances and support. Indications are that the restrictions and anxieties stemming from the pandemic have only intensified the conditions generating workplace stress.

When considering career choices, individuals evaluate multiple factors, such as location, salary, prestige, personal interests, job requirements, growth opportunities, and social circumstances. Personal priorities will vary, but the information tools for a reliable assessment of employment decisions are ubiquitous. In 1430 England, it is unlikely that a blacksmith's adolescent son would be investigating other appealing occupations. Apprenticeship training on shaping metals would usually begin at ages seven to thirteen. William would most likely learn the trade from his father, and sister Emma's options were even more limited. In contrast, members of digitally literate Generation Z possess unique personal ambitions and previously unfathomable alternatives. Aligning future teacher aspirations with campus needs (e.g., coaching, mentoring, and research) supports recruiting, retention, and student learning. Upgrading the teaching profession warrants restructuring the models to align with financial and personal agency goals.

SUBSTANDARD REMEDY

In responding to the steadily declining number of education graduates, districts have been forced to compensate by employing more long-term substitutes, American College Test (ACT), and emergency-certified teachers. Long-term subs' effectiveness in most classroom situations ranges from overseeing worksheets to babysitting. Schools are fortunate if residual learning occurs. Emergency certification is a limited and temporary measure enacted by districts to deal with local shortages of certified teachers. Candidates receive a one-year employment permit, sometimes renewable, while they work toward long-term authorization. As of this writing, only seven states with critical shortages issue emergency teaching certificates.

Alternative Certification Program (ACP) is a sanctioned program with distinct requirements in each state. Nationally, school districts hire about 20 percent of new teachers (38 percent in Texas) from ACP programs. ACP provides a path to teaching for someone with an earned bachelor's degree but without a teaching credential. An ACP program design comprises a contractual teaching assignment for candidates while they simultaneously take required preparation courses.[13] The authorizing institutions have mentors who observe classroom performance, provide evaluations, and assist candidates in preparing for the required state exams. ACP programs have increased exponentially over the past few decades, filling the void left by fewer college education graduates.

An initial concern with ACP programs is the internal incentive for quality control. For-profit, non-IHE (institutions of higher education) organizations enroll about 68.2 percent of participants with limited oversight.[14] The expanding scope of certification institutions, particularly those with commercial interests, increases the instances of unacceptable applicants. Mulvihill and Martin surveyed the issues in the state of Indiana:

Some are good programs and follow a valid itinerary to licensing. Others are misguided attempts based on good motives, and some are out and out disingenuous, like the popular online program that promised in its advertising that the program would "lead to" an Indiana teaching license, when in fact, graduates were licensed by another state and then had to apply for a transfer license in Indiana.[15]

The NCTQ evaluates the integrity of ACP programs providing teacher preparation and publishes grades for institutions. While many participants become outstanding teachers, historically the learning curve takes more time, and fewer remain in the profession. The quality of ACP preparation can differ widely by the establishment. All but four states (Oregon, Wyoming, Utah, and Alaska) allow for alternative certification programs, but "only 13 states have regulations that require all alternate route candidates to demonstrate the necessary content knowledge before admission into a program."[16]

A University of Texas study reported that "the odds of retaining a teacher who holds an alternative certification were 14-22% less likely than the odds of retaining a teacher with a standard certification."[17] Carver-Thomas and Darling-Hammond's research found that teachers coming into the profession through ACP programs were 25 percent more likely to leave a campus than teachers entering through a traditional university certification program.[18] At the national level, forty-six states allow teachers to enter the profession through an alternate route, "compared to only a few 30 years ago."[19] This shift in staff resourcing has negatively impacted turnover rate and instruction quality.

TEACHER SELF-ESTEEM AND JOB SATISFACTION

Employee job satisfaction translates to higher productivity and lower turnover. Forward-thinking businesses wisely invest in employee development and offer progressive challenges to keep staff members engaged and productive. Twenty-first-century business prototypes understand the evolving workplace and the value of promoting employee well-being, resulting in improved quality of work.[20] According to a 2018 UK Essays' survey study:

> When people are not feeling fulfilled in their job or career, their self-esteem can suffer as a result. When people feel valued and fulfilled at work, they are more able to go above and beyond what is asked of them, which lends to a feeling of accomplishment and more confidence.[21]

A person's self-concept and self-worth are to varying degrees influenced by their career role. The UK Essays study referenced above found "a positive correlation between job satisfaction and self-esteem."[22] The Bureau of

Labor Statistics stated that in 2018, members of the US workforce averaged 34.5 hours per week at their jobs. In contrast, an NCES survey reported that full-time teachers spend an average of 50.9 hours a week on teaching and other school-related activities, 45.5 percent more than the typical employee.[23] Granted, teachers have extended time during the summer as well as a winter break. However, despite extended recesses, a teacher's work expectations and time requirements are unrelenting in order to meet student needs during intense semesters.

Insufficient life-work balance and failure to meet goals often lead to frustration, complacency, and even burnout. For many individuals, a career is an integrated component of their self-esteem and identity. Estimating and visualizing one's fit in a particular career is part of the decision-making process of entering a profession or remaining employed in a particular position.

Individuals in "professional" careers display a broad spectrum of attitudes toward personal job satisfaction. As stated earlier, the pandemic has influenced half of US workers to reevaluate their career goals. Teachers' stress level during Covid-19 was the highest in decades, with attrition rates yet to be determined. A total of 40 percent of new teachers were already leaving the classroom within their first five years of employment.[24] Annually, 8 percent of teachers leave the profession, another 8 percent move to other schools, and over 50 percent quit teaching before reaching retirement eligibility.[25] Such an elevated level of instability is undeniably damaging to student achievement. At its core, high teacher mobility is an imminent warning sign of systemic deficiencies.

All professions evolve within changing cultures and economies. New fields emerge while others (e.g., home economics) become obsolete. Necessary knowledge and skillsets continuously advance—and the pace will only accelerate. The public image of teaching as a profession is positive. Surveys indicate that "more than 70 percent of Americans have trust in public school teachers today."[26] While this appears impressive, what are the specific characteristics that the public associates with "trust"? If the confidence is in traditional order and safety, the compliment is shallow. The community deserves a heightened awareness of the trajectory both for the teaching establishment and the future needs of students.

The connotations of the word "professional" are varied and often ambiguous to interpret. Employees in a plethora of "professions" differ in numerous respects. Dietitians, electricians, accountants, attorneys, and scientists belong to that designated affiliation. Several commonalities separate professionals from other employees. Members of a profession earn a living from an occupational activity with specific attributes. Abbott delineated seven universal features characteristic of a profession. Those standard traits include the following:

- a professional association
- a cognitive base
- institutionalized training
- licensing
- work autonomy
- colleague control
- code of ethics[27]

Professional positions vary in salary and prestige depending on the national and local culture. Meeting the above criteria has little relevance in the modern workplace, however. Labels and classifications that at one time evoked a recognized social status are less distinct. Blue-collar, white-collar, exempt, non-exempt, professional, and paraprofessional are outdated terms with increasingly vague collective meanings. When used as an adjective, the "professional" label is an expectation of competence and ethical standards in expertise. Abbott's "traits" only identify the unique similarities and differences from other occupations under broad categories. Successive generations care less about institutional definitions and more about career possibilities. While a secure income remains a priority, other concerns have altered attitudes about careers. How am I treated, and am I respected? How am I learning and growing? Do I have a life outside work? Furthermore, am I making a difference?

Present-day applicants seek career fulfillment and personal agency. High-performance standards are viewed as a welcome challenge in career aspiration; undaunted, one takes greater risks for the prospect of superior rewards. Raising the criteria and expectations for a cognitive base, institutionalized training, and licensing will attract high-achieving talent. Strengthening requirements and corresponding supportive work culture are essential for transformation.

CONCLUSION

Agatha Christie "assumed the burden of a profession" by accepting responsibility and high standards. Belonging to a profession is no guarantee that employees act the part, "exhibiting a courteous, conscientious, and generally businesslike manner in the workplace."[28] In upgrading the portrait of teachers as authentic professionals, new rigorous standards are essential for admission and continuance. These criteria at the state level should involve input from multiple education leaders, including public school teachers, administrators, university professors, and state education representatives.

In 2003, Ravitch reported that both colleges of education and state education departments concurred that teachers need more extended periods of pedagogical training. The emphasis was on elevating education as a profession, imitating law and medicine with their stellar entry criteria. Teachers must be both well-educated and well-trained in practice. For teaching to become a respected and burgeoning profession, entry and performance standards must be based on a solid foundation of compelling research.[29] This ideal is only possible by investing in the restructured model, one that includes continuous growth, personal advancement, revamped salary structures, and a contingent of teachers serving as pedagogues and scholars.

As a group, teachers meet the criteria of a "profession" by definition but are too often perceived as being on the fringes. Teaching has little career leverage as a required high-demand position in current society. The National Education Association and American Federation of Teachers made notable gains for their constituents in the second half of the twentieth century (e.g., due process, class size, and instructional resources). At the same time, the unionization movement may have hindered teachers' professional stature. Teachers' association with union ideology evokes comparisons to autoworkers and images of strikes. Union protection of the least competent 20 percent of teachers damages the potential for excellence for all other teachers.

Revamping teaching will require incremental phases, diligent oversight, and patient persistence. Innovation is necessary when a system has remained dormant for decades, and the enthusiasm for membership in a profession has waned. Contemporary processes compel resilient justification, collaborative planning, and fair measures for accountability. Education is vital for economic prosperity, intellectual capacity, and humanistic leadership. For authentic professionalism, schools require a structure and culture that builds agency, cultivates pride in teaching roles, and rewards performance. If districts facilitate an enticing educational ecosystem, the teachers will come—and they will stay.

NOTES

1. National Center for Education Statistics, 2021.
2. "College Graduates by Major," 2019.
3. Buttner, 2021, 3.
4. Flaherty, 2020.
5. Hargreaves & Fullan, 2012.
6. Ingersoll et al., 2018.
7. "Driven by Data," 2021.
8. Will, 2019.
9. "Driven by Data," 2021.
10. "Frustration in the Schools," 2019.
11. "Pulse of the American Worker Survey." 2022.

12. "Burn-out an 'Occupational Phenomenon,'" 2019.
13. DeMonte, 2015.
14. Yin & Partelow, 2020.
15. Mulvihill & Martin, 2019, 1.
16. National Council on Teacher Quality, 2020, 2.
17. Reyes & Alexander, 2017, 5.
18. Carver-Thomas & Darling-Hammond, 2017.
19. National Council on Teacher Quality, 2020, 1.
20. Litchfield et al., 2016.
21. "Relationship between Job Satisfaction and Self-Esteem," 2018 1.
22. "Relationship between Job Satisfaction and Self-Esteem," 2018 1.
23. "Schools and Staffing Survey, Public and Private Teachers," 2013.
24. "Why Do Teachers Leave?" 2016.
25. "Teacher Turnover: What You Need to Know," 2020.
26. Chen, 2020.
27. Abbott, 2014.
28. "Professional," Merriam-Webster.com, 2021.
29. Ravitch, 2002.

Chapter 3

Authenticating Teacher Agency

There is no passion to be found playing small—in settling for a life that is less than the one you are capable of living.

—Nelson Mandela

To achieve systemic excellence, the progression of a teaching career requires financial security, resilient support, and growth opportunities. Too many bright young students do not consider teaching a tenable vocation. An alarming number of new teachers become so frustrated with conditions that they exit early. Demoralizing circumstances can undermine the spirit of once-promising teachers. Disillusioned and realizing their limited employment options, they choose to settle for complacency. When nearly 45 percent of new teachers leave the profession within the first five years, the problem is systemic.[1] The National Commission on Teaching and America's Future estimates that the cost of recruiting, hiring, and training new teachers has reached $7.3 billion annually.[2] Transforming the profession has an economic rationale running parallel to an educational equity justification.

THE NEXT GENERATION

Students contemplating careers weigh all readily accessible information. The outlook for future teacher cohorts is considered relative to personal aspirations, values, and perceptions. Younger generations often prioritize work-life balance and flexible hours over salary. Recent surveys find that competitive salaries are still compelling, but Millennials (b. 1980–1996) and Generation Z (b. 1997–2015) prefer to work in fields with accommodating schedules and growth opportunities.[3] This shift in attitudes represents a preference for personal time relative to work careers. The confines of entrenched school teaching schedules and limited growth prospects are fundamental barriers to recruiting future teachers.

Opportunity, gender, socioeconomic status, peers, parental attitudes, and school guidance affect employment options and resulting choices. Changing culture and perception of a profession extends beyond influencing the mindsets of the next generation. Al-Bahrani et al. reported that parental wishes most strongly influence teenagers' aspirations.[4] A national survey on the public's attitudes toward the public schools reported that "fifty-four percent of parents would not like one of their children to take up teaching in the public schools as a career."[5] Survey data indicate a much lower desire for promoting a teaching career when compared to other prospering nations with more supportive educational structures (e.g., Finland and Singapore).

Students who expressed interest in teaching shared their reasons, including enjoyment of working with children and young people (60 percent), wanting to make a difference and give back to their community (51 percent), being inspired by one or more of their teachers (42 percent), or having a passion for a specific subject (41 percent).[6] Altruistic purpose is not an impediment for most applicants at the beginning of their careers. One survey reported that 57 percent of Millennials want their work to affect the world positively. Another 50 percent would even accept a reduced salary if they believed their work was "making the world a better place."[7] Generation Z is one of the most socially conscious peer groups in recorded surveys, with four out of five respondents believing that their efforts "could change the world for the better."[8]

Harnessing the social equity passions of today's youth is a starting point for appealing to potential new teachers. Extending the range of career alternatives involves building frameworks for employment needs such as security, flexibility, and growth opportunities. Capitalizing on inherent humanistic desire with supportive structures is part of the strategy to entice prospective teachers. Capturing the hearts of talented prospects is a manageable hurdle, but convincing their pragmatic minds is more challenging and requires a collaborative strategy. Education is dependent on new generations, and an astute rationale for recruitment must target the personal attributes that incentivize.

Those entering a teaching career are not discernibly prioritizing the accumulation of wealth. Nevertheless, reports of teachers working second jobs to make ends meet intimidate prospective educators. The Economic Policy Institute reported that almost one-third of new teachers have a second job. When including other jobs *within the school system* (e.g., student activity sponsorship, coaching), the percentage of educators increases to 59 percent.[9] Like about 70 percent of teachers nationwide, author Matt began his career with undergraduate loan debt, to which he added when completing a master's degree. The family budget was tight, with a starting salary in 1978 of $11,000. Along with a desire for additional leadership responsibilities, income was a factor influencing his decision to become a school administrator after sixteen years of teaching.

The National Center for Education Statistics reported that "between 1999–2000 and 2015–16, average student loan debt for master's degree completers increased by 71 percent for master of education degrees (from $32,200 to $55,200)."[10] Teachers have some advantages in canceling loan debt when working in high-poverty schools thanks to certain loans. However, managing debt while subsisting on a low fixed income is a financial hardship for many teachers. The Biden administration canceled $5.8 billion in student loan debt in 2021 for over 300,000 borrowers. This type of action is particularly constructive in altering overall conditions and enticing anyone considering a teaching career.

An additional factor affecting career choice is gender stereotypes. Pre-K-12 classroom teachers are about 75 percent female. Having more male teachers does not directly impact students' academic results. However, other rewards from shifting percentages benefit *all* students. McGrath et al. reported four distinct advantages of gender balance on campuses:

- Male and female teachers contribute to children's gender knowledge.
- The presence of both male and female teachers in classrooms allows students to learn from teachers whom they perceive as being similar to themselves.
- Having a diverse workforce of teachers can enhance decision-making processes and drive positive outcomes.
- The presence of male teachers may help promote alternative, non-violent, and gender-equitable versions of masculinity.[11]

Even within subject areas, stereotypes inhibit the teacher pool from expanding. There is a disproportional college gender disparity in science, technology, engineering, and math (STEM) majors. Societal typecasting exacerbates the teaching shortages in these subjects. However, students' view of STEM subjects as primarily male careers is slowly changing. The number of women graduating in STEM fields increased from just over 140,000 in 2009 to over 200,000 in 2016.[12] The percentage has grown by highlighting successful women as relevant role models, providing encouragement, and building confidence through developing skillsets. Early counseling should be integrated with planning to encourage prospective teachers, along with incentives for more females to matriculate into STEM programs from grade school through college.

When recruiting teachers, applicant pool diversity must be part of the conversation. All students deserve quality instruction from diverse, competent teachers in nurturing campus cultures. The imbalance of racial and ethnic teachers supporting students with a like heritage is well documented. In 2015, almost 80 percent of young teachers (aged 25–34) in the United States were white compared to about half the enrolled students. The student-to-teacher ratio for Hispanics was 24 percent students to 9 percent teachers, and for African Americans, it was 13 percent to 8 percent.[13] Proactively collaborating with university education departments can mitigate this disproportion to advance student achievement.

> Research indicates that minority students do better contemporaneously in school—and likely in the long run as well—when they are exposed to teachers of their same race or ethnicity. As a consequence, the underrepresentation of minority teachers relative to the proportion of minority school-aged students could be having the effect of limiting minority students' educational success.[14]

As society changes, educators should respond to cultural norms by yielding to the expectations of future teachers and the evolving demographics of students. An educational ecosystem that is progressive and flexible helps meet the requirements of both.

An educational orthodoxy that reinforces teachers' intrinsic desires and accommodates life-work balance is necessary to compete with the more progressive private sector. Randstad recently investigated the reasons workers stay with their current employers and found that 58 percent of workers feel their companies lack the growth opportunities that would make them stay long term.[15] Teachers work in one of the most limited professions for internal maturation and advancement. With 8 percent already leaving the classroom every year,[16] designing an appealing ambience in education is more than ever imperative.

KEEPING THE CURRENT

The scope of transformation extends beyond prospective teachers. Augmenting the repository of new talent is the long-term prescription for elevating the teaching profession. The more immediate imperative is creating the conditions for current teachers to remain passionate, committed, and thriving. While moving toward these lofty objectives, examining the root causes of teacher disillusionment may lead to solutions. Why do some experienced teachers lose their enthusiasm? Although practical reasons are frequently cited (e.g., salary and commuting distance), campus culture carries the most weight regarding attitudes toward work. A feeling of isolation in the classroom leaves too many teachers discouraged. Complacency can quickly ensue when a teacher is dissatisfied but realizes few other viable options exist. The longer one is employed, the more daunting it is to let go of one's investment in a pension. The last five years preceding retirement should not be purgatory for teachers—or their students.

When disillusionment and complacency become the norm, can the situation be reversed? A total of 71 percent of the US workforce admit that they remain in their current jobs because it is easier than starting something new.[17] Loss of passion can translate into reduced productivity. The consequences vary according to employment. If an assembly line employee has excessive absences, the company may call up the next person without affecting its bottom line. On the other hand, the repercussions of one apathetic teacher in education can be life altering. Allowing minimal effort or indifference to pervade a classroom is not an option.

An agonizing dilemma for any principal is deciding whether a complacent teacher can be revitalized or needs to be removed from the classroom. If the person in question was previously an accomplished teacher, a growth plan, coaching, and support would be an advisable first strategy. A teacher who never connected with or added value to students warrants a more straightforward course of action. Viable systemic approaches for these scenarios are presented in chapter 5, which deals with evaluations. The mandate for principals regarding the many competent, experienced teachers is to fairly cultivate growth, passion, and purpose, thereby fending off complacency.

Organizing multiple advancement options and pathways will strengthen teacher recruitment, development, and retention over their careers. Teacher pathways align with intrinsic motivation theory as significant drivers of systemic educational advancement. The sequential paths begin with extensive support, feedback, and guidance toward "earned autonomy." As principals verify increasing classroom competence, teachers achieve greater independence and leadership responsibility.

A teacher's ability to provide quality service to diverse learners is contingent on both mindset and skillset. A teacher's determination can grow a student's skills. Commitment to operate at a high level through perseverance, knowledge, and social interaction strengthens individual agency. Aptitude in personal attributes is not "set" (as was once believed with IQ) but is highly influenced by life conditions. For teachers, the classroom environment and career opportunities are pivotal. Although shaped more substantially at an early age, the agency is a fluid capacity that can expand throughout life.

Motivation theories suggest an innate human tendency to move toward personal betterment. Psychologists Deci and Ryan's Self-Determination Theory associates autonomy, competence, and relatedness as constructs for personal motivation and self-actualization.[18] Pink supported these findings, identifying three motivational components: autonomy, purpose, and mastery.[19] With a campus culture better attuned to teachers' social-psychological essentials, they can amplify personal agency. The Peak Performance Center identified six employee outcomes associated with autonomy (see figure 3.1).[20]

Younger employees change jobs more frequently than did preceding generations. Associated with the Covid-19 pandemic, "the great resignation" saw more than 4 million employees quit their jobs in April 2021 alone.[21] If teachers begin working toward autonomy early in their careers, the average tenure can increase, reversing the downward trend and providing stability for pre-K-12 education. The six residual qualities in figure 3.1 are the very antitheses of complacency. Teacher pathways can act as an incubator to sustain an educator's passion. The continuity and longitudinal experience that stem from extending the careers of inspirational teachers advance students, especially those most at risk of being disenfranchised.

School districts could learn from another public institution: the US armed forces. The military transitioned from the draft (instituted in 1940) to an all-volunteer operation on July 1, 1973. The survivability of an elective military was seriously questioned by opponents, who were later proved wrong. All

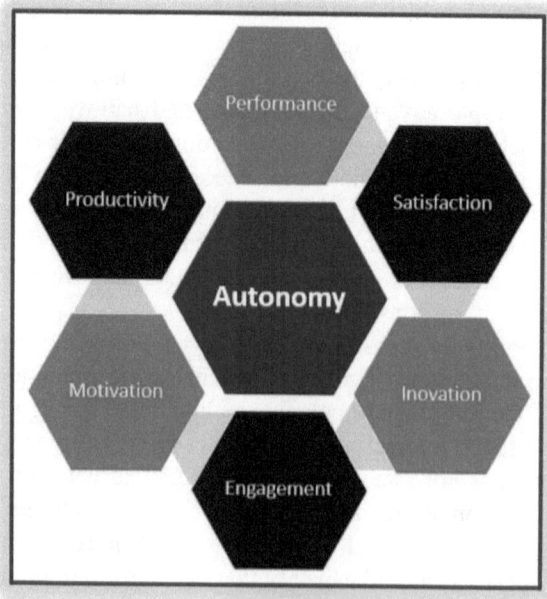

Figure 3.1   Benefits of Autonomy from the Peak Performance Center. *Source*: The Peak Performance Center. (2021). Autonomy improves our performance. Retrieved from https://thepeakperformancecenter.com/business/performance-management/autonomy-improves-performance/.

military branches already had a hierarchal ranking system for progressive authority and responsibility. With a self-imposed imperative for global defense predominance, the government instituted innovative enticements that ensured continuity. Some of the progressive benefits of securing the military's pool of recruits include the following:

- room and board, including meals;
- highly competitive pay and benefits packages;
- enlistment bonuses;
- advanced enlistment rank opportunities;
- tuition reimbursement for semester hours, graduate credits, and credits toward a master's degree or doctoral degree;
- special and incentive compensation to address specific manning needs;
- specialized military schools (e.g., aviation, medical, leadership); and
- retirement benefits after twenty years.

The national concern for a successful volunteer military resulted in enterprising measures for persuasion and stability. Our service members place their lives on the line for their country and deserve every incentive listed above. Parallel anxiety over a diminishing teacher pool should stimulate comparable strategies. Teachers contribute in an equally decisive capacity to promoting national welfare. Multiple reports project that the nation will confront a significantly higher teacher demand in five to ten years. Simultaneously, districts require more employees to hold higher-level qualifications. Like the military's actions, proactive planning in the education arena is necessary to avoid a fast-approaching crisis.

CONCLUSION

Cognitive and behavioral studies lead to a better understanding of motivation. Maslow's ubiquitous hierarchy of needs builds from a base of physiological requirements, then psychological ones, and finally, self-fulfillment. His thinking was modified over several decades, becoming less rigid and recognizing that his pyramid progression is not always linear.[22] Psychologists point out that educational level and social context also impact an individual's inclination toward a particular level. One generally accepted premise is that people move on to higher phases when lower-level needs are met. In our post-industrial society, US citizens have the time and informational access to reflect and grow in more complex personal needs such as self-esteem, cognition, aesthetics, and self-actualization.

Basic human needs, wants, and desires evolve. Some of the physiological, safety, and survival anxieties experienced a few generations ago have diminished nationally, making way for newfound purposes. External influences such as advertising and social media mold an individual's wants and desires, sometimes unconsciously. A preference or desire can become an emotional need, prompting someone toward a resolution to maintain equilibrium.[23] Successful organizations recognize that providing employees with a range of possible career options to advance their aspirations is mutually beneficial.

In some ways, teachers' work environments still resemble Henry Ford's industrialized assembly line. Overdependence on the conformity of rules, instructional dogma, and rigid schedules work against innovation and also sacrifice contemporary teachers' propensities. Educational institutions cannot compete for talent with a growing number of employers offering progressive venues for workers. In reversing undesirable teacher attrition and declining interest from talented prospects, educational leaders must construct an ecosystem that fosters growth and self-fulfillment. Teacher pathways are pivotal cornerstones in this system. Strikwerda cites several pragmatic reasons why organizations should create career paths:

- Retain your best employees;
- Give employees a sense of purpose;
- Attract top achievers;
- Increase the cumulative ability, experience, and diversity in your workforce;
- Create an employee-centric culture; and
- Compete with other employers in your market.[24]

Freedom and personal choice are a hallmark of our national culture. As more individuals spend less time on basic needs, the ambition for self-determination intensifies. Even historically marginalized groups, recently excluded from particular jobs, now explore a more expansive range of career choices. Contemporary work culture, individual mindsets, and employment options differ profoundly from those of a generation ago. Teacher agency, having the "capacity to act or cause change,"[25] is central to a professional resurgence. Authentic teacher dignity and stature emerge by creating the conditions to comply with their nascent motivations. An educational system that recognizes and accommodates the modern teacher's aspirations will be a cornerstone for flourishing schools.

NOTES

1. Ingersoll et al., 2018.
2. Carroll, 2018.
3. Bernazzani, 2021.
4. Al-Bahrani et al., 2020.
5. Downey, 2018, 3.
6. Croft, Guffy & Vitale, 2018.
7. Hendrikse, 2020, 18.
8. Ibid.
9. Garcia & Weiss, 2019.
10. Cornman et al., 2018.
11. McGrath et al., 2019.
12. Feldman & Richter, 2019.
13. Lindsay, Blom, & Tilsley, 2017.
14. Figlio, 2017, 5.
15. "Your Best Employees Are Leaving," 2018.
16. "Teacher Turnover: Stayers, Movers, and Leavers," 2015.
17. "Your Best Employees Are Leaving," 2018.
18. Ryan & Deci, 2000.
19. Pink, 2011.
20. "Autonomy Improves Our Performance," 2021.
21. Hume, 2021.
22. McLeod, 2020.
23. Stosny, 2013.
24. Strikwerda, 2022, 2.
25. Littlejohn & Foss, 2009, 27.

Chapter 4

Embracing Research

> Research is an organized method for keeping you reasonably dissatisfied with what you have.
>
> —Charles F. Kettering, engineer and inventor

Teaching may be an art, but the practice should simultaneously become a burgeoning science, keeping pace with accelerating change. The desire "to sponsor and carry out scientific research for the benefit of humanity"[1] motivated Charles Kettering to establish his foundation in 1927. A renowned inventor holding 186 patents, Kettering believed deeply in the potential of scientific research. The Kettering Foundation continues his legacy as the institution's work has gradually moved toward a "focus on democracy, particularly the role of citizens."[2] Proponents of controlled studies, such as Kettering, have influenced the growth of applied research in government, industry, and universities as a vital agent for progress.

Since gaining credibility during the Enlightenment, the scientific method has enhanced the human condition through systematic investigation in multiple disciplines. A striking irony in pre-K-12 education is that teachers who promote the scientific method are rarely involved in the controlled study of their instructional practices. Teachers continuously learning about learning seems intuitive, but this process rarely occurs, especially in a standardized way.

Teachers should improve their craft through methodical observation, data collection, and analysis of student achievement. The most consequential student group (56.6 million students in 2020) is pre-K-12. Ongoing research should be routine in the institutions responsible for this extensive population's knowledge and skill acquisition. A better understanding of how students learn is the contiguous study of pedagogy. This school-age cohort comprises the most impressionable education group when the capacity for learning and the potential for behavioral guidance is optimal.

In post-secondary institutions (19.6 million college students), research is at the forefront for all faculty members: "publish or perish." Business success is linked to sizable investments in product and market research. Without commercial studies of its customer base, a business is merely guessing at its chances of success. Doctors receive ongoing training for their profession from the latest findings in peer-reviewed studies. To retain credibility among patients, physicians are expected to remain abreast of current medical developments. The medical profession's progress is widely supported by rigorous university studies, Food and Drug Administration stewardship, and the pharmaceutical industry's research. At the same time, however, pre-K-12 teachers have virtually no stipulations to conduct or participate in educational

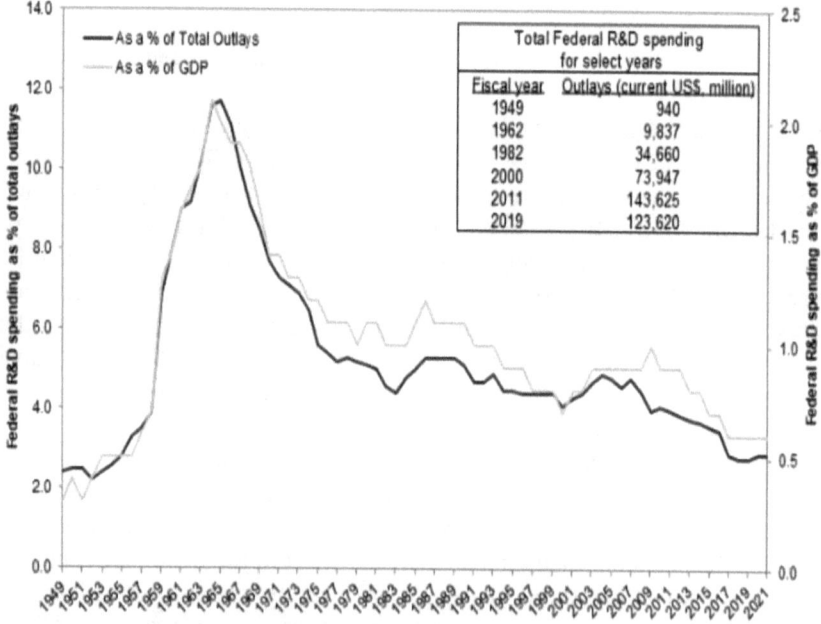

Figure 4.1 **US Federal Government Research and Development (R&D) Spending Percentage of GDP over Sixty Years.** Image produced by ProQuest as part of ProQuest Social Science Premium Collection database. www.proquest.com Image published with the permission of ProQuest. Further reproduction is prohibited without permission. *Source*: Pethokoukis, J. (2020). US federal research spending is at a 60-year low. Should we be concerned? Retrieved from https://search.proquest.com/docview/2400721181.

research. The limited requirements for teachers' annual professional learning fall woefully short of comparable progress using inquiry methods.

Google and Amazon built and maintained their businesses in large part through continuous research. Company leaders have ongoing access to accurate data for millions of products, services, and information about their competitors. Entire departments are devoted to investigating the efficacy of innovative practices or new products. Google supports an entire division dedicated exclusively to artificial intelligence. Amazon surpassed all global companies in research and development (R&D) in 2018 with investments of about 22.6 billion dollars.[3] Successful businesses use strategies derived from R&D, which have demonstrated unquestioned marketing success.

The United States has not sufficiently recognized the need for investment in educational research to spur continued economic and societal progress. Government spending to generate new knowledge and create innovative technology is crucial to collective advancement. Yet the gross domestic product (GDP) percentage for research is the lowest in sixty years (see figure 4.1).[4] Private institutions continue to prioritize R&D funding but focus on areas affecting their bottom line.

Federal spending on R&D reflects national interests. The relative global standing indicates priorities and future competitiveness in select areas. UNESCO's Institute for Statistics annually tracks the percentage of GDP spent on R&D by country. In the most recently reported data, the US government ranked ninth in terms of percentage of GDP outlay (see table 4.1).[5] The current comparative status raises compelling questions about national priorities and their implications over time.

Table 4.1 Percentage Share of the Gross Domestic Product Spent on Research and Development

		Research and Development Expenditures (as % of GDP)	
Rank	Country	Most Recent Year	Most Recent Value
1	Israel	2018	4.95
2	Korea, Rep.	2018	4.81
3	Switzerland	2017	3.37
4	Sweden	2018	3.34
5	Japan	2018	3.26
6	Austria	2018	3.17
7	Germany	2018	3.09
8	Denmark	2018	3.06
9	United States	2018	2.84
10	Belgium	2018	2.82

Source: UNESCO Institute for Statistics, 2021

Countries vary significantly in terms of where research funds are dispersed. The targeted area(s) for research spending is another salient topic for deliberation. Studies in the social disciplines, education included, are criticized for being less robust than those in the sciences. This assessment is a legitimate critique for several reasons. Two impediments are (1) restrictions on using the scientific method with human subjects and (2) a general distrust of recommendations in the social sciences.[6] Fundamentally, the United States has never prioritized educational research at the levels of science, health, technology, or the military.

Educational research in the United States languishes due to a scarcity of funding relative to other areas (see figure 4.2).[7] Federal and state investment in studies is recurrently political, and government control too often serves narrow electoral goals. Research funding is heavily skewed toward the physical sciences (i.e., astronomy, physics, chemistry, and earth sciences). Our nation would serve everyone, not only education, by balancing its priorities. The welfare and well-being of society are correspondingly enhanced through studies in the social sciences, including psychology.

Studies in education primarily investigate student learning, teacher pedagogy, and learning ecosystems. The variables associated with these three

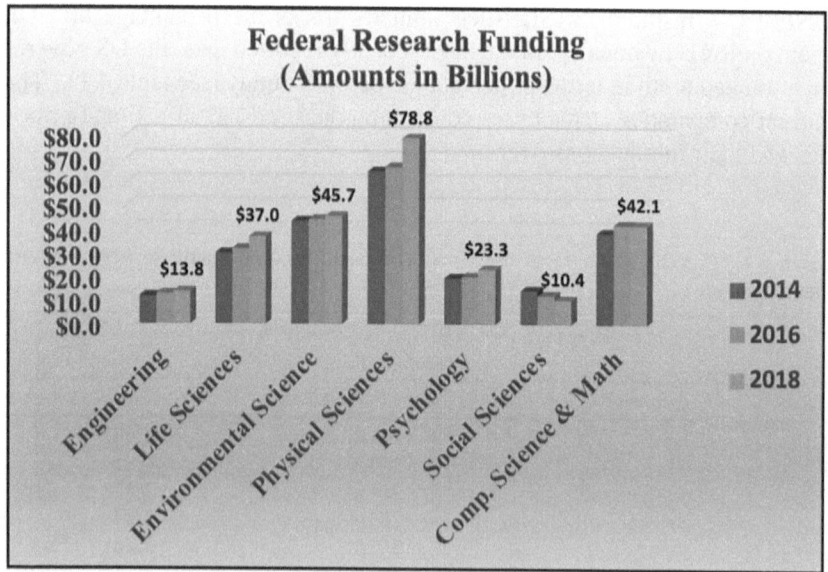

Figure 4.2 Trends in Federal Science Funding, by Discipline. All figures are in billions of dollars for 2015. *Source*: Belluz, J., Plumer, B., & Resnick, B. (2016, September 7). The 7 biggest problems facing science, according to 270 scientists. Vox. Retrieved from https://www.vox.com/2016/7/14/12016710/science-challeges-research-funding-peer-review-process.

categories interconnect with philosophy, psychology, sociology, neurology, and environmental science. Findings in one discipline often lead to advances in another. Although basic research in a discrete field should not be decreased, there is a growing trend for cross-disciplinary research.[8] Ohio State professor Amy Youngs outlines some of its benefits.

- Provides an understanding of complex social challenges and community responses to issues such as climate change, migration, poverty, mass incarceration, and addiction that require a multifaceted approach to solve.
- Combines disciplinary breadth with the ability to collaborate and synthesize varying expertise.
- Enables researchers to reach a wider audience and communicate diverse viewpoints.
- Encourages researchers to confront questions that traditional disciplines do not ask while opening up new areas of research.
- Promotes disciplinary self-awareness about methods and creative practices.[9]

Business and industry frequently cite deficiencies in employee competencies from public school graduates. As they endorse research in their organizations, it would serve their bottom line to champion the same approach in school systems.

Teachers may review a limited sample of current teaching and learning studies in college methods classes. However, undergraduate preparation programs generally do not include courses on *conducting* research practices. Many teachers would welcome participation in research as a personal growth opportunity, but this would require additional time and a supportive culture. A researcher's mindset adds another dimension to a teacher's impact on learning. Teachers intuitively look for motivational tools and instructional strategies. The ideal setting for responsible experimentation is a lab school. The importance of research continues to grow in non-educational professions, as reflected in their increasing budgets. Campus teachers should become part of this invaluable trend because it accelerates progress.

LAB SCHOOLS

A laboratory school, sometimes referred to as a demonstration school, is managed by a university or college. The various purposes of a campus include training future teachers, educational research, open observation, and professional development. Lab schools embrace evidence-based pedagogy. Educators incorporate scientific observation, data collection, and analysis to refine specific components of teaching and learning. The analytical process leads to theories, better-quality instruction, and recommendations for replication in other schools. Clinical student teachers receive invaluable field experience guided by master teachers and professors. These prospective teachers begin their careers by experiencing an investigative growth mindset linked to pedagogy.

Not a recent idea, laboratory campuses have existed since the seventeenth century in Europe and Japan.[10] In 1896, John Dewey opened a laboratory school in Chicago. The University of Chicago Laboratory School continues today as a distinguished pioneer school of the progressive education movement. Dewey believed that his experimental school would initiate a reform movement leading to an enlightened democratic society. However, as conceived by Dewey, problem-based learning experienced pushback from staff. Using experimental practices, creative thinking, and learning by discovery was an exceedingly foreign pedagogy and a problematic cultural change. Frustrated teachers often resorted to practices such as lecturing, explaining, and repetition to convey the desired knowledge and skills.[11]

Most lab schools are private, with universities establishing their demonstration purpose. Some public labs schools operate much like charter schools, with the university providing sponsorship. For over fifty years, under three different names, the International Association of Laboratory and University Affiliated Schools (IALS) has endorsed current and prospective campuses. IALS supports about sixty member schools with various grade configurations. The organization's purpose is described on its website:

> IALS is an international association of laboratory and university affiliated schools engaged in practices of teacher training, curriculum development, research, professional development, and educational experimentation for the purpose of supporting member's schools and as a voice speaking for the improvement of learning for all children.[12]

A collaborative lab campus may have a unique emphasis depending on community demands. Beyond an implicit research commitment, some standard components include the following:

- teacher preparation in an inquiry-based culture under the tutelage of master teachers;
- curriculum development as a result of a controlled investigation;
- professional learning as a result of a controlled investigation;
- scheduled visitation for those interested in replication; and
- opportunity for teachers to earn expanded autonomy.

Ideally, selected campuses are diverse and include economically disadvantaged students. An underlying principle is for lab schools to serve all students with a commitment to equity.

Student Selection Process. Zoned neighborhood students are entitled to attend their home campus if they choose. A lottery should be conducted if the campus is a new district magnet or if additional seats are available for a zoned campus. Lotteries are blind and randomized, but many rules must be established to weigh lottery odds, set percentages, and prepare to defend decisions. Thoughtful discussion of goals and preparing for contingencies are prerequisites for success. Documented procedures are necessary when unhappy parents appeal placements, and they will. Some discerning questions to answer when establishing lottery proceedings include the following:

- What is the entry grade, and will seat openings be available in successive years?
- How will the lottery treat historically disadvantaged students?
- What is the procedure for a waitlist if one is not selected?
- How will siblings of students currently enrolled at the school be considered?
- Will district employees be given special consideration for their children?
- Will out-of-district applicants be given consideration?
- What is the calendar, and when are the deadlines?
- How many district choices will be allowed per family?
- What is the process of moving to second or third choices?

Although this list is not exhaustive, it could assist district departments in designing a maintainable system. Lottery procedures strengthen sustainability if they receive official school board approval.

Teachers should not be criticized for the absence of controlled classroom study nor express opposition to its inclusion. Most campuses and classroom settings are not designed to analyze instructional practices or expand a research mindset. Expanding laboratory schools as an alternative model would increase the efficacy of both teaching and learning. New models in the public sector are viable with state support. The conditions for a newly conceived lab school include organic university partnerships, regulated structures, and an openness to innovation. In addition to generating relevant research for public education, master teachers expand their knowledge, clinical teachers develop in optimal pedagogic environments, and students receive leading-edge instruction.

LAB SCHOOL COLLABORATION OF INSTITUTIONS

Three institutions play contributing roles as partners in operating a lab school, with the possibility of a fourth member. The key players who provide checks and balances include the state department of education, the local university, and the community school district. Under the right circumstances and with a memorandum of understanding (MOU), some advantages may derive from the support of an educational resource company. The working relationship between the campus and higher education faculty is of substantive consequence. True synergy requires a daily presence and communication from both contributors for the campus to realize its purpose.

University professors are sometimes faulted for living and working in ivory tower isolation. Teachers dealing with various classroom issues, limited time, and accountability burdens are criticized for disregarding current educational theory and research. State education departments are often disparaged as an extension of the dominant political party's agenda. Although there is some truth to these denunciations, partiality can be reduced subsequently with a collaborative purpose. Thinking beyond routine work silos with mutual goals can create the necessary focus to revitalize education for the sake of future generations.

The proposed lab model should progressively operate with newly selected staff from day one. Converting an existing campus, leadership, and staff is ineffectual. Even with extensive training, imposing an alien classroom model on an existing group of teachers invites incoherence. The optimal strategy is hiring a pioneering faculty with aligned conviction. An entire year of planning and staffing is worth the investment. The one downside is depleting teacher talent from other campuses for the systemic longitudinal benefits.

State Department of Education (SDE). The success of lab schools begins with the endorsement and support of the SDE. As an authoritative institution, the SDE sanctions the rationale and articulates the student benefits. State validation empowers superintendents, school boards, and university leaders to proceed with some assurance of sustainability. The SDE leadership is also fundamental to coordinating such a consequential educational endeavor. Exclusively focused on student learning, the initiative must be removed from political or commercial influence. By establishing a lab school advisory committee, the SDE brings objectivity in selecting proposals and aligning with the vision.

Unlike previous lab schools, state coordination enhances the project scope. The SDE can utilize their research department and state databases to make broad recommendations. The advisory committee would establish the guidelines for startup grants, decide on allocated resources, and determine a study's continuance. A process of applications for state grants and their renewal safeguard thoughtful planning for dedicated partnerships and worthy research projects.

If a state allocates fifty lab campuses, the grant committee can address a representative balance of investigations with geographic location, grade levels, academic subjects, and local district deficiencies. All state lab schools can develop future teacher talent and offer professional learning. The difference from prior lab campuses lies in the expanse of coordination for unique controlled studies. Individual campuses should investigate a wide range of topics (e.g., neurological development, socialization, motivation), but they all relate to one overarching theme: How can we improve instruction and learning? The committee stewardship of grant approval maintains quality rationales, compelling study designs, and eliminates redundancy in contributing to the initiative's objectives.

If a specific instructional methodology, formative assessment tool, or supplemental software program displays efficacy, the SDE committee can extend the sponsorship or replicate it at another campus. The recommendations from controlled studies may lead to upgrading the state curriculum standards. The initiative may also improve state-endorsed professional learning, target state resources, and validate approved lists of educational vendors' materials. State endorsement and leadership are crucial to remolding public attitudes toward the structure of lab schools.

Local University. The university's laboratory school role includes leadership as a research institution for investigation integrity. Professors assume academic responsibility for study design, correlation with related studies, methodology, unbiased data collection, robust analysis, and recommendations. A prerequisite for university partnership is an established education department that prepares teachers. Grant writing expertise at most universities can also result in funding to sustain faculty members based at the lab campus.

The university's commitment to the partnership is essential to success and sustainability. Daily boots on the ground are expectations for collaboration with teacher-researchers, observation of interaction with students, and conducting valid studies. This author has seen approved grants for campus-university labs degenerate into occasional professor drive-by visits. Having a pre-determined schedule and designated space for university faculty assists in securing an effectual co-partnership.

Local School District. The local school district supports the operational logistics, staff-student recruitment and selection, and budget for the designated campus. The most auspicious and consequential district decision is selecting the principal and leadership team. A University of Chicago study correlated a principal's ability to create a vibrant learning culture with maximum student gains. The decisive components identified for establishing campus culture were (a) instituting systems for supporting teachers to support students, (b) sustaining shared leadership among staff, and (c) monitoring the work of teachers and leaders in the school.[13]

Dynamic principals also attract and retain effective teachers at rates higher than their campus colleagues.[14] Selecting a principal early in the process offers the advantage of comprehensive planning, diligent hiring, and training of an exceptional team. The lead time to work with university staff holds additional benefits: clarifying roles, coordinating schedules, conducting community meetings, and procuring appropriate research tools. Before opening the doors to students, the organizational time invested prepares the innovative culture for success.

Educational Resource Company. In some situations, an educational resource company's participation yields mutual rewards. An MOU is a necessary guarantee of mutual acceptance of the company's role and supports objectivity in the research. Without compensation, the partner company will provide:

- books, tools, materials, software;
- professional training on resources;
- technical support; and
- ongoing adaptation of resources based on teacher input.

Progressive feedback from students and teachers on engagement and achievement establishes a loop for new or revised resource usage. After a designated period of verified significant gains, the state can authorize the company to act as an approved resource vendor. The state could also purchase products at scale and endorse them as free supplemental resources for all state schools.

The company's partnership and investment are a calculated risk. However, the gamble enhances the business's public credibility, while product sanctioning raises its stature. Objective validation of products from a state-endorsed lab school can increase sales. Moreover, successful participation with selected companies potentially stimulates public-private cooperation to enhance student achievement.

Federal Endorsement. With multiple bureaucratic and political constraints, the federal Department of Education (DOE) is at a disadvantage in managing programs with complex and nuanced issues in each state. DOE's influence is invaluable in affirming educational innovation through new structures in a cooperative role. Federal grants support all states and should incentivize and encourage sharing models. The sphere of compelling national leverage also includes promoting success stories, advancing public understanding of research in lab schools, and protecting district equity.

RAISING THE LEVEL OF EDUCATIONAL RESEARCH

Education master's theses and doctoral dissertations are prevalent in universities nationwide. While worthy contributions, these studies tend to be descriptive, limited in scope, and are rarely replicated in different settings. Research advantages in lab schools include superior internal controls, extended observation time, institutional funding, and potentially larger sample sizes. While a university candidate determines a thesis or dissertation topic, in contrast, approved lab school investigations are selected according to their potential to address practical and equity issues.

The state establishes guidelines for an appropriate study in a school setting at designated lab campuses. Parental consent is a prerequisite for student enrollment. Some investigation designs are not suitable for the classroom. For example, double-blind placebo-controlled studies are the most reliable design in science. To eliminate bias, neither the control nor the experimental groups know which is receiving a particular treatment. These "gold standard" study models are difficult to implement in schools for ethical reasons. By design, some deserving students may be denied valuable instruction.

Lab schools are still prudent venues for research without excluding students from promising pedagogic methods. Correlational research procedures can compare participating students to those at other district campuses or in statewide databases. Qualitative and quantitative methods provide a critical lens for reflecting on data. Principals, professors, and teachers can join forces in harnessing practitioner savvy and a critical inquiry thought process. Based on objective data collection and analysis, sensible decisions are made to discard, expand, adapt, or replicate over entire calendar years.

Data-driven instruction is a recent outgrowth of high-stakes testing and accountability in schools. Stemming from policies such as the No Child Left Behind Act, unfortunately, the corresponding implementation cycle was used primarily for test preparation. Lab schools should establish a broader perspective for pre-K-12 teaching and learning as research models. Whole-child development considers the related constructs of memory, executive function, social-emotional learning, engagement, and motivation. With lab schools, teachers at other campuses have a prototype for investigating learning. They are encouraged to utilize an inquiry mindset in approaching their craft. The pervasive goal is to provide teachers with the opportunity for continuous growth and leadership in an evolving educational ecosystem.

Social psychologist Kurt Lewin is credited with introducing the prototype of "action research." His work in the late 1930s promoted "systematic enquiry for all participants in the quest for greater effectiveness through democratic participation."[15] Lewin's process included the discussion of problems with subsequent group decisions for adapted treatment. His methodology is characteristic of an ongoing cycle of fact-finding, critical reflection, planning, and revised action. The typical campus has no infrastructure to conduct research comparable to lab schools. However, exemplar lab school models are paragons other schools can emulate in embracing the ideology of systematic investigation.

Chapter 4

CONCLUSION

Having worked for over four decades in public schools, I have seen too many academic programs implemented using unsubstantiated notions and with crossed fingers. Educational product vendors easily prey on campus principals experiencing accountability anxiety and seeking a panacea. Some companies present "field studies" of their new resources, touting student achievement. I have examined countless internal "research" reports and found most of them to be blatantly biased and self-serving. A product study must be impartial and then successfully replicated with larger populations. Invested public funds should meet higher standards than inflated pseudo-studies. *Controlled* studies must replace rose-colored assumptions and random acts of vendor salesmanship.

Statistical power is the probability that a treatment effect will lead to an expected event (hypothesis test). Successful experiments should achieve a statistical power of 80 percent or better. Consumers want a high degree of certainty that something will consistently work. The confidence level for a predicted seven-day weather forecast is about 80 percent, that an MMR vaccine protects against measles is 97 percent, mumps at 88 percent, and rubella at 97 percent. The probability that Amazon will deliver your package on time is about 96 percent. Raising parental confidence in instructional efficacy and learning in school should correspondingly be linked with ongoing objective research and reliable data.

A dynamic teaching force is indispensable for student well-being, equity, and national progress. However, the teaching profession now operates in a precarious state amid rapid societal changes, severe talent deficits, and limited innovation. In planning for transformation, a rational strategy first articulates attracting and retaining teachers through an engaging work environment. Lab schools led by venerated teacher leaders are central to this nascent vision. Embracing research emanates from a sound philosophy regarding the value and potential of the educational system.

Accelerating the revitalization of education with integrity and equity requires a kinship with the scientific method. Through controlled studies, educators can discern the optimal integration of disruptive tools, such as social media, adaptive learning software, smartphones, gaming, virtual reality, and virtual schools. Lab schools are a rational blueprint for sequential progress. Upper-level master teachers serve as practitioners and researchers in collaboration with university staff. Small-scale pilot studies investigate instructional delivery and student development, building confidence with consistent, replicated results. Lab models generate an inquiry-based culture and facilitate a trusted infrastructure that galvanizes teachers. Beyond the job enticement through leadership positions, teacher-researchers' long-term cultivation elevates the entire profession's stature.

NOTES

1. Kettering Foundation, 2021.
2. Ibid., 2021.
3. "Ranking of the 20 Companies with the Highest Spending," 2021.
4. Pethokoukis, 2020.
5. "Research and Development Expenditure," 2021.
6. Solovey, 2019.
7. Belluz, Plumer, & Resnick, 2016.
8. Bridle et al., 2013.
9. Youngs, 2021, 2.
10. Haag, 2017.
11. Phillips, 2014.
12. "International Lab Schools: Who We Are," 2021.
13. Allensworth & Hart, 2018.
14. The New Teacher Project, 2012.
15. Adelman, 1993, 7.

Chapter 5

Meaningful Teacher Evaluations

> True genius resides in the capacity for evaluation of uncertain, hazardous, and conflicting information.
>
> —Winston Churchill

Akin to citizens assuming their physicians are reputable, students deserve and should expect high-quality teachers. While the former may influence life or death (along with minor ailments), the latter enduringly influences life's quality. Unfortunately, patients fare better with their doctors than economically disadvantaged students do with their teachers. Treatments for a broken arm, a cut requiring stitches, or a middle-ear infection are consistent across races and economics (provided the family has access to medical care). A teacher's contribution is more complex, as it addresses whole-child development. Education has yet to progress significantly in the class divide based on socioeconomic conditions. Receiving a public education and societal readiness are not mutually exclusive.

The potent antidote for educational inequity is value-added teachers. Identifying these teachers is a formidable task for administrators. In my experience, stewarding accurate and reliable teacher evaluations is the most challenging assignment for principals. Principals consistently rate nearly all teachers as effective,[1] even when student performance suggests otherwise. The New Teacher Project's publication *The Widget Effect* found that "less than 1 percent of teachers were being rated as unsatisfactory."[2] District systems provide no adequate control for the widespread inflation of evaluations.

Over the past fifteen years, multiple states have invested in developing and field-testing high-quality, researched teacher assessment tools in order to reform the evaluation process and improve validity. This effort represents progress, but educators should recognize that the instruments are only *one* part of a blueprint for enhancing authenticity. Evaluations will continue to be inflated without additional support systems. School districts often do not acknowledge the powerful influence of personal and social context when assigning a rating. Societal norms such as age, gender, race, and community social standing influence individual judgment (e.g., a teacher is a board member or a school administrator's spouse).

A principal's appraisal training should include reviewing relationships in a social and ethical context. Discussing simulated cases can assist administrators in understanding how to avoid any perception of inappropriate behavior. It is essential to be astutely aware of conflicts of interest relating to favoritism, nepotism, maintaining professional distance, or even grooming teachers for a campus leadership role. Adjusting to altered relationships may require guidance when moving from a teacher to a principal role. In conducting evaluations, it is judicious to avoid any possibility that assumptions about crossing professional boundaries could be made.

Teacher evaluations are a crucial responsibility for all principals. The primary purposes of evaluations are teacher accountability and growth; secondary reasons are related to strategic assignments and leadership roles. Principals will naturally undergo internal conflicts when weighing the ramifications of being entirely fair and objective with self-preservation. Despite the new instruments and training, ratings have changed very little. Kraft and Gilmour's interviews with principals identified four "coping and rationalizing behaviors" that explain their excessively high appraisal scores:

- Time constraints—Lack of time was the most frequent reason for not giving a teacher a low rating. Rating a teacher as being below proficient required intensive amounts of time to document their performance in support of their professional growth.
- Teachers' potential and motivation—Principals felt that new teachers were still learning and that it was unfair to rate them as being below proficient if they were working to improve their pedagogy.
- Personal discomfort—The most challenging part of the job is probably delivering those difficult messages, and not everyone can do that. An unsatisfactory rating could lead to teachers losing their jobs.
- The challenges of removing and replacing teachers—Principals mentioned that they also sought to avoid the "long, laborious, legal, draining process" of evaluating a teacher. They also expressed their hesitancy to initiate dismissals due to fear of having to hire an even lower-quality replacement.[3]

Administrators excel at simulated evaluations using video lessons of unknown teachers. Training occurs in a protected setting with no downside to being objective and honest. Without additional guardrails, principals will persist in taking the path of least resistance when it comes to actual classroom evaluations. Fair and objective evaluations are a cornerstone of transforming the teaching profession despite logistic or social obstacles. Confidence in this component is fundamental to credibility and success. Public acceptance of new systems for teacher pathways, master teachers, and differentiated salaries are predicated on valid evaluations.

Principals must take a holistic view stemming from multiple data sources such as planning, content knowledge, instructional alignment, instructional delivery, student relationships, and classroom culture (domains). Evaluations happen in the context of diverse student populations and differing community expectations. Every teacher has a unique skillset, and diagnosing domain strengths and growth areas helps the principal serve as a competent coach. Proficiency with each phase—observing, recording, and providing feedback—requires objectivity, dedication, and courage.

Ultimately, the principal's credibility and student learning are at stake with every appraisal. Teachers often know their colleagues' appraisal history from informal campus conversations. Master teachers become resentful when undeserving colleagues receive high ratings. Underperforming teachers assume their practice is adequate and become less open to feedback. Over the longer term, teachers desire and deserve to earn respect thanks to the integrity of the appraisal process. Another obligation of a competent principal is to ensure reliable evaluation standards among assistant principals on the same campus.

Controlled collaborative systems can assist educators in better approaching legitimacy in dealing with the challenges of meaningful appraisals. Counteracting the "coping and rationalizing behaviors" described earlier, principals benefit from comparative data, on-campus calibration, and feedback from their supervisors. A cycle for valid teacher evaluations (figure 5.1) aims at a fair and consistent process. The five components include (1) a quality appraisal tool, (2) ongoing calibration training, (3) comparative data analysis, (4) collaborative walk-throughs with coaching, and (5) using multiple measures.

QUALITY APPRAISAL TOOL

The No Child Left Behind (NCLB, 2002) legislation made schools and districts accountable based on state student assessment scores. Race to the Top (RTT) in 2009 extended that accountability to teachers based on varying state percentages of student scores. RTT funding included incentives for developing meaningful teacher evaluation instruments. States worked to refine tools and include student performance as a part of the cumulative score. Other refinements addressed the requirements for appraiser qualifications, the

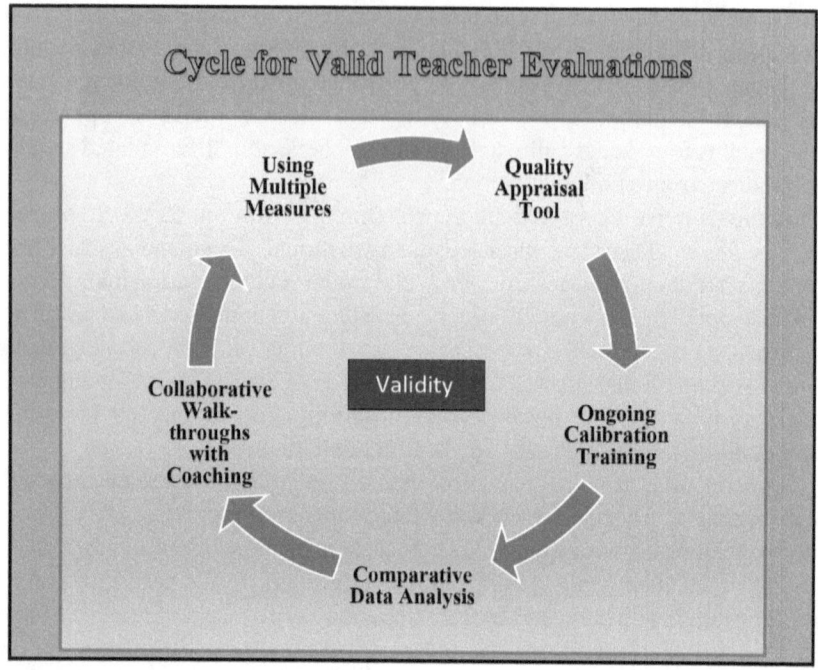

Figure 5.1   Cycle Components for Validity in Teacher Evaluations, Weber, 2022. *Source*: Self-created.

scheduling of teacher observations, methods for collecting data on classroom practice, and incorporating wide-ranging evidence for rating teacher performance. Listed in table 5.1 are the eight teacher evaluation policies recommended in the RTT application.

A 2014 evaluation brief by the National Center for Education Evaluation reported findings derived from interviews with administrators from forty-nine states and the District of Columbia, which included the following:

- States, on average, reported requiring less than half of eight teacher evaluation policies aligned with RTT priorities.
- States reported that teacher evaluation policies were most aligned with RTT priorities focused on using multiple measures to evaluate teacher performance (thirty states), using multiple rating categories to classify teacher performance (thirty-one states), and conducting annual evaluations (twenty-five states).
- States reported teacher evaluation policies were least aligned with RTT priorities focused on using evaluation results to inform decisions regarding career advancement (one state) and compensation (six states for annual salary increases and five states for performance-based compensation).[4]

Table 5.1 Race to the Top (RTT) Teacher Evaluation Criteria.

Design and implement rigorous, transparent, and fair evaluation systems for teachers.
1. State required multiple measures of performance to evaluate teachers in tested and nontested grades and subjects.
Differentiate effectiveness using multiple rating categories that take student achievement growth into account as a significant factor and are designed with teacher involvement.
2. State required a minimum number of rating levels (two) be used to classify teacher performance.
3. State required districts to use student achievement growth to evaluate some or all teachers and specified the extent to which it must factor into teacher evaluations.
Conduct annual evaluations that include timely and constructive feedback and provide teachers with data on student achievement growth for their students, classes, and schools.
4. State required that evaluations of all teachers (probationary and nonprobationary) take place at least annually.
Use evaluations to inform decisions about staff development, compensation, promotion, tenure, certification, and removal of ineffective teachers.
5. State required that teacher evaluation results be used to guide decisions about professional development.
6. State required that teacher evaluation results be used to guide decisions about dismissal.
7. State required that teacher evaluation results be used to guide decisions about compensation (including annual salary increases or performance-based compensation).
8. State required that teacher evaluation results be used to guide decisions about career advancement.

Source: National Center for Education Evaluation, 2014.

The Every Student Succeeds Act (ESSA) of 2015 stepped back from RTT evaluation goals. States were granted autonomy on whether to include student outcomes in ratings. Autonomy was given to innovate, develop, and implement state evaluation systems. In 2015, more than half of all states (twenty-seven) required annual, summative feedback to teachers. By 2019, only twenty-two states maintained this requirement. ESSA failed to address the relevant concerns to improve the teacher appraisals that were fundamental to the accountability movement.[5]

Those states that enhanced evaluation specificity using rubrics made progress in accurately documenting observable behaviors. Rubric descriptions for each domain and sub-domains (dimensions) are concisely articulated on a matrix with varying proficiency levels. With explicit descriptions of observable behaviors, principals can improve consistency and better justify their teacher ratings. Danielson's Framework for Teaching[6] and the Marzano Causal Teacher Evaluation Model are two widely studied and respected observation systems.[7] These prototypes are implemented as the recommended appraisal models in multiple states and utilized in independent school districts across the country. The Danielson rubric incorporates a four-point scale, while Marzano uses a five-point scale. Forty-one states require an evaluation with at least three rating categories as of 2019.[8]

The Texas Teacher Evaluation and Support System (T-TESS) has been the state's recommended system since 2016. After three years of piloting and

Table 5.2 Texas Teacher Evaluation and Support System (T-TESS), Domain 2, Dimension 4

INSTRUCTION DIMENSION 2.4	DISTINGUISHED The Teacher:	ACCOMPLISHED The Teacher:	PROFICIENT The Teacher:	DEVELOPING The Teacher:	IMPROVEMENT NEEDED The Teacher:
Dimension 2.4 Differentiation The teacher differentiates instruction, aligning methods and techniques to diverse student needs. **Standards Basis:** 1C, 1F, 2A, 2B, 2C, 3C, 4A, 5A, 5C, 5D **Sources of Evidence:** Pre-Conference, Formal Observation	• Adapts lessons with a wide variety of instructional strategies to address individual needs of all students. • Consistently monitors the quality of student participation and performance. • Always provides differentiated instructional methods and content to ensure students have the opportunity to master what is being taught. • Consistently prevents student confusion or disengagement by addressing learning and/or social/emotional needs of all students.	• Adapts lessons to address individual needs of all students. • Regularly monitors the quality of student participation and performance. • Regularly provides differentiated instructional methods and content to ensure students have the opportunity to master what is being taught. • Proactively minimizes student confusion or disengagement by addressing learning and/or social/emotional needs of all students.	• Adapts lessons to address individual needs of all students. • Regularly monitors the quality of student participation and performance. • Provides differentiated instructional methods and content to ensure students have the opportunity to master what is being taught. • Recognizes when students become confused or disengaged and responds to student learning or social/emotional needs.	• Adapts lessons to address some student needs. • Sometimes monitors the quality of student participation and performance. • Sometimes provides differentiated instructional methods and content. • Sometimes recognizes when students become confused or disengaged and minimally responds to student learning or social/emotional needs.	• Provides one-size-fits-all lessons without meaningful differentiation. • Rarely monitors the quality of student participation and performance. • Rarely provides differentiated instructional methods and content. • Does not recognize when students become confused or disengaged, or does not respond appropriately to student learning or social/emotional needs.
	STUDENT-CENTERED ACTIONS ←――――――――――――――――――――――――――――――→ TEACHER-CENTERED ACTIONS				

Source: Texas Education Agency, 2016.

study, the rubric was purported to be internally consistent at both the domain and dimension levels.[9] This appraisal tool was selected as an example due to the author's experience converting its ratings to numeric weights. With four domains and sixteen dimensions, the rubric includes five levels of competence: Improvement Needed, Developing, Proficient, Accomplished, and Distinguished. Table 5.2 presents the T-TESS rubric for Domain 2 (Instruction), Dimension 4 (Differentiation).[10]

A quality appraisal tool is crucial for fair, consistent, and justified evaluations. When professional advancement and monetary gains are contingent on evaluations, the specific framework used is scrutinized and subject to criticism. A sanctioned instrument faithfully used protects the principal from grievances. Principals need to feel supported; however, the primary rationale in selecting a quality appraisal tool is its position as the first component for unbiased accuracy.

ONGOING CALIBRATION TRAINING

The calibration process is where appraisers convene to discuss the performance of employees and achieve agreement on performance appraisal ratings.[11] Consistent calibration across a school district is the centerpiece of evaluation accuracy and fairness. Effectively differentiating among high, average, or low performers is a prerequisite for assigning consistent ratings. Reliability across a district clarifies teacher standards and expectations for excellence. The system builds trust and currency from stable implementation if appraiser calibration is successful.[12]

The frequency of calibration training is contingent upon the observation and examination of data. All administrators have required training with the appraisal tools prior to use. Less experienced principals may need frequent refresher sessions. The most stable criteria for revisiting calibration training are comparative data analysis and collaborative walk-throughs with coaching. These two steps counterbalance the inherent tendency to inflate the evaluations of familiar teachers.

Simulated evaluations using videos with group discussion and scoring provide a cursory understanding of the rubric. Because appraisal frameworks often include multiple domains and even more dimensions, internalizing the instrument takes study and practice. As a principal, I needed ten to fifteen scored observations to feel comfortable with the Texas Teacher Evaluation and Support System (T-TESS) appraisal tool. Understanding and mastering the complex instrument is fundamental but does not ensure evaluation validity.

COMPARATIVE DATA ANALYSIS

Unfortunately, most guidance for implementing a teacher's evaluation tool ends after the mandated training. Expecting cogent district calibration from a single preparation session is a miscalculation. When preparing new drivers, a video and written assessment are deemed inadequate preparation before handing over the keys to a car. Licensing includes a state-approved driver education course with minimum hours of driving practice. The analogy is not far-fetched, given teacher evaluations' implicit inflation and career implications. A persuasive stimulus for appraisal accuracy is introducing peer comparisons. Principals have an innate desire to know how they compare or contrast with their mainstream colleagues. In 2018, my department had an opportunity to test this premise.

Comparative teacher rating data were shared during a presentation at a principals' meeting. A slide show exhibited the previous year's group evaluation data. On a scatter plot, principals could see the overall mean and domain rating scores with unnamed schools. Individual appraiser folders were distributed with their campus data to inform them of relative placement. Additional frames showed clusters of schools by performance brackets compared to evaluation data. Without embarrassing any one principal, many experienced an epiphany on calibration.

Using the Texas T-TESS appraisal tool, the hypothetical Smith-Jones Academy example (table 5.3) illustrates the type of data report for enhancing calibration. District and campus ratings are juxtaposed for review using raw scores for the four domains. This sample triggers thoughtful questions because of the apparent statistical anomalies.

This self-created report may appear exaggerated, but the scoring ranges from campus to campus are frequently extensive. I have seen extreme aberrations: for example, teachers rated a perfect 5.0 with a class where students showed no growth. In the Smith-Jones report, three unexpected data points raise questions. Why does an unsatisfactory campus have such high teacher evaluations? Why are the mean campus results significantly higher than the

Table 5.3 Texas Teacher Evaluation and Support System (T-TESS) Calibration Comparison Report

Hypothetical Report—Smith-Jones Academy		
4 Domains / 16 Dimensions	District	Campus
1.1 Standards and Alignment	3.20	4.55
1.2 Data and Assessment	3.05	4.91
1.3 Knowledge of Students	3.16	4.2
1.4 Activities	3.06	3.9
2.1 Achieving Expectations	3.09	4.12
2.2 Content Knowledge and Expertise	3.15	4.61
2.3 Communication	3.14	4.77
2.4 Differentiation	3.04	4.88
2.5 Monitor and Adjust	3.08	4.12
3.1 Classroom Environment, Routines, and Procedures	3.36	4.57
3.2 Managing Student Behavior	3.37	4.68
3.3 Classroom Culture	3.34	4.55
4.1 Professional Demeanor and Ethics	3.53	4.63
4.2 Goal Setting	3.39	4.73
4.3 Professional Development	3.37	4.76
4.4 School Community Involvement	3.45	4.85

Campus Aggregate Score: 4.56
Campus Accountability Rating: Unsatisfactory
District Aggregate Score: 3.24

Numeric Scale Improvement Needed = 1   Developing = 2   Proficient = 3
Accomplished = 4   Distinguished = 5

Appraiser Aggregate Scores
Principal 3.52
Assistant Principal 4.86

district? Why is there such a difference between the principal's and assistant principal's ratings? Unusual circumstances may justify some of these variances, but a review of the campus calibration by appraisers is warranted for future validity.

Principals realizing their actual evaluation position, proximal to colleagues or an outlier, paves the way for improving consistency. With administrators no longer residing in a campus silo, a broader perspective raises the expectation for a coherent rationale behind designated scores. There may be sound justifications for a particular campus having exceptionally high or low teacher ratings. Nevertheless, the district now has another level of transparency. This heightened awareness readies principals for feedback, reflection, and coaching. Principals have appreciatively reported that comparative evaluation data analysis has helped them grow professionally.

COLLABORATIVE WALK-THROUGHS WITH COACHING

Conversations between the district supervisor and campus appraisers are scheduled to examine student data, teacher classroom behavior, the appraisal rubric, and ratings in greater depth. Working together to deconstruct relationships among these factors can lead to more reliable standards. Examination of student data extends beyond state exam passing percentages. Other pertinent indicators include growth measures, student grades, behavior management data, lesson planning, and student surveys. Aggregate data analysis should also delineate according to grade level, discrete subjects, and student demographics.

Collaborative walk-throughs and scripting with the principal and supervisor are practical and efficient ways to improve calibration. Another administrator with no personal connection to the teacher is more inclined to diagnose teacher-student interactions objectively. An immediate superior brings in another layer of accountability. Having the primary evaluator observe instances of a principal executing one of their most critical responsibilities has implications for impending careers. Earnest discussions involving professional transparency assist district leaders in guiding principals' growth by using evaluation tools reliably.

Increased competence with any appraisal tool comes with practice. Emphasis on a more comprehensive evaluation process requires principals to spend enough time in the classroom. Some districts mandate a minimum number of classroom visits to prevent "one snapshot" observation occurrences. Without stipulating an ideal length, instructional observation time is considered by most to be a high-value activity for principals. Many districts follow Elmore's Instructional Rounds model, with teams of administrators concentrating on one problem of practice.[13] Personal growth extends beyond proficiency with the instrument. Administrator time spent in the classroom advances one's understanding of instructional standards, individual students, and the learning culture.

USING MULTIPLE MEASURES

Over the last two decades, states have gravitated toward using test scores and student growth in teacher evaluations. Isolating growth is theoretically an approach thought to be impartial and may appear a justifiable way to evaluate. Skilled instructors have a tangible impact when they move most classes to a higher level. Schools can then accurately identify the best teachers and assign them to highly at-risk students. The problem is that value-added measures in isolation are unreliable, even with subjects such as reading and math that use consecutive-year scale scores. According to Darling-Hammond et al., value-added measure assumes that student learning is measured by a given test, is influenced by the teacher alone, and is independent from the growth of classmates and other aspects of the classroom context. None of these assumptions is well supported by current evidence.[14]

Passing rates from test scores are an even less stable indicator of teacher efficacy. Viewed over time and in the context of specific student groups, administrators should consider testing data and qualitative measures. However, no one instructional facet accurately captures authentic teacher effects. Districts hire principals to lead and make reliable decisions for their campus. As student guardians, elite campus leaders possess the conviction and tenacity to be ethical and consistent with evaluations.

Standardized student surveys of teachers can serve as a relevant component of teacher evaluation systems. Studies of objective student feedback surveys have found a high correlation with student learning gains.[15] A student may spend up to a thousand hours in the classroom with a teacher, compared to a few hours with a principal. Students are overwhelmingly honest and deserve a voice in their education. As an additional component of multiple measures, student surveys contribute to teachers' summative evaluation ratings being fair and comprehensive. In 2019, thirty-one states either required or allowed the inclusion of research-based student surveys as part of teacher evaluations.[16]

Evaluating the complex facets of teacher performance is not an exact science. In "approaching" validity, using multiple measures significantly improves the probability of getting it right. Multi-domain appraisal tools contribute to understand the holistic contributions to student success. Principals must also consider teacher behaviors outside formal classroom observations. More implicit contributions may include parental engagement, after-school tutoring, grade-level leadership, or extra-curricular sponsorship. Another attribute of skilled leadership is incorporating qualitative factors contributing to a campus learning culture.

Teacher evaluation is key to establishing confidence in an elevated teaching profession. Including multiple data sources provides a more insightful context for a teacher's contributions. Additional factors can also be correlated with student outcomes, helping us understand the root causes of variations in achievement. School leadership has historically failed to meet high standards with teacher appraisals.[17] Educators espouse the importance of understanding the "whole child." With more extensive evidence, the same premise applies to teachers.

CONCLUSION

The legitimacy of evaluation scores cannot be overestimated in constructing a new education structure for building teacher professionalism. They provide the basis for personal and professional growth leading to improved performance. Trusted appraisal data is the girder that sustains credible teacher pathways and programs. As the main load-bearing beam, there can be no allowance for group inflation, arbitrary scoring, or personal partiality. Teacher salary, prestige, and student advancement are all at stake. Emphasis is on quality assessment tools and reliability training matters, but the process is incomplete and vulnerable without additional safeguards.

A district cycle for valid evaluations incorporates five components that reinforce consistent campus standards. Principal perception when conducting formal appraisals will always include inconsistency due to human bias. Unwarranted charitable ranking of teachers may result in principals being liked, but in essence, principals are practicing rationalization and avoidance. The strength and stamina to objectively observe, provide feedback, and fairly score instructional delivery do not come naturally to most administrators. A validity cycle provides the reinforcement and collective conscience for district authenticity.

Accurate identification is a prerequisite for placing the most qualified teachers with the highest-need students. Responsibly determining teacher leadership roles, differentiated compensation, and strategic deployment are all contingent on two data sources: student progress and accurate evaluations. The identification system must be accepted and trusted for its impartiality. As principals demonstrate appraisal competence over time, less coaching is required, allowing for greater autonomy.

Winston Churchill's standard of the "true genius capacity" required for evaluations with "uncertain and conflicting information" could be applied to appraisers of teachers. This specific principal responsibility is daunting but also has a maximum educational impact. Recent legislation to discern variance in teacher capabilities has not yielded the desired accuracy. Inflated teacher evaluations persist. Principals are making quality judgments about other public servants' abilities. Campus teachers may be subordinates, but they are also indispensable professional colleagues. Evaluating the essence of a teacher's influence on students over time requires safeguards: systemic assistance for principals. Fair and precise appraisals are possible with checks and balance processes, additional time, and coordination.

NOTES

1. Loewus, 2017.
2. Weisberg et al., 2009, 6.
3. Kraft & Gilmour, 2017.
4. "State Requirements for Teacher Evaluation Policies," 2014.
5. Ross & Walsh, 2019.
6. Danielson, 2009.
7. Marzano, 2017.
8. Ross & Walsh, 2019.
9. Lazarev et al., 2017.
10. Texas Education Agency, 2016.
11. Caruso, 2013.
12. Ibid.
13. Elmore, 2009.
14. Darling-Hammond et al., 2012, 8.
15. Ross & Walsh, 2019.
16. Ibid.
17. Kraft & Gilmore, 2017

Chapter 6

Teacher Pathways

> An empowered organisation is one in which individuals have the knowledge, skill, desire, and opportunity to personally succeed in a way that leads to collective organisational success.
>
> —Stephen Covey

Teacher pathways are an integral element when constructing a succession process for classroom excellence. Losing an incredible teacher is a hardship for any campus. Principals often feel blindsided when teachers leave. I remember the frustration during months of searching for competent replacements throughout the long summer. The following hypothetical example is all too commonplace.

Ms. Garza and Ms. Washington have taught fifth grade in adjacent rooms for thirty-five years. They are recognized throughout the community for their creative and inspiring pedagogy. In May, they jointly announced their retirement to an unsuspecting faculty. Other teachers at the campus are resigning or transferring for various reasons, but they are not "irreplaceable," like this fifth-grade duo. The New Teacher Project (TNTP), defines an *irreplaceable* as a teacher "so successful they are nearly impossible to replace." The study continues, noting that "when an outstanding teacher leaves a low performing school, it can take up to 11 hires to find one teacher that reaches the same level of quality."[1] Similar scenarios occur every year in most school districts.

School districts cannot afford to occupy principal's time continuously contending with staffing dilemmas. A succession plan considers best- and worst-case attrition probability and the appropriate responses. Talent management departments should have timelines and specific guidelines for recruiting, selecting, onboarding, developing, advancing, and retaining teachers. Regardless of these systems, simulating and responding to severe staffing issues becomes unsustainable when the well of prospects is empty. Teacher pathways build the layers of insurance for maintaining instructional quality even in years of drought.

Teacher pathways directly confront the "root cause" of the waning numbers of new teachers. The two main reasons students avoid teaching careers are salary and the opportunity for career development.[2] These concerns have diminished the overall number of education majors, especially among the highest-performing college students.[3] Counteracting this trend, specialized roles with steadily expanded responsibility can create an ecosystem of self-determination. Associating each position with increased status and salary builds a culture of professionalism. Teachers being viewed as education leaders by their peers favorably alters self-perception. A system of earned autonomy creates a more attractive workplace, a desirable portrayal of teachers, and a talent influx.

Enriching programs for personal growth (e.g., master's degrees, residencies, and leadership training) align with prospective responsibilities within teacher career pathways. For example, the pathway outlined in figure 6.1 illustrates a model designed to (a) convey the value placed on teacher

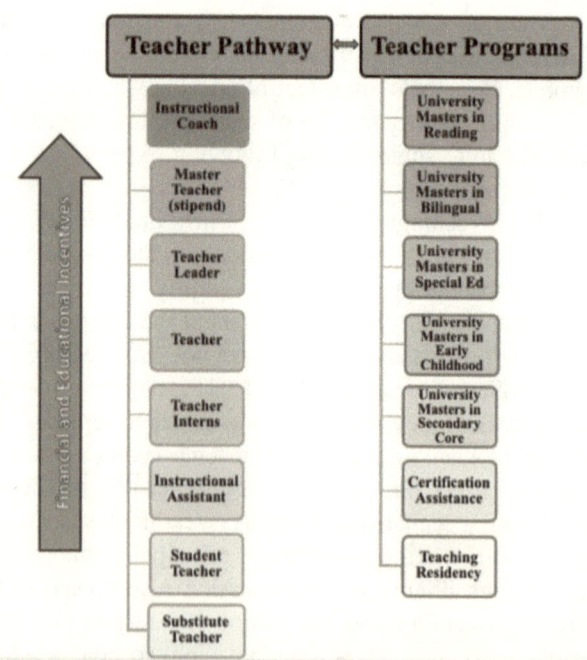

Figure 6.1 Potential District Teacher Pathways and Programs. Weber, 2020. *Source*: Self-created.

leadership through talent investment, (b) build a talented pool of internal teachers, (c) retain current talented teachers, and (d) attract potential external candidates. District communication of a coherent vision assists prospective applicants in their decisions to apply. Sustaining and nurturing the model motivates current teachers to persist in commitment. Over time, support for teacher empowerment culminates in a district reputation that generates loyalty and longevity.

Teacher pathways and programs are analogous to the business model of an organizational chart. Prospective and current educators can vividly visualize career advancement with supportive options for professional growth. Employees understand how roles contribute to the district's overall success and the opportunities to build skillsets for new positions. The talent management website links each role or program with specific details, including job descriptions, expectations, salary, and selection criteria. A congruent principal pathway further expands choices for teachers inclined toward campus leadership. The abstraction of working as an under-compensated second-grade teacher for the next thirty years is diminished and replaced with dynamic career possibilities.

Planning for teachers' succession must consider normal attrition, high-need certifications, and emergencies. More extensive time, energy, and strategies are necessary for recruiting critical-need positions (e.g., special education, secondary math). Updating plans at set intervals is ongoing, as staffing data constantly change. Another salient planning factor is calculating each year's future student enrollment projections. The ultimate goal is the continuity of prepared teacher candidates, ensuring instructional stability for student attainment. Revamping district culture goes beyond filling vacancies and minimizing talent deficits. It works toward a transformational and self-sustaining prototype of progressively upgraded talent.

School districts work with partners to establish the frameworks to grow the quantity and quality of teacher talent. Faculty at local universities are integral colleagues with their programs and research. Resources from state and federal education departments and private foundations are attainable as seed funding for innovative projects. Partnership grant applications from school districts and universities are more persuasive than independent requests from either organization. A collaborative district-university plan addresses external and internal pools, databases, ongoing analytics processes, staff diversity considerations, and campus compatibility. Automated software integrates with human capital management platforms to track pathways and provide reports that enhance efficiency in a talent department.

Articulated requirements for extra time and additional responsibilities assist individuals in making choices for life-work balance. Some roles associated with stipends require negotiation and prorating to encourage the proper equilibrium for teachers. Flexibility and empathy for personal lives reinforce the credibility of a district's mantra of respecting employees. The cumulative establishment of trust leads to earned autonomy and recognition of professional stature.

TEACHER PROGRAMS

Program opportunities for teachers incentivize growth, maintain stability, and develop expertise across all grades and subjects. Tailored to local district needs are master's degree cohorts, clinical teaching residencies, certification assistance, and teacher-leader training. My program model in figure 6.1 is one example, and similar structures have been successful in other districts. Enrollment into any specialized degree or residency is contingent upon funding and the number of applicants meeting the selection criteria. Candidates selected in district-sponsored programs commit to three years of employment post-completion. Combinations of state "grow your own" grants, private foundation contributions, and local funds targeted for high-need campuses can sustain yearly cohorts.

Master's Degrees. Master's degree partnerships with universities address three serious teacher supply issues: high-need certifications, talent retention, and instructional skill development. As illustrated in figure 6.1, the district-supported master's degree programs for reading specialists, bilingual education, and special education help attract and retain teachers. Master's degrees in secondary core subjects like math and science also respond to a fourth issue: the need for dual-credit (DC) teachers. The selection rubric for matriculation weighs experience, evaluations, and student performance data. For most, rewards for completion would be a salary step increase and an enhanced skillset leading toward becoming a teacher leader or master teacher.

Linking training programs to pathways creates a unique model tailored to the necessities of a district. Master's degree programs for non-critical teaching positions are less prudent, but stipends built into the salary structure incentivize additional degrees and certifications. Teachers ineligible for programs can still participate in the teacher pathways. Master teachers are invaluable contributors to student agency in all subject areas. Rubrics to substantiate performance merit will vary; nevertheless, the value of all teachers is communicated across the district.

A primary aspiration for master's degree partnerships is growing capacity in high-need instructional areas. High schools have conspicuous staffing needs. A national movement for expanding DC courses has struggled to find teachers. Eligible high school students who complete DC classes simultaneously receive academic high school credit and college hours for an approved course. Offering DC courses is an equity-based approach to assisting low-income students, but a severe shortage of credentialed DC teachers is the main barrier to success. Increasing the pool of DC faculty through master's degree partnerships expands students' opportunities to transition into college and save considerable tuition expenses.

The degree and course prerequisite policies for teaching DC courses are inconsistent across states but are moving toward raised standards. Greater consistency with instructor qualifications enhances the probability that universities will accept DC courses toward future degrees. Astute districts should think long term and make provisions for teaching degree plans that conform with the imminent higher requirements. The largest DC regional accreditor for high school teachers and college faculty members is the Higher Learning Commission. In 2015, the Commission upgraded its policy requiring instructors to have a master's degree in their teaching specialty, or at least eighteen graduate-level credit hours within that specialty.[4]

Negotiation and agreements with post-secondary institutions guarantee the legitimacy of dual-certified high school instructors and preapproved courses. More students deserve guidance to enroll in advanced classes (i.e., DC, Advanced Placement, International Baccalaureate). Traditional high schools underestimate too many bright students; low expectations and complacency should not deprive them of career opportunities. The prospect of early college credits with rigorous courses generates empowering post-secondary options.

Financial assistance is an inhibiting factor for post-secondary enrollment, with 70 percent of students graduating with loan debt.[5] By reducing this fear, students with dual credits significantly increase their probability of post-secondary graduation. A Columbia University study tracked more than 200,000 high school students and found that "88 percent of dual-enrollment students continued in college after high school, and most achieved a degree or transferred within six years."[6] As a point of comparison, 42.8 percent of all persons between ages sixteen and twenty-four were *not* enrolled in school in 2018.[7] Supporting and cultivating high school teachers' completion of master's degree programs will make DC courses viable and, moreover, expand an educated workforce.

Master's degree sponsorship for early childhood, reading specialists, bilingual education, and special education respond to establishing equity for the most at-risk students. Quality teacher leaders in these specialized roles are the foremost change agents to close achievement gaps and accelerate learning. With universities tailoring some courses for campus needs (e.g., dyslexia, inclusion), these degree programs prepare master teachers for leadership.

Teacher Residency Programs and Internal Staff Assistance. Figure 6.1 includes preparation programs for substitute teachers, instructional assistants

(IAs), and student teachers. Many districts fail to consider the untapped internal talent, lacking only sponsorship to thrive as teachers. With reasonable job accommodations and covering university costs, these employees already have a relationship with the district and demonstrate better retention rates. Conventional partnerships with local universities sponsor verified prospects from these three groups.

Certification assistance is not limited to prospective teachers such as substitutes and IAs. Incentives for current internal and external teachers include sign-on bonuses and assistance with certification costs and preparation. Leveraging teachers in critical-need areas to attain another certification is discussed in chapters 10–12. A two-year promissory commitment to teaching SE, ECE, or bilingual with an option to return to a former position after two years would work to the teacher's financial advantage. Simultaneously, the stability of instruction is reinforced for the campus and students.

Other possibilities for teacher residencies are external commercial organizations. Institutions such as Urban Teachers and the Relay Graduate School of Education expand the scope of intern applicants nationally. Residents enter with bachelor's degrees, then earn master's degrees and certification under the guidance of skilled educators. These programs have solid track records of recruiting skilled and diverse teaching talent. My working collaboration with a Relay partnership was productive in expanding the secondary core teaching pool with above-average retention rates.

Teach for America (TFA) corps has been an alternative certification program supporting high-poverty districts since 1990. My personal experience with TFA has been constructive in recruiting many talented teachers into classrooms. The challenge persists with TFA retention rates and the finder's fee of $3,000 to $6,000 per teacher. Connecting with community partners for financial support and steering TFA employees into teacher pathways helped diminish these issues. TFA has also worked to accommodate districts to prioritize finding teachers in acute-need areas.

PATHWAY ROLES

Pathways are aligned with programs but are not mutually exclusive. An excellent teacher can progress to a teacher leader, master teacher, or instructional coach based on their students' performance and evaluations. The pathway's integrity in assigning expanding responsibility is predicated primarily on the validity of evaluations. External candidates can be considered for teacher leadership roles based on their past student data. In these cases, diligence with background reviews and demonstration lessons improves the probability of auspicious selections.

Substitute Teachers. Creating pathways for substitute teachers is a practical investment. Principals recognize and appreciate reliable and competent substitutes. Many substitutes have college degrees, and others have significant college hours. While state education agencies may only require a high school diploma to serve as a substitute, it is common for districts to set a minimum number of college credits, an associate's degree, or a bachelor's degree as a prerequisite. Principals are best situated to recommend subs. Those exhibiting strong instructional potential and student-centered relationships should be considered for recruitment. Substitutes serving long term during teacher leaves of absence would have applicable student achievement data for additional review.

Working with local universities to establish a certification pathway for vetted substitute teachers contributes to each educational institution. Certain agreements would be necessary to assist a capable substitute toward teacher certification (e.g., MOUs with the university, commitment documents). Assisting with certification and signing on a known quality substitute has a high probability of favorable returns. Most principals prefer to hire someone they have observed working effectively with children rather than an unknown first-year teacher. For the substitute, an opportunity to more than double their income and receive benefits is ample motivation to sign a multiyear commitment to remain with a district.

Alternative Certification Teachers. Nationally, school districts hire about 20 percent of new teachers from alternative certification programs (ACP). ACP provides a path to teaching for someone who has earned a bachelor's degree but does not have a teaching credential. Program design involves a contractual teaching assignment for candidates while simultaneously taking requisite preparation courses.[8] The authorizing institution assigns mentors who observe candidates in the classroom, provide evaluations, and help prospects prepare for compulsory state certification exams. AC programs have increased exponentially, filling the void with reduced college education graduates.

Many of those alternatively certified become outstanding teachers, but the learning curve historically takes more time, and fewer remain in the profession. The quality of alternative certification preparation can differ widely according to the institution. Organizations like the National Council on Teacher Quality (NCTQ) evaluate the integrity of AC programs that provide preservice teachers preparation and publish grades for institutions.[9] Texas alone has over 200 approved alternative teacher certification programs, and some organizations are dubious. Districts expand the credible applicant pool by applying NCTQ ratings, tracking data, and building partnerships with reputable establishments.

A University of Texas study reported that "the odds of retaining a teacher who holds an alternative certification were 14-22% less likely than the odds of retaining a teacher with a standard certification."[10] This hiring supply shift has negatively impacted the turnover rate and instruction quality. The Learning Policy Institute reported a significant teacher turnover discrepancy between ACP and traditional programs at the national level. A report by Carver-Thomas and Darling-Hammond found that teachers coming into the profession through AC programs were 25 percent more likely to leave a campus than those entering through a traditional university certification program.[11]

Apprehensions aside, ACP teachers are necessary for districts to fill vacancies. The current shortages are a byproduct of a failure to elevate the teaching profession. Provider ratings and thorough district screening are acknowledged requisites for ACP hires, but the attrition rates cannot be ignored. Under the guidance of a compensated teacher leader, mentorship can assist new ACP teachers in moving toward an accomplished career. ACP employees benefit even more than traditional education majors with mentors due to their reduced preparation time and field experiences.

Student Teachers. In 2015, the American Institutes for Research reported that "about 80 percent of new teachers complete a traditional teacher preparation program."[12] This critical candidate pool has been diminishing as a primary source for new teachers. Increased diligence in furthering student teaching programs is wise, considering their comparative history with other preparation systems. Student teachers have a higher success rate than alternative programs. A Midwestern Higher Education Compact study found that traditional teacher preparation was superior to ACP in a teacher's instructional knowledge, self-efficacy, and retention at all levels, except for kindergarten.[13]

Considering teacher shortages and the competition among districts for new teachers, cultivating trust and outreach to universities is paramount. Detailed student teacher handbooks, early strategic placement with proven teacher leaders, and ongoing communication will build trust. Personal connections attract student teachers in high-poverty communities who would otherwise be drawn to wealthier suburban school districts. Conversations with university leaders are vital to articulating district needs for coursework alignment. Sharing projections based on historical data will assist universities in guiding more students in need areas. As the Learning Policy Institute reported, many districts reflect national trends in vacancies. With teachers of mathematics, science, and special education, the annual turnover rate exceeded 13 percent. The attrition rate among those teaching English to students who speak other languages is about 19 percent.[14]

Placement criteria with teacher leaders mentoring student teachers must be purposeful and consistent. The campus principal must endorse the teacher leader and provide guidance. University supervisors appreciate the thoughtful placement of their graduates and school district support. Most importantly, the district earns the reputation of furnishing a high-quality clinical experience for student teachers. To reinforce this level of excellence, it is also appropriate for the teacher leader to earn a stipend for expert mentoring.

Socializing student teachers as part of the district's educational community is a rational recruiting strategy. A welcoming orientation, classroom visits by administrators, and a celebratory lunch near the end of an assignment are a few possibilities that would promote a familial district ecosystem. Talent departments working with the university to set up mock interviews help build student confidence. Some districts hold early job fairs and invite student teachers to interview directly with principals. Based on attrition projections, offering initial teaching contracts to mid-year graduates serves school systems, particularly in acute-need areas.

Engaging in creative activities and events can foster a deep connection between student teachers and the district. Frequent reassuring communication and hosting social gatherings are worthwhile investments. If particular events work well, they are easier to replicate in future semesters. Some student teachers will be recruited for clinical intern positions, but all student teachers must be nurtured as candidates for district positions. Over time, the district's reputation for professionalism and encouragement will spread and create a reliable conduit for the recruiting pipeline.

Instructional Assistants (IAs). Texas only requires that an IA earn thirty college credit hours. Most individual districts require more than the state minimum, and after reviewing my staff data in 2016, I was surprised by the findings. More than 100 district instructional assistants had earned bachelor's degrees, and many were close to completing a degree. These experienced employees emerged as natural candidates for pathway inclusion. Supporting a skilled IA toward teacher certification warrants certain agreements (e.g., MOUs with the university, commitment documents). Like proven substitutes, assisting with certification and hiring a known, quality IA is a safe decision. With a minimum-size cohort, universities will work with districts to be flexible in scheduling and sometimes offer reduced tuition.

An additional benefit from the investment is that most IAs work in higher-need areas (e.g., early childhood, special education, and bilingual education). Hence an IA becoming a successful teacher is even more viable than the pathway available to substitute teachers. Seasoned assistants have a practical understanding of demanding classroom responsibilities. Some experienced IAs have an in-depth knowledge of instructional methods and resources. An IA could double or triple his or her salary, while the district reaps the reward of its commitment to a high-need position. Veteran IAs enjoy another incentive: they have already invested eligible time in the state retirement system.

Clinical Teaching Interns. The conventional path to becoming a teacher is to progress through a bachelor's program in education and student teaching for one semester. California's requirement of 600 hours is almost double that of other states, which is equal to two full semesters. Most student teachers pay full-time tuition and perform unpaid campus duties; moreover, some colleges prohibit them from holding an outside job. Regrettably, completing a non-education degree and becoming a teacher through alternative certification is financially advantageous. Reacting to the teacher shortage and the declining number of education majors, some states offer support for student teachers as a mitigating strategy. A full-year clinical teaching internship is a superior option for students and districts.

In 2018, the Texas Education Agency made a regulation revision allowing local districts and universities to substitute the one-semester student teaching requirement with a full-year paid teaching internship. The San Antonio Independent School District (SAISD) leveraged instructional assistant funding to create high-need clinical intern positions the following year, subsequently retaining those teachers. The model implemented by SAISD cited several advantages:

- financial support for the intern (salary of $25,000);
- extended preservice experience with a high-quality mentor teacher leader or master teacher;
- higher quality initial instructional support for students;
- three-year commitment to teaching in a high-need position; and
- savings with new teacher onboarding (about $21,000 for an urban district).[15]

Examples of innovative student teacher incentives are being explored across the nation. Indiana created stipends in 2020 for student teachers in special education and secondary math or science up to $4,000.[16] Oklahoma decided to use $12.75 million in federal relief funding to pay eligible Oklahoma student teachers for their work in 2021–2022 through 2023–2024. This program provides an estimated 1,300 student teachers up to $3,250 in payments each year.[17] The Arizona Teachers Academy initiative offers student teachers full-tuition scholarships and access to post-graduate induction services. In return, "academy-funded educators commit to teaching in an Arizona school, public or charter, for as many years as they received funding."[18]

Other isolated state-district initiatives like those above demonstrate a willingness to pilot creative ideas. While helpful, more is necessary to reverse an unrelenting teacher shortage. For sustained progress, unambiguous structures send a compelling message of valuing teachers. Clinical teaching interns can effectively replace current instructional assistant positions. Roles typically include critical-need areas such as early childhood, special education, or bilingual education. Benefits are evident for both the clinical teaching interns and the district.

Expanding cohesive, compensated clinical teacher pathways to secondary positions offers the benefits mentioned above: incentives, quality mentorship, addressing critical needs, and retention. Monitored data help to ensure cost-effectiveness and academic efficacy. An eventual transition from student teaching to full-year internships for *all* education majors could be a catalyst for transforming the teaching profession. The advantages described in the SAISD pilot could work to reduce barriers and strengthen the continuity in motivating and preparing teachers.

Teacher Leaders. Teacher leaders serve as department chairs, community outreach liaisons, campus committee chairs, or mentors for new teachers. Elementary reading specialists can serve as grade-level chairs and deliver professional development in teacher leader roles. Other teacher leaders could receive stipends for serving as coordinators for a multi-tiered system of support or as college advisors for high school students; the possibilities are extensive. The positions are part of a merit-based ladder encouraging a growth mindset and collaborative support for students. Leadership responsibility is rewarded with expanded pedagogic autonomy and financial compensation.

A teacher or teacher leader may hesitate to consider pathways and programs due to competing personal events. Flexibility and empathy for private lives reinforce the district's principle of respecting teachers. As individuals progress through unique stages and life changes (e.g., working on a degree, illness, pregnancy, military service), adjusting for individual needs strengthens a healthy campus culture. Being adaptive offers room for teachers to accept degrees of responsibility. Provided a teacher is effective with students, short-term accommodation equates to long-term loyalty.

District and campus administrators instill a culture whereby all teachers are leaders, and continual personal growth is expected. Supervisors work to promote the value of individual professional learning. Pathways can reinforce career pride and help shape attitudes for advancement. Each level can build new skillsets and confidence as teachers explore finding professional satisfaction and personal agency.

Master Teachers (MTs). Master teacher programs are a more recent approach to teacher recruitment, retention, and instructional productivity. An MT initiative conforms with motivation theory and endorses raising the stature of the teaching profession. This expert level is the apex for those desiring to preserve their work with students while serving as esteemed instructional leaders. An MT who is eligible for the uppermost compensation and autonomy focuses on mentoring interns, imparting effective pedagogy, and conducting research. (I elaborate on the diverse roles of campus MT in the next chapter).

Instructional Coaches (ICs). ICs appear in both the teacher and campus leadership pathways. ICs have greater leeway to follow their talents and passion as an integral connection between principals and teachers. As stated in the previous chapter, an instructional coach's purpose is to provide teachers with on-site coaching and job-embedded professional development. Serving as a coach is an incredible content growth opportunity, especially when working with multiple grade levels and subjects. Coaches serve by guiding teachers with demonstration lessons, collaborative planning, and student data analysis.

The sourcing for coaches is both internal and external. A distinct advantage in selecting from the internal teacher pool is familiarity with a candidate's skillset. Principals are ideally positioned to identify teachers with the instructional acumen, interpersonal finesse, and organizational capability to thrive as a coach. While MTs guide prospective educators and supervise research, ICs mentor current teachers. For a successful MT, moving to a coach position should be a seamless transition of responsibilities.

Retired Teachers. Retired teachers are not a part of the pathway model. However, they can notably contribute to the broader district teacher succession plan. One strategy to address shortages and long-term absences is to create a priority substitute pool of retired teachers at a higher daily compensation rate. The implementation may require legislative changes because of differing state statutes for retirees. A rigorous reentry standard is necessary for such a program to be effective. Criteria could include a set threshold on past teacher evaluations and student performance data.

Bringing back retired teachers is becoming a more common practice in districts with high numbers of vacancies. Endorsed by superintendents, several states, including Illinois, have recently worked to relax some restrictions for retired teachers to counter severe shortages.[19] Districts should limit hiring retired teachers to those with exemplary records and those who can teach high-need subjects. Allowing veterans to return to the classroom without penalty for their retirement is educationally and economically sound. The state could allow a percentage of positions based on enrollment, geography, and demographics. Reinstating former teachers is a temporary solution for school districts but far better than a scenario where student learning stops or regresses with rotating or less capable substitutes.

CONCLUSION

The inherent premise behind the pathway structures is to enhance motivation to become and remain a teacher. Bolstering future generations' aspirations to enter the profession correspondingly promotes the public perception of teachers. Numerous psychologists have formulated theories of motivation to explain certain aspects of human incentives to achieve (e.g., Maslow, Vroom, Locke). Some combination of intrinsic (satisfying human needs) and extrinsic (rewards or penalties) factors prompts individual actions. Elements of each are embedded in the pathway model to empower and reward teachers.

Upgrading the repository of teacher talent is inextricably linked to an ecosystem where job satisfaction is prevalent. Teachers drive student success, and empowered teachers enrich the school system. The desire to become a career educator proliferates when the essential monetary and psychological requisites are systemic. This chapter's epigraph, Covey's endorsement of an "opportunity to personally succeed," applies to teacher pathways and "leads to collective organisational success." One of Covey's most referenced habits, "begin with the end in mind,"[20] is, in this context, a remarkably inspiring school system.

NOTES

1. The New Teacher Project, 2012, 2-4.
2. Croft, Guffy, & Vitale, 2018.
3. Hargreaves & Fullan, 2012.
4. "Criteria for Accreditation," 2022.
5. TheBestSchools Staff, 2020.
6. Fink, Jenkins, & Yanagiura, 2017, 1.
7. Hanson, 2022.
8. DeMonte, 2015.
9. "NCTQ Databurst," 2020.
10. Reyes & Alexander, 2017, 5.
11. Carver-Thomas & Darling-Hammond, 2017.
12. DeMonte, 2015, 4.
13. Jang & Horn, 2017.
14. Carver-Thomas & Darling-Hammond, 2017.
15. Weber, 2021.
16. "Student Teaching Scholarship for High-Need Fields," 2021.
17. "OSDE Using $12.75 Million in Relief Funds," 2021.
18. "Arizona Teachers Academy," 2021, 1.
19. Vercelletto, 2019.
20. Covey, Collins, & Covey 2020, 8.

Chapter 7

Master Teachers in Distinctive Roles

> Teaching is a noble profession because it is the mother of all professions. Teaching should be ranked alongside other professional fields such as Law, Engineering and Medicine among others.[1]
>
> —Ann Oparah, educator

Like numerous other educators, I fondly remember specific inspiring teachers. With no previous interest in English Language Arts (ELA), Mrs. Sprandle was, by serendipity, my ELA teacher as a junior and senior in high school. She had a charisma that excited her classes about writing and literature. Motivated to extend my time with her, I also enrolled in her elective Shakespeare course. Mrs. Sprandle was near retirement, petite five-feet tall, with wide glasses and a theatrical voice. I was an average, quiet student primarily interested in music.

She kindled my curiosity to explore new boundaries. Embedded in my memory is a paper I wrote on Iago's motivation for malfeasance in *Othello* and memorizing soliloquies from *Macbeth* and *King Lear*. Previously, I tolerated my ELA classes and cared little for writing. Her exemplar model as a master teacher helped alter my thinking about education and profoundly influenced my decision to attend college. Incidentally, serendipity was one of Mrs. Sprandle's "words to know."

Some teachers have a gift for connecting with and engaging students. Thompson describes "turnaround teachers" as those with the capacity to nurture potential, instill resiliency, and encourage a desire to pursue goals. She writes that a prerequisite to teaching for a growth mindset is having one.

> When they exhibit a growth mindset, they're more likely to establish high expectations for students, make instruction engaging and offer extra help when

necessary. Unlike individuals who convey fixed mindsets, teachers with growth mindsets genuinely believe each of their students is capable of learning the covered material, and they use strategies to unlock hidden potential.[2]

Turnaround teachers in the proposed pathways of this discourse are labeled "master teachers." They may teach different grade levels or subjects, but their commonality is competence, respect, and influence as teacher leaders. Master teachers (MTs) possess and instill a growth mindset and ownership of learning. Occupying the pinnacle of professional progression, two categories of MTs contribute to the envisioned ecosystem: pedagogue and researcher. Both the art and science of instruction are represented in this teacher echelon.

MASTER TEACHER AS PEDAGOGUE

The largest consortiums of MTs are the pedagogues. Their prototypical contributions are twofold: (1) working with the most at-risk students and (2) mentoring developing teachers. Many will perform these assignments simultaneously. New teachers initially perform more successfully when they student teach with an effective teacher mentor.[3] Student teachers, clinical interns, and beginning teachers can accelerate their progress when learning from a MT.

The initial and most requisite assignments are the premier practitioners. In alleviating teacher shortages, the pool for MT pedagogues must be more extensive than for researchers. Furthermore, few teachers entering the profession are trained in conducting studies or expressing interest in that area. Recurring reasons for becoming a teacher include a desire to work with young people, being of service, material benefits and security, time compatibility, enthusiasm for creativity, the ability to influence others, and even the desire for authority.[4] Notably absent as a motive for teaching is "contributing to a body of knowledge about instruction and learning." Cultivating interest and aspiration to become an MT researcher will take time and community inculcation.

In the core subjects (reading, mathematics, science, and social studies), MT pedagogues are scheduled to work with the most at-risk students on campus. States identify precise criteria for students identified as at-risk of dropping out of school (e.g., retained, failing multiple subjects, limited English, homeless). However, campuses are best equipped to determine student needs and placements. The MT program endeavors to re-engage, motivate, and close learning gaps through optimal teacher-student alignment and scheduling. MTs certified in special education and bilingual education work to challenge historically marginalized students. Exceptional MTs in the arts, foreign languages, career and technology, and other subjects set high standards of excellence for all students.

San Antonio Independent School District (SAISD) Program. SAISD instituted a Master Teacher Initiative (MTI) in the fall of 2017, designating approximately 270 master teachers to work with at-risk students. By the fall of 2019, the number had neared 600. Student performance data from the Measures of Academic Progress (MAP) and the State of Texas Assessments of Academic Readiness indicated encouraging gains for students working with the MTI. The innovation may have been a significant variable in SAISD moving from a state rating of F in 2016 to a B in 2019.

SAISD's MTI, designed to build instructional equity and improve student performance, was first launched in the district's lowest-performing schools by identifying, recognizing, and rewarding high-quality teachers. SAISD supported accelerated teaching and learning experiences with model classrooms and resources for selected MTs. Each campus submitted a master teacher plan to address unique needs and goals. After plan approval, principals were allowed to interview and hire a designated number of sanctioned MT candidates.

MTs received supplemental compensation in their monthly paychecks, with principals signing off on work time. Stipends had two components: (1) employment for additional days and (2) extended instructional time during the school year (estimated at an additional five hours per week). The system allowed flexibility in prorating time and days for individual circumstances. Scheduling accommodations for personal life situations were positively received and appreciated by MTs.

MTI stipends were financed from a five-year Teacher Incentive Fund (TIF) grant and local budget resources. While making some modifications throughout the grant period, the initiative's fundamental structure remained intact, with MTs positively influencing student growth. The dilemma, like many auspicious initiatives, is fiscal sustainability. SAISD was fortunate to have a funding segue with the state Teacher Incentive Allotment (TIA) discussed in the subsequent section.

SAISD's decision to select high-performing teachers *prior* to the school year for performance-based stipends has advantages. This approach is preferable to rewarding campus individuals at the end of an academic year, the predominant practice with TIF grants. The standard TIF model has districts dividing allotted award funds at year's end if a campus meets articulated goals. Post-performance monetary distribution decisions often raise questions of discrepancies between campuses, suspicions of favoritism, and jealousy among staff members.

Years earlier, as a middle-school principal, I was tasked with distributing ex post facto TIF bonuses of different amounts to staff, including custodians and cafeteria workers. Such decisions are arbitrary and sometimes made after receiving a previously undetermined award. In my experience, teachers perceived advanced vetting of MTs with well-defined criteria and providing a stipend for additional time as fairer. MTs also realized that stipends were not a property right. Continued MT designation was contingent upon credible performance and principal recommendation for the following year.

Texas Teacher Incentive Allotment (TIA). The TIA was initiated in 2019 to incentivize exemplary teachers with the opportunity to earn a six-figure salary. A primary TIA objective is to retain highly effective teachers at traditionally hard-to-staff schools. The program was established by House Bill 3, a comprehensive public school funding bill ratified by the 86th Texas Legislature. TIA established three progressive levels of teachers with increasing allotment ranges:

- Recognized—Allotment: $3,000–$9,000; Average = $6,181.
- Exemplary—Allotment: $6,000–$18,000; Average = $12,576.
- Master—Allotment: $12,000–$32,000; Average = $22,537.[5]

State biennium funds allocated for TIA were $86,642,177 for the fiscal year 2022 and $187,227,013 for the fiscal year 2023. The anticipated number of TIA teacher designations for 2022 by level was 1,427 master, 2,587 exemplary, and 3,125 recognized teachers. Projected TIA designations for 2023 were 3,455 master, 5,867 exemplary, and 5,631 recognized teachers.[6]

Teachers are approved for TIA awards through two different sanctioned methods. Any teacher in a Texas district earning National Board Certification (NBC) is eligible for the recognized status. The second selection option is when a local district's teacher designation system is accepted through a multi-step application process with the Texas Education Agency (TEA). No district limits are set on the number of teacher selections with either application procedure. TEA contracted with Texas Tech University to monitor the quality and impartiality of local teacher determination systems.[7]

With initial study funding from the Carnegie Foundation, the National Board for Professional Teaching Standards began issuing NBC designations in 1994. Over two decades of research have shown that NBC teachers positively impact student achievement. Thirty states have implemented policies encouraging teachers to pursue certification in response to these favorable studies. The National Board Resource Center at Stanford University reports that NBC has also helped with teacher retention, developing teacher leaders, and building communities of learners pursuing excellence.[8]

Teachers can earn board certification in twenty-five areas across sixteen disciplines from pre-K through grade 12. After course study, standards are assessed on four components: Content Knowledge, Differentiation in Instruction, Teaching Practice and Learning Environment, and Effective and Reflective Practitioner. The total cost of certification is $1,900, and teachers must complete maintenance of certification every five years.[9] Starting in 2019, Texas school districts could request fee reimbursement from TEA for their NBC teachers who attained certification, renewal, or certification maintenance. Promoting the NBC program is warranted and, with district incentives, optimistically will expand beyond the current 1 percent of TIA teachers.

TEA used layered formulas (see table 7.1) to incentivize teacher procurement and retention in hard-to-staff schools, specifically rural and high-poverty areas. House Bill 3 in 2019 established economically disadvantaged census blocks with five tiers, assigned funding weights to each tier, and required an annual review of the census block data. The state department recognized that national guidelines for poverty are antiquated and overly broad. Federal Title I funding distribution offers no nuance for degrees of poverty. Equal funding for rich and poor schools does not translate to fairness for student needs. TIA utilized the TEA tiers for district funding, with rural and highest block schools receiving additional weights.

Almost all (99 percent) approved TIA teachers were recommended by local district systems with data validated by Texas Tech University. After the first two years, the initiative designated 4,610 teachers, 1.2 percent of all state teachers (see table 7.2). The multiplier's effect on stimulating teacher procurement in low socioeconomic and rural districts is inconclusive. The proviso for determining "success or failure" is impossible without a reference for comparison. A total of 40 percent of all approved districts were classified as rural, and Title I campuses with NBC teachers comprised 43 percent of campuses. With such an established baseline of data, the time is opportune for targeted goals and revised strategies toward defined objectives.

Table 7.1   Possible Funding Amounts at a Glance, reproduced from the TEA website. The maximum allotment funding amount is $32,000, and the highest student tier level is 5.

Designation	Base	Multiplier	Tier Student Point Value	Non-Eco-Dis X 0	Tier 1 X 0.5	Tier 2 X 1.0	Tier 3 X 2.0	Tier 4 X 3.0	Tier 5 X 4.0
Recognized	$3,000	$1,500	Non-Rural	$3,000	$3,750	$4,500	$6,000	$7,500	$9,000
Recognized	$3,000	$1,500	Rural	$4,500	$6,000	$7,500	$9,000	$9,000	$9,000
Exemplary	$6,000	$3,000	Non-Rural	$6,000	$7,500	$9,000	$12,000	$15,000	$18,000
Exemplary	$6,000	$3,000	Rural	$9,000	$12,000	$15,000	$18,000	$18,000	$18,000
Master	$12,000	$5,000	Non-Rural	$12,000	$14,500	$17,000	$22,000	$27,000	$32,000
Master	$12,000	$5,000	Rural	$17,000	$22,000	$27,000	$32,000	$32,000	$32,000

Source: Teacher Incentive Allotment, 2022.

Table 7.2 Texas Teacher Incentive Allotment (TIA) Distribution

School Year	State Teachers	TIA Teachers	TIA Distribution Percentage	Recognized	Exemplary	Master
2019–2020	363,121	3,976	1.10	2,449	1,100	427
2020–2021	369,395	634		317	224	93
2-year Total		4,610	1.20	2,766	1,324	520

Total TIA Districts (from TIA District Map)

Total Texas School Districts	TIA Districts	Percentage	Rural	Selected %	Non-rural	Selected %
1029	240	2.3	106	44	136	56

TIA National Board-Certified Teachers

	2019–2020	2020–2021	2019–2020	NBC Totals
Rural Campuses in Texas < 2000 & < 20%				
Number at Rural Campuses	32	16	32	48 (11.3%)
Number at Non-rural Campuses	283	93	283	376 (88.6%)
Total	315	109	315	424 (100%)
Title 1 = Poverty Level over 40%				
Number of Title 1 Campuses	121	62	121	183 (43%)
Number of Non-Title 1 Campuses	121	62	121	183 (43%)

Source: Texas Education Agency, 2022.

The progressive strategy by TEA to ameliorate the teacher shortage is commendable. Although the program launch has been underwhelming, TEA deserves some latitude given the severe education disruption due to the pandemic. TIA's innovative approach seeks long-term education solutions by incorporating the researched NBC option and innovative frameworks. The program also considers Self-Determination Theory constructs of autonomy, competence, and relatedness to intrinsically motivate teachers.[10] With TIA's unrealized potential, the hope is for TEA to anticipate the capricious politics of state governance with the next legislative session.

In 1984, Texas' HB 72 established a four-step career "ladder" for public school teachers and librarians. Selected for a level-three teacher bonus in 1990, I was motivated to invest extra time to advance my career. Long story short: level four never materialized, and the career ladder was abolished in 1993, due to insufficient state and local funding. TIA is more fully developed than its predecessor almost forty years ago. Hopefully, history will not repeat itself, and overseers understand they are beholden to the inclinations of state governance. Preparing for the inevitable questions when budget debates commence is essential. Continuous data collection, student progress monitoring, transparent evaluation reports related to objectives, and pragmatic program modifications will place TIA in a position to justify the continuation of its worthwhile endeavor.

Talent Transfer Initiative (TTI). The US Department of Education released a two-year study of a master teacher model involving ten school districts. The TTI pilot program provided stipends to high-performing teachers, matching them with struggling campuses. TTI successfully attracted value-added teachers, and students exhibited growth for both years in reading and math (more significant in the second year):

> The Talent Transfer Initiative (TTI), used in districts across the country, offered $20,000, paid in installments over a two-year period, to the highest-performing teachers if they transferred into and remained in designated schools with low average test scores. This program successfully attracted high-quality teachers to low-performing schools, had a positive impact on elementary student tests scores and on teacher retention rates during the payout period, according to a 2013 study.[11]

Sign-on bonuses, stipends for high-need subjects, and stipends for low-performing campuses can serve as temporary remedies. Competitive shifting (e.g., removing excellent teachers from Brooklyn to help Harlem) is not a sustainable staffing formula for education. The TTI met the primary objectives of the pilot studies. However, only 5 percent of teachers offered the incentive chose to transfer to lower-performing schools, and "retention in these schools returned to the status quo once the two-year incentive period ended."[12] Although the initiative provides some promising model features, long-term success requires a stable funding source.

Opportunity Culture Initiative (OCI). The OCI program was first piloted in the Charlotte-Mecklenburg School District (CMS) in Charlotte, North Carolina. In this program, high-quality teachers are responsible for more students. "Teachers who have demonstrated effectiveness with student learning are named 'multi-classroom leaders'— they lead a teaching team, provide on-the-job coaching to their teachers, and still do some teaching themselves."[13] These teacher leaders produced learning gains equivalent to those of teachers in the top quartile in math and nearly that in reading.[14]

Since piloting in CMS, Opportunity Culture has expanded to ten states and thirty-eight different school districts. The initiative's website offers models, funding sources, case studies, and multiple resources.[15] A report by the American Institutes for Research and the Brookings Institute included 15,000 students and approximately 300 teachers and reviewed data for CMS, Cabarrus County Schools, North Carolina, and Syracuse (New York) City School District:

> Students' math gains were statistically significant in all seven of the researchers' statistical models. Reading gains were statistically significant in six of the seven models. The researchers' findings indicate that gains in Opportunity Culture classrooms were substantially higher than those in schools with no Opportunity Culture roles, and in Opportunity Culture schools prior to the implementation of these roles.[16]

Participating principals have reported improved teacher retention rates along with student achievement gains. This model, where MTs lead teams of their colleagues and earn additional pay, has demonstrated considerable potential for education systems. Reflecting the program's appeal, in 2018–2019, Chicago Public Schools, the nation's third-largest school district, began implementing Opportunity Culture models.

PHASE-IN FOR LONG-TERM EFFICACY

Over an extended career, I have worked under ten different superintendents and observed frequent leadership changes in other districts. The average tenure for a school district CEO is three to six years, depending on the state and district size.[17] The brief leadership incumbency, coupled with immediate accountability expectations, often works against long-term system progress. Superintendents realize their grace period is fleeting. Intense energies are commonly exerted to improve state test scores, raise graduation rates, and maintain school-board relations. Actions are not necessarily based on research for student development. The superintendent has likely exited by the time investment in early childhood education reshapes student performance (about five years).

Counterbalancing short-term superintendent strategies for survival and phasing in an MT initiative is an opportunity for building a protracted system. Piloting MT implementation with the teachers assigned to pre-K through second grade is the most cost-effective and instructionally compelling approach. Closing learning gaps as students pass through successive grades becomes more challenging. Re-engaging and accelerating students in the early grades strengthens the entire district. Adding proportionately more MTs in upper grades as students advance with improved readiness skills is a reasoned strategy. The incentive for outstanding upper elementary teachers transferring to lower grades also mitigates the shortage of qualified early childhood applicants.

All students deserve quality instruction. Consequently, districts should take advantage of an expedient MT placement at any grade. While allowing for practical flexibility, the emphasis on early childhood MTs will enable more significant progress over time. Reducing the shortage of early childhood teachers, combined with the instructional and economic rationales, supports this overarching strategy. The recent models discussed (SAISD, TIA, TTI, OCI) present several viable approaches for MT pedagogues and team leaders. The second proposition, MTs as partners in research, has few prototypes but offers substantial promise.

MASTER TEACHER AS RESEARCHER

The master teacher as a researcher is the most unfamiliar and non-traditional position in this proposal. For education skeptics, consider this statement by humanitarian Nelson Mandela: "It always seems impossible until it's done."[18] If educators are to embrace research, as discussed in chapter 4, master teacher-researchers (MTRs) are indispensable. Partnerships with universities are part of the equation, but teachers must steward an expanded role by internalizing an inquiry mindset. MTR time is evenly divided between teaching and conducting approved studies with placement in a laboratory school.

Pilot lab schools collaboratively led by MTRs and resident university professors may comprise less than 5 percent of district campuses. State funding continues for those campuses demonstrating results and publishing recommendations. Schools not meeting target goals must re-apply or restructure. Valid findings that apply to improving teaching and learning are readily shared. Ideally, studies influence state representatives to sponsor education legislation removed from politics. The success of MTR programs and lab schools should later reduce the substantial remediation costs of struggling students.

Clinical teaching interns are groomed under the MTRs and resident professors following a competitive selection process. Orientation begins early in the undergraduate teacher preparation program. An inquiry mindset becomes a central goal for the next generation of teachers. Too often, undergraduates only seek a "manual of answers" for how to teach effectively. A scholarly cadre of MTRs investigates and verifies student development, wishing to understand the behaviors and practices that advance education. Growing the pool of MTR candidates requires revised college preparation programs and retraining current teachers within school districts.

Purposeful interactions and continuity between pre-K-12 schools and post-secondary institutions are mutually beneficial. Data discussions allow analysis, reflection, and planning for student development over a twenty-year continuum. Compartmentalizing student achievement with horizontal snapshots by grade and subject is an expedient news item but has limitations in predicting student success. Vertical analysis of student progress is more comprehensive and insightful. Educators have much to learn from each other by correlating multiple factors for longitudinal student progress. Equitable education should follow student advancement into adulthood and societal assimilation.

A rubric for MT selection would include multiple factors with percentage weights. Suggested fields include a minimum number of years of experience (e.g., two), degrees, certificates, the past two years' evaluations, student performance data, and principal recommendations. District criteria for choosing candidates and position postings will vary according to unique circumstances (e.g., budget, student needs, applicant pool). The system can succeed if the district demonstrates consistency in the selection process and expectations for MT continuance.

CONCLUSION

Mrs. Sprandle, the master pedagogue, and Mr. Analytics, the master researcher, are examples of preeminent teachers who are shining models of aspiration. They redefine teachers as professionals and as respected, competent, and well-compensated individuals. If you build a better role model, more students will desire entry as teachers. Provided there is trust for maintaining auspices, momentum will approach critical mass. Critical mass is defined as "a size, number, or amount large enough to produce a particular result."[19] That result is enthusiasm and buy-in for a compelling teaching career.

MTs established in a well-defined pathway genuinely compare to full professors at a university. In academia, the sequence of positions typically progresses from a graduate student, teaching assistant, assistant professor, associate professor, and finally full professor. Some full professors receive a "distinguished" designation that includes a higher salary, greater prestige, and more time to concentrate on their research. The contrast is substantial when paralleling the supply and demand status of pre-K-12 and university applicants. A 2020 survey found that early-career researchers required at least fifteen job applications for college faculty positions to receive a single offer.[20] Imagine if that teacher application ratio applied to an inner-city public school.

A reconceived teacher paradigm, emulating influential organizations incentivizing employees, resembles a pyramid with MTs at the pinnacle. Manifesting the MT position contributes to three objectives: (1) boosting desirability for the teaching profession, (2) augmenting the inquiry mindset in educators, and (3) improving equity and general efficacy for students. The first objective directly drives the other two. Accentuating MTs that burgeon from coherent pathways promotes higher standards for all teachers. Ms. Ann Oparah's belief that teachers should be "ranked alongside other professional fields such as Law, Engineering and Medicine"[21] may come to pass progressively with nascent structures. An elite plateau of MTs, duly recognized and rewarded, is but *one* salient component in elevating the entire teaching profession.

NOTES

1. Oparah, 2019.
2. Thompson, 2016, 1.
3. Goldhaber et al., 2020.
4. Alexander, Chant, & Cox, 1994.
5. "Teacher Incentive Allotment," 2022.
6. Eighty-Seventh Texas Legislature Regular Session, 2021.
7. "Teacher Incentive Allotment," 2022.
8. National Board Resource Center, Stanford University, 2022.
9. "National Board for Professional Teaching Standards," 2022.
10. Ryan & Deci, 2000.
11. Glazerman et al., 2013, xxv.
12. Bradley & Green, 2020, 362.
13. Will, 2018, 1.
14. "Opportunity Culture Overview," 2019.
15. "Opportunity Culture Student Outcomes," 2019.
16. Barrett, 2018, 2.
17. "Hire Expectations: Big District Superintendents Stay in Their Jobs," 2018.
18. Mandela, 2001.
19. "Critical mass," Merriam-Webster.com/dictionary, 2022.
20. Notman & Woolston, 2020.
21. Oparah, 2019.

Chapter 8

Recasting Teacher Unions

> Organizations can't serve two gods ... They serve one. And in the case of teachers' unions, it is the interests of their members. Period.
>
> —Rod Paige, former secretary of education

> There are teachers' unions around the country realizing they want to improve standards of the profession, improve the quality of their profession, and ultimately attract the best and the brightest to their profession. The vast majority of teachers are dedicated and committed.1
>
> —Antonio Villaraigosa, former mayor of Los Angeles

In my opinion, teachers deserve an enhanced societal status, higher salaries, and expanded resources to perform their invaluable mission: educating our children. Having worked for sixteen years as a teacher, having a spouse who worked thirty-two years as a teacher, and now with a son in his seventh year of teaching, the educators in our classrooms have my respect and empathy. Their powerful influence on society is only partially realized—and the possibilities remain uncharted. Creating an ecosystem for the teaching profession to flourish is essential to achieving a world-class vision of education. So, where do teacher unions fit within the overarching goal of better preparing future-ready students?

TEACHER UNIONS IN THE UNITED STATES

Labor unions have had an indelible influence on the professional stature of teachers over several generations. Founded in 1857, the National Education

Association (NEA) represents 3 million members, and the American Federation of Teachers (AFT), established in 1916, supports another 1.7 million members. The NEA is the largest labor union in the United States. Until the mid-1950s, the NEA primarily represented public-school administrators and college faculty. For the past sixty years, they have reconstituted the organization to align with the AFT and primarily represent teachers. Both the NEA and AFT wield substantial policy and political weight at the local district and national levels.

During the evolution of unions, a legislative milestone that expanded their dominion was Congress ratifying the National Labor Relations Act (NLRA) in 1935. This statute protected the rights of employees to organize and engage in collective bargaining (CB) with private employers. The NLRA was historic because it sought to rectify the power imbalance between employers and employees. That same year, the NLRA authorized the National Labor Relations Board to provide oversight in administering the provisions of the Act.

Public employees, including teachers, were first granted CB rights in 1962 when President Kennedy signed Executive Order 10988. Public-sector statutes established boards comparable to the NLRA to manage compliance with the laws. The industrial labor model was replicated in organizing public labor procedures despite the differences among the constituents. Over the past half century, "private-sector union membership has declined precipitously," while public union membership has remained stable.[2] Data from 2020 verifies that the NEA/AFT now constitutes more than half of the total public-sector union participants and approximately one-quarter of all union affiliates in the United States.

A collective bargaining agreement (CBA) constitutes a binding legal contract between a union and the school district. Teachers have a right to join and advocate for their profession through unions utilizing a CBA. Unions play a lawful role and rightfully fight for dedicated teachers in classrooms. Via due process, they have protected teachers from arbitrary negative consequences. Teacher unions have fought for classroom conditions that have also benefited students (e.g., class size reduction, instructional resources). While some negotiated teacher unions' attainments have been constructive for education, some critics contend that particular demands have impeded innovation and student academic progress. Given the societal value of a superlative educational system, teacher union advocacy in education requires guardrails. The scope of teacher union activity has more substantial societal ramifications than that of the blue-collar union workers in many other jobs. Therefore, the ethical imperative is to examine the impact of union activism on teachers, students, and the educational system.

Teacher unions played a significant role in shaping school policy and practice for much of the twentieth century. The NEA and AFT have experienced upswings and declines in political influence. They have advocated for raising teacher salaries, improving classroom working conditions, and protecting teachers' due process rights. The NEA/AFT political base is primarily the Democratic party, and its collective voice continues to resonate nationally. In 1972, the NEA established a far-reaching and persuasive political action committee. One notable accomplishment of the NEA was their influence in establishing the US Department of Education in 1979.[3]

Individual states' level of CB capacity spans a broad national spectrum. García and Han grouped states into four categories based on whether (1) CB is legal and mandatory for employers and (2) unions can require nonunion members to pay agency or fair share fees. Agency fees oblige nonunion members benefiting under CB to remunerate the union for nonpolitical activities. Table 8.1 identifies states that the authors classified by level of CB influence. Employers in the twenty-three "High-CB" states are required to bargain with the union and allow mandatory agency fees for nonunion members. The eleven states in the "Mid-CB" group had mandatory bargaining laws but barred compulsory agency fees. The "Low-CB" group includes nine states where local school districts choose whether or not to sign CBAs. Lastly, the seven states in the "No-CB" group prohibit CB rights for teachers.[4]

During the last decade, the pendulum has swung further toward limiting union power. Legislators in the mid-level CB states of Idaho, Indiana, and Tennessee and the high-level CB states of Michigan and Wisconsin

Table 8.1 Collective Bargaining Levels by State

States with No to High Levels of Collective Bargaining (CB) Rights for Teachers				
States with High-Level CB		States with Mid-Level CB	States with Low-Level CB	States with No CB
Alaska	Montana	Florida	Alabama	Arizona
California	New Hampshire	Idaho	Arkansas	Georgia
Connecticut	New Jersey	Indiana	Colorado	Mississippi
Delaware	New Mexico	Iowa	Kentucky	North Carolina
Hawaii	New York	Kansas	Louisiana	South Carolina
Illinois	Ohio	Nebraska	Missouri	Texas
Maine	Oregon	Nevada	Utah	Virginia
Maryland	Pennsylvania	North Dakota	West Virginia	
Massachusetts	Rhode Island	Oklahoma	Wyoming	
Michigan	Vermont	South Dakota		
Minnesota	Washington	Tennessee		
	Wisconsin			

Source: García & Han, 2021, 4.

"launched unprecedented initiatives extensively restricting or entirely prohibiting the CB rights of public-sector employees, including public school teachers."[5]

Another recent setback for teacher unions involved their influence on nonunion employees. In 1977, the Supreme Court decision of *Abood v. Detroit Board of Education* supported the use of agency fees. Four decades later, the Supreme Court overturned the ruling from *Abood* in *Janus v. American Federation of State, County, and Municipal Employees Council*. The recent ruling stated that agency fees violated the constitutional free speech rights of nonunion members. This legal decision dealt a severe financial blow to the NEA and AFT.

Lieberman emphasized the value of "curbing excessive union power while maintaining a viable system of teacher representation."[6] Teacher unions are not inherently good or bad, but the checks and balances must always support the overall vision for student achievement:

> It is safe to predict that whatever policy is placed on bargaining tables, the union position will be based on what is good for the teachers and/or the union. I do not say this because teachers and their unions are more self-serving than other interest groups. My reason is that despite having convinced themselves to the contrary, the teachers and their unions are no less self-serving than the interest groups they routinely revile as greed-orientated exploiters.[7]

The paramount consideration in balancing power for teacher unions should be the residual effect on children's learning. The quality and *equality* of education for all children is the foremost priority. Unfortunately, decisions continue to emanate from partisan politics rather than what is best for students, teachers, and educational systems.

All requests made on behalf of teachers must be examined in the context of student success. Any failure affects adults if union members produce goods or services exclusively for profit. However, students suffer if teacher union goals do not align with academic progress. All students may have the right to an exceptional free public education, but they do not have the bargaining representation to fight for their learning conditions. In multiple CBA scenarios, there is a discernable conflict of interest between teacher union requests and the best interests of students.

Cowen and Strunk examined over three decades of research on the impact of teacher unions in the United States. Despite unions' long-standing negotiation tenure, the limited research indicates that union bargaining has yielded unsubstantial outcomes for educational advancement. The authors found a "preponderance of empirical evidence" suggesting that strong teacher unionization is correlated with augmented district expenditures, teachers' salaries, and, notably, experienced teachers' salaries. The union-related impact on academic performance found that "differences in student outcomes [are] mixed, but suggestive of insignificant or modestly negative union effects."[8]

Unions cannot simultaneously oblige two masters: they serve their card-carrying members. Moreover, the rhetoric often attempts to connect teachers' desires with children's well-being for self-serving interests. The general rhetoric of correlated teacher-student mutual welfare lacks integrity. Unions often ascertain that states with more substantial CB have superior student performance, but the moderate correlation is likely due to other factors, particularly family income. The interests of union members have always been and will continue to be paramount. The first step in finding a common-good resolution for CB is delineating the interests of teachers that may not be aligned with those of students. Well-defined parameters of negotiation topics serve not only to protect students but also to raise the public perception of teachers.

TEACHER TENURE

Teacher tenure protecting "bad teachers" is the most contested issue between management and unions. Teacher quality is the primary factor for a child's long-term success.[9] Consequently, contracts containing seniority rules that hinder firing ineffective teachers are highly contentious. The eventual solution to a complex situation warrants consideration from several perspectives. Learners require safeguards from the damaging aftermaths of incompetent teachers. If the evidence is conclusive, decisions should favor students.

At the same time, educational systems require a fair and consistent system to ensure due process protection against misguided administrators. Documentation must be thorough when it comes to non-renewal. A third factor, often overlooked, is the supply and demand of teaching faculty. After many years of struggling to recruit and hire teachers and reflecting on the inauspicious projections of future vacancies versus new applicants, I arrive at a sobering conclusion: management is not in an ideal position to be inflexible.

In the 1952 case of *Adler v. Board of Education of the City of New York*, the Supreme Court asserted "that school authorities have the right and the duty to screen the officials, teachers, and employees as to their fitness to maintain the integrity of schools as a part of ordered society cannot be doubted."[10] The obligation to students and communities requires modifications in teacher evaluation efficacy, contractual progression toward tenure, and rules for a reduction in force (RIF). The recommendations to validate teacher evaluations in chapter 5 are critical to successfully managing tenure. If *all* teacher evaluations were reliable and well-documented, the system would not allow ineffective teachers to progress to tenured status. Proactive prevention is an underutilized strategy. Analogous to keeping students engaged to prevent classroom behavior problems, authentic teacher evaluations avert the potential "dance of the lemons."

Over the last decade, several states passed legislation making teachers revert to probationary contracts if they were rated "ineffective." Other states passed statutes that repealed tenure entirely.[11] Reserved customarily for new teachers, individuals on probationary contracts may not have the right to appeal or request a hearing ordinarily available to teachers with term or continuing contracts. Recent actions by states to mitigate or eliminate tenure entitlements stem from the obstacles involved in removing a harmful or ineffective teacher. School districts are frequently reluctant to initiate dismissal proceedings because of the extensive documentation, time demands, and expenditure. Discharging a teacher "could take anywhere from two to almost ten years and could cost $50,000 to $450,000. All the while, these grossly ineffective teachers were left in the classroom."[12]

However, states must be cautious and not over-legislate, given the current supply and demand context. Diminishing teacher protections will not support districts in attracting the substantive new talent sought for impending vacancies. DeMitchell recognizes the importance of achieving tenure equilibrium: "Protection of teachers from arbitrary and capricious dismissals serves the public good," while "the status quo regarding tenure practices is not in the public interest."[13] Raising standards for obtaining tenure can be accomplished through fair processes that appeal to most constituents. Although school leaders must still demonstrate just cause for termination, the rules require alteration. This author believes that the modifications suggested below better protect students, safeguard effective teachers, and assist administrators throughout a district:

1. *Extend the probationary teacher period to four years.* After two years, teachers who receive distinguished evaluations may be moved to a term contract (tenure). If principals are thorough in completing valid evaluations, novice teachers will be coached up or coached out. Teachers who do not receive proficient assessments (a 3 on a 5-point scale) in their final two probationary years will not be retained for tenure.
2. *Eliminate continuing teacher contracts.* A continuing contract automatically renews every year. The additional protection requires a written administrative proposal for termination, a vote by the board to accept that request, and sending the employee a notice of the proposal. A separate appeal process follows these steps. Term contracts will provide the necessary safeguards for due process rights and tenure security if performance is acceptable.
3. *After receiving an unsatisfactory performance evaluation, a tenured teacher is automatically given a probationary contract the following*

year. The teacher would be entitled to request a hearing and a vote by the school board as a final determinant to alter the contract. The district will reinstate the term contract if the teacher receives a proficient evaluation the following year. Continued poor performance on the probationary contract would result in termination after one year.
4. *The last-in and first-out process for a RIF include an amended formula.* The ranking would be based on (1) certification and (2) an equal weight of years of service and performance evaluations. Teachers with more years of experience would always be at an advantage, but incorporating their classroom efficacy could alter their seniority status.

Having additional years for probationary contracts would allow principal supervisors the time to examine the consistency of teacher evaluations. Success is predicated on those supervisors holding principals accountable by being in classrooms, recognizing accomplished pedagogy, and having the courage to appraise teachers honestly. Assuming these recommendations are implemented with integrity, only efficacious teachers would be granted tenure. When teachers legitimately earn tenure, and many subsequently advance to become master teachers, it occasions the elevation of the profession.

LOCAL SCHOOL BOARD AUTHORITY

School district boards and administration have distinct responsibilities to serve the community's educational needs. A board's clientele is far more extensive than the employees' union. In addition to students being a priority, their obligation extends to parents, educators, public taxpayers, and state officials. A reasonable equilibrium with all constituents is only possible if local school boards remain independent as representatives. School boards should be protected from special-interest lobby influence, which includes teacher unions.

The local board of trustees establishes school districts' policies and day-to-day governance. Local boards' control of public schools is a staple in the United States, with origins dating back to the Massachusetts Bay Colony of the mid-seventeenth century. The overwhelming majority of school board members, over 94 percent, assume power from district community elections. They serve as citizens' representatives, but their delegated authority stems from the state's constitution and laws.

Beckham, Wills, and Weeks describe the multiple duties of local board members, which include developing policies, rules, and regulations to control the operation of the schools and system organization. Trustees approve administrative recommendations for school sites, school finances, equipment purchase, staffing, attendance, curriculum, extracurricular activities, and other day-to-day functions within the district's boundaries. Boards may also be authorized by the state to "levy taxes, invest resources, initiate eminent domain proceedings, acquire land, and assume bonded indebtedness."[14]

Like teacher unions, local school boards are inherently neither good nor bad and require checks and balances. Serving a local district in a governing role motivates trustees to seek office, not monetary gain. The most recent National School Board Association report found that most school board members receive no annual compensation:

- A total of 75 percent of small-district school board members receive no salary.
- Less than 40 percent of large-district school board members work more than forty hours per month on board-related duties in return for a salary.[15]

While trustees may not receive a salary and their role involves many hours of civic work, there are countless personal objectives underlying running for a school board position. One candidate may consider being a trustee a stepping stone to attaining political office, while a hot-button issue may incentivize another as a trustee. Along with these and various other motives, many citizens have an exclusively altruistic desire to serve the community and its students.

Thanks to the electoral endorsement of their community, board members are empowered to make decisions. Ideally, from a parliamentary viewpoint, they safeguard a school district's mindfulness of the principles and attitudes of their local community. Local values must also conform to state laws. Remaining impartial and abiding by their limits often become issues for trustees. Aside from hiring the superintendent, all personnel recommendations derive from the fair hiring practices of the administration. Issues arise when board members overstep their defined roles and supersede the superintendent's leadership.

As with governance at every level, examples of leadership from local officials range from dynamic to ineffective and, at times, even corrupt. Fortunately, state oversight systems are in place to intervene in unwarranted decisions or remove school boards if necessary. Often-cited concerns include the meager eligibility requirements for school board members. The five standard qualifications for school board members in most states are the following:

1. Being a registered voter.
2. Being a resident of the district that the individual is running to represent.

3. Having at least a high school diploma or a certificate of equivalency.
4. Not being a convicted felon.
5. Not being a current employee of the district or related to a current employee in that district.[16]

Considering the board's scope of governance, onboarding tutelage with legal policy, curriculum standards, and financial accountability should be a requisite for board service. Nevertheless, there is little national consistency for trustee member induction, and state-to-state requirements for training vary significantly.

Training, political limitations, and more refined policies enhance an unbiased board relationship with teacher unions. Unions are prominent lobbying groups with both internal and external insight. Trustees with a partisan relationship with union leaders diminish impartiality and, at worst, invite collusion. The following three suggested proposals serve to cultivate principled and equitable leadership for local boards:

- Require yearly standardized training or exit exams for all trustees on their duties and responsibilities.
- Prohibit school board candidates from receiving union endorsements and funding, as this is an explicit conflict of interest.
- Ensure detailed guidelines for due process are in place to safeguard teachers from school administrators' arbitrary or excessive exercise of power.

With authority to negotiate, local board members must meditate on union requests in the context of district, student, and community interests. Basic expectations for trustees include understanding their role as well as serving with the ethics and objective courage to reach agreements for the public welfare.

A PRAGMATIC MODEL

Contemporary opinions are diverse and often polarizing regarding the relevance and virtue of teacher unions. The epigraphs at the beginning of this chapter exemplify that dichotomy. Union leaders frequently state that what is favorable for teachers also benefits students. With a contrary and extreme viewpoint, Education Secretary Rod Paige in 2004 compared the NEA to "a terrorist organization."[17] Such unsubstantiated generalizations and insults serve little purpose. However, an analysis of the effect of union bargaining on stakeholders is crucial to educational progress. Citizens should consider three questions in making systemic recommendations for the role of teacher unions in pre-K-12 education:

- What components of teacher unions help or hinder student learning?
- What components of teacher unions help or hinder educational progress?
- What components of teacher unions help or hinder professional teacher status?

Determining teacher unions' limitations as hybrid and unique organizations is society's ethical responsibility. As opposed to blue-collar Teamsters, United Auto Workers, or United Steelworkers, teachers are (1) under public state governance and (2) meet the standards of a profession. Teachers are exempt employees removed from timeclocks and operate under different regulations than the Fair Labor Standards Act. When negotiating, the process should not reflect the traditional "industrial union versus management" playbook.

Toch et al. described the conventional manual laborer's goals, "where winning workers big checks for the shortest possible hours has been the aim and quality of the product is considered management's worry."[18] The assumption that public unions represent similar goals diminishes teachers' public esteem. DeMitchell questioned a teacher union's use of an industrial labor model for CB, noting "Four themes emerge from the analysis of harm—blind protection, the work of unions, divisiveness, and the union label." Social status is inferred from the observed behavior of groups and their members. With some union actions, public perception of teachers becomes more closely associated with *hourly laborers* than *professional employees*.[19]

Union leaders and government officials will have different perspectives on governance structures, salary, working conditions, and teacher non-renewal. The negotiating system can function more effectively if (1) bargaining issues are further delineated and (2) elected trustees objectively moderate disputes with teachers and students in mind. If a resolution is impossible, the state should appoint an arbitration group to make decisions. Strikes affecting students and families should be eliminated as an option.

LIMITING BARGAINING TOPICS

Teacher unions' pursuits potentially help or hinder student learning, educational progress, and professional teacher status; hence they warrant examination. Bargaining issues viewed in this context begin with student safety and academic progress and reflect teachers' professionalism. Some policies should intentionally be written in general terms to allow for unforeseen circumstances. Campuses require the flexibility to respond to immediate day-to-day dilemmas in the best interest of the student body. Stanford professor Terry Moe delineated some of the policy requests from teacher unions that may fail to safeguard students:

- Rules specifying complicated, time-consuming grievance procedures to be followed for dismissing a teacher;
- Rules prohibiting some percentage of standardized test results as a component of evaluations using multiple measures;
- Rules prohibiting formal "growth plans" for teachers with "developing" or "improvement needed" evaluations (two lowest on a 5-point scale);
- Rules limiting the number of faculty meetings and their duration;
- Rules limiting the number of minutes teachers can be required to be on campus before and after school;
- Rules limiting the number of courses, periods, or students a teacher must teach;
- Rules limiting the non-teaching duties that teachers can be asked to perform, such as yard duty, hall duty, or lunch duty;
- Rules limiting the number of parent conferences and other settings in which teachers meet with parents;
- Rules giving administrators no flexibility regarding class size;
- Rules giving guaranteed preparation times of a specified number of minutes per day;
- Rules giving teachers who are union officials time off to perform union duties;
- Rules limiting teaching assignments and transfers;
- Unions as an organization engaging in political endorsements of the school board candidates. Individual teachers should independently vote their conscience without coercion.[20]

Administrative guidelines for principals and schedulers are recommended and appropriate, rather than hard-and-fast rules that stifle the ability to accommodate students. Excluding union-imposed work restrictions like the topics above provide campuses with the necessary flexibility to respond to the dynamic needs associated with poverty, mobility, multiculturalism, and high rates of student trauma.

Union requests should be assessed and categorized as reasonable or incompatible with a student-centered campus. Teacher unions would still be advocates for teacher-specific issues (e.g., salary, classroom resources, safety). Outstanding teachers place student welfare first and would understand the rationale for modification. They also have ample career options, so savvy principals can accommodate tenure longevity.

CONCLUSION

Public institutions differ considerably from private businesses, particularly educational institutions. The essential purpose of small businesses and corporations is to amass profit; they cater to select customers that sustain their bottom line. In education, on the other hand, personal compensation matters, but the clientele is not exclusive. Accountability is for every child that walks in a classroom door. Public and private unions must also respond to employers in distinctly different ways. In a 1937 letter to the National Federation of Federal Employees, President Franklin Roosevelt wrote the following:

> The desire of Government employees for fair and adequate pay, reasonable hours of work, safe and suitable working conditions, development of opportunities for advancement, facilities for fair and impartial consideration and review of grievances, . . . is basically no different from that of employees in private industry . . . but meticulous attention should be paid to the special relationships and obligations of public servants to the public itself and to the Government. . . . The process of collective bargaining, as usually understood, cannot be transplanted into the public service. It has its distinct and insurmountable limitations when applied to public personnel management.[21]

Roosevelt also considered strikes by public unions an obstruction of government. "Between 1960 and 1974, there were more than 1,000 teacher strikes involving more than 823,000 teachers."[22] Union walkouts are damaging to students along with teachers' image; fortunately, strikes have declined in recent years.

In adapting teachers' CB to a contemporary model, the process begins by recognizing its functional differences from the industrial model. Authentically considering children as a priority in CB involves examining issues through an altruistic lens. As a repurposed organization, the union responds to wide-ranging challenges as the champion of both teachers and students. Expanding the vision for broad educational advocacy raises the public's perception of unions and the teachers they represent.

Perhaps in the not-too-distant future, the structure and prestige of teachers as a profession will make unions obsolete. US society has not historically viewed teaching as a preeminent vocation, and unions provided a resolute voice to improve inadequate conditions. Today, however, industrial-style negotiations, like the assembly-line classroom, are obsolete. Accelerating knowledge, academic expectations, and adapting for contemporary classrooms evince the salient need for a prominent class of teachers. In keeping with education's transition, unions must work to change their model and image. Rebranding entails leaving the blue-collar union mantra behind and embracing public service beyond solely representing teachers. Union demands for uniformity must be replaced with an openness to flexibility in responding to ever-widening heterogeneous classroom demands.

Teachers' association with traditional unions can create ambiguities. Can the designation "professional" coexist with a union's membership philosophy? Is teaching a distinguished career or a job to support basic needs? The complex reasons for employment are part of our self-concept. A reasonable salary is essential but rarely a teacher's primary motivation. Reconciling the discord with teacher identity will be a formidable task if unions adhere to the "us versus them" mentality.

The term "professional" implies unselfish service. Its etymology dates from the "Late Latin *professus*, past participle of *profitēri* which meant to profess, confess." In Middle English, the word "*profes* [is] an adjective meaning having professed one's vows." Professionals describe "those who 'professed' their skill to others and 'vowed' to perform their profession to the highest standard."[23] Professionals also represent specific knowledge and expertise. Acquired training and skills are utilized to assist others in a particular field. In serving students, the collaboration between teachers and administrators is fundamental in a complex learning ecosystem.

Teacher unions have historically advocated conforming to rules and mistrusting management. When trust is minimal, union members assume that the only means of protection is an agreement that dictates the minutiae of responsibility and often handcuffs principals. If unions' CB strategy is predicated on the opposition, the repercussions can disable the necessary teamwork for student achievement. The dilemma of professionalism versus unionism cannot be resolved until negotiation topics are better delineated. Rather than demonizing unions, the appreciable solution is for state legislative leaders to reframe the role of unions as partners, with student welfare as the centerpiece.

Soliciting teachers' inclusion in pertinent discussions of instructional decisions, purchasing resources, wages, and other topics better serves educational systems. Their frontline expertise with content, pedagogy, and classroom social dynamics is an irreplaceable resource. However, teachers should not be made to feel reticent or cornered by misaligned dogmas. Unconstrained unionist protection tarnishes the teaching profession, while a well-balanced confederation promotes optimal customer service. The progressive remodeling of teacher unions clarifies and confines bargaining issues in light of their bearing on students.

NOTES

1. Villaraigosa, 2021.
2. Robson, Pennington, & Squire, 2018, 13.

3. Hawley & Jones, 2021.
4. Garcia & Han, 2021.
5. Garcia & Han, 2021, 4.
6. Lieberman, 2000, 274.
7. Ibid. 278.
8. Cowen & Strunk, 2015, 1.
9. Opper, 2019.
10. *Adler v. Bd. of Educ.*, 1952, 493.
11. DeMitchell, 2020.
12. DeMitchell & Onosko, 2016, 610.
13. DeMitchell, 2020, 164.
14. Beckham, Wills, & Weeks, 2020, 2.
15. National School Board Association, 2018.
16. Meador, 2019, 1.
17. Paige, 2004.
18. Toch et al., 1996, 64.
19. DeMitchell, 2020.
20. Moe, 2012, 174–75.
21. Roosevelt, 1937.
22. Robson, Pennington, & Squire, 2018, 24.
23. Balthazard, 2015, 1.

Chapter 9

Reimagining Professional Learning

Never let formal education get in the way of your learning.

—Mark Twain

As a long-tenured educator, my perception of professional learning (PL) was that school districts' approaches lacked philosophy and coherence. The state and district set a prescribed number of PL days. Sometimes the district would manage the structure and content, while at other times, the campus principals had complete autonomy. Over the years, some thought-provoking or practical presentations helped me grow as a teacher and administrator. Nevertheless, the required training was often compliance-related, redundant, non-applicable, or a veiled staff meeting. I never embraced the ubiquitous "warm-up" games as part of the ritual. The economical "one trainer for the entire district" usually failed a majority of attendees. Organizers and presenters performed their PL obligation responsibly, but I was left with one persistent question: Is the PL for teachers meeting the purpose of enhancing student learning?

The Boston Consulting Group (BCG), sponsored by the Bill and Melinda Gates Foundation, conducted a survey-interview study on professional development for teachers. The participants included more than 1,300 teachers, PL leaders in education agencies, principals, and PL providers. The 2014 report findings were consistent with my own experiences. Some of the core information included the following:

- A total of 18 billion dollars is spent annually on professional development;
- A typical teacher spends sixty-eight hours each year—more than a week—on PL activities typically directed by districts. When self-guided PL and courses are included, the annual total comes to eighty-nine hours;

- Few teachers (29 percent) are highly satisfied with current professional development offerings;
- Few teachers (34 percent) think professional development has improved;
- A large majority of teachers do not believe that professional development is helping them prepare for the changing nature of their jobs, including using technology and digital learning tools, analyzing student data to differentiate instruction, and implementing the Common Core State Standards and other standards;
- Professional development formats strongly supported by district leadership and principals, such as PL communities and coaching, are currently not meeting teachers' needs; and
- Principals share teachers' concerns about the efficacy of PL.[1]

The same report found that teachers and administrators essentially agree on what they would like to experience with PL. Training should be relevant, interactive (hands-on), sustained over time, treat teachers like professionals, and be delivered by someone who understands the classroom experience. Additionally, teachers with more choices reported higher satisfaction with their most recent PL.[2]

RATIONALE FOR TEACHER PROFESSIONAL LEARNING

The Learning Policy Institute defines effective professional development as "structured professional learning that results in changes in teacher practices and improvements in student learning outcomes."[3] PL is a universal structure for school systems, recognizing the need for continuous improvement with "the individual teacher seen as the most influential factor within the school for learner outcomes."[4] In principle, as teachers' skills advance, their effect on student learning becomes more effectual. In common practice, PL can become an exercise in compliance if educators' strategies do not reflect an evolving culture. Netolicky suggests reevaluating the purpose of teacher PL:

> [The study] recommends that the definition of professional learning be broadened, that teachers and schools think more expansively and flexibly about what it is that transforms educators, and about who drives and chooses this learning. Schools and systems can work from their own contexts to design and slowly iterate models of professional learning, from the bottom up and the middle out.[5]

Communities and schools should expect that the 18 billion dollars invested yearly in PL is advancing teacher practices and, in turn, student learning. However, states lack the systems to monitor, collect data, or determine PL's effect on performance. Are state and local PL investments translating into improved teaching and learning? A report by Jaquith et al. examined PL requirements in four states. Their research suggested several elements to advance state success with PL. These recommendations included:

1. A common and clearly articulated vision for professional development that permeates policy and practice;
2. Effective monitoring of professional development quality;
3. Mentoring and induction requirements that are linked to and create a foundation for ongoing PL;
4. An infrastructure of organizations for facilitating professional development; and
5. Stability of resources.[6]

These proposals are realistic suggestions for progress. State and district cooperation, coupled with guidelines for principals and teachers, can foster their implementation. An electronic state platform where all teachers enter their annual PL training hours would enable monitoring and correlation studies with their research department.

INTEGRATION OF PROFESSIONAL LEARNING FOR ELEVATING TEACHERS

With an abundance of opinion books in print, PL is a popular topic for education authors. The objective of this chapter is *not* to delineate an extensive framework but rather to consider PL as an integrated component of a comprehensive plan for teachers. Four ideas are proposed to incorporate teachers' structured learning to advance the profession. These propositions are categorized as (1) functional structures, (2) connections to research, (3) connections to pathways, and (4) PL communities.

Functional Structures. All teachers have unique needs, and the survey consensus is that districts need flexibility. A functional structure avoids the extremes of top-down requirements versus a smorgasbord of elective choices to meet an arbitrary number of hours. It involves a few simple systems with collaboration between principal and teacher. The approach distinguishes between compulsory PL and individual plans that allow discretion.

In the districts where I worked, annual compulsory training included sexual harassment and emergency response procedures. The entire faculty would sit through a state-produced video, sometimes the same video for consecutive years, and then everyone would sign a verification document. These types of mandated PL for all teachers should comprise asynchronous online classes.

Teachers only need a time frame to complete and perhaps electronic reminders. Whether completed during a school planning period or at home, teachers possess valuable flexibility. Material can be broken into modules with a few questions at the end of each section. This approach improves the likelihood that teachers assimilate content. The school district meets legal requirements with an electronic signature.

Conferences to determine discretionary PL provide a principal with a forum to astutely guide staff as the campus instructional leader. In a typical scenario, assume all teachers must complete twelve hours of PL beyond those mandated by law. Many options are available in district-approved catalogs, college courses, or conventions. The goal is for selections to legitimately enhance a teacher's knowledge and pedagogic skill in their craft. Neither complete district control nor unconditional teacher choice in PL will likely accomplish optimal results. The functional suggestion is collaborative planning, pairing principal and teacher.

A master teacher may require minimal PL guidance, whereas a novice may not know what he/she does not know. A PL system supporting flexibility with internal guardrails can promote meaningful teacher development. I propose establishing a consultation process that considers experience and performance in the classroom. At the beginning of a school year, a conference would determine the individual teacher's most appropriate twelve discretionary hours of PL. These conversations would include coaching toward pathways, discussing long-term career goals, and, lastly, decisions for the current year. A suggested sequence would include the following:

1. The teacher completes a template listing the desired annual PL courses with a brief rationale on how the courses will improve their skills and benefit students.
2. The teacher meets with the principal, who reviews the proposal and discusses choices relative to the teacher's observations and evaluations.
3. The principal can either sign off on the proposal, suggest enrolling in a program, or request that the teacher revise the proposal based on acknowledged areas of needed improvement.

In most cases, experienced teachers with evaluations above the proficient level will receive approval. Novice, less experienced, and other teachers needing support receive valuable guidance and coaching to build competencies. A principal may recognize an obvious shortcoming with classroom management or content knowledge. A competent leader understands their responsibility for teacher development using honest dialog and relevant PL counsel. With a culture of campus trust, teachers will accept feedback and work on personal growth, anticipating a future of expanded autonomy.

Connections to Research. In a 2018 review of seventy-five studies, Ping, Schellings, and Beijaard reported that PL is not a well-researched topic, despite the abundant literature in print. The review found few quantitative, large-scale studies on this subject. The accessible research reports on teachers' PL are primarily small-scale, unfunded, and practice-based. The summary stated that "research on teacher educators' professional learning appears to be a growing field of interest but fragmented in focus."[7] Other conclusions from their analysis found that

- there is no clear knowledge base essential for teacher educators' work;
- teacher educators undertake different activities from which to learn; and
- they generally experience the need to learn to do their work as teacher educators.[8]

Given the substantial funding, collecting data and studying the impact of PL is both wise and fiscally responsible. The state departments of education (DOE) are best situated to lead this initiative, assisting local districts in providing better-informed guidance to teachers. The suggested functions for a state DOE include the following:

- Solicit bids, codify, and generate an approved online catalog of approved PL courses. A selection committee would review proposals from universities, private non-profits, and commercial resources; for example, Learning Forward, Michigan Virtual, and Connecticut's State Education Resource Center.
- Offer unlimited free online courses for all state education employees.
- Develop a statewide repository to collect PL data and include a section for survey ratings and suggestions from participants.
- Conduct correlation studies with courses and other teacher-student variables.

Providing an accessible venue for all educators with a feedback system for ongoing improvement allows principals and teachers to have confidence in courses and gives them flexibility. With large statewide data samples, robust studies can compare PL courses with classroom results (e.g., behavior management, social-emotional development, reading). Annual updates and competition for state contracts can lead to an optimistic prognosis for quality.

Local districts should also contribute to research as part of lab school work. As discussed in chapter 4, one component of lab schools is analyzing professional learning through controlled investigation. These campuses can incorporate study results for selected PD training and provide visitation opportunities to other educators interested in replication. Research sharing between state and local entities collectively contributes to an inquiry mindset for all educators.

Connections to Pathways and Programs. Pathways and programs should be integrated with functional structures to optimize the interoperability among district goals, enhanced pedagogy, teacher longevity, and PL. Aligning PL with teacher pathways adds additional choices while contributing to the professional status of teachers. Master's degrees, certifications, reading credentials, and other programs satisfy teacher growth goals and position them for promotion and increased compensation.

Principals assume a pivotal counseling role in conversations with teachers and approval of discretionary PD. Not all teachers will be ready for or committed to a district pathway. Notwithstanding those who are unprepared, the progression of pathways and programs is substantially contingent on a campus leadership endorsement. The principal's contribution includes reflecting on the potentiality of teaching talent, awareness of available opportunities, and working with district administration to support participation.

Professional Learning Communities. Vibrant professional learning communities (PLC) within a campus add to the cohesiveness of teacher development. Not necessarily credited for PL hours, accruing PLC time codifies pedagogic learning, with ancillary advantages being instructional alignment and school esprit de corps. Serviss articulated some of the positive aspects of PLCs, which include the following:

1. PLCs allow educators opportunities to directly improve teaching and learning.
2. PLCs build stronger relationships among team members.
3. PLCs help teachers stay abreast of new research and emerging technology tools for the classroom.
4. PLCs help teachers reflect on ideas.[9]

Doğan and Adam's recent critical analysis of PLC studies support previous research findings. The authors reviewed thirteen international empirical studies on PLC. Their findings show that "participation in PLCs resulted in improved teacher practice and increased student achievement."[10] The study provided specific examples of what improved teacher practice and the impact on students. Recommendations articulated specific research designs to enhance the quality of PLC studies.[11]

Several recognized books by Richard DuFour and colleagues (e.g., *Revisiting Professional Learning Communities at Work*,[12] *Learning by Doing*[13]) delineate widely used PLC protocols and practices. Teachers, like their students, are social learners. Individual and collective growth through PLCs is a constructive pursuit for any campus. A successful process to mold culture transpires through the planning and resourcefulness of the principal. The vision and guidance persist until legitimate ownership of a PLC is predominantly by teachers. The end product of this endeavor is a "culture of collaboration" with an ongoing focus on questioning and learning.[14]

A significant factor in PLC success is the administrator's ability to schedule common planning time for select teachers during regular school instructional hours. Feasible, organized meetings can happen at any time agreed upon by the participants. However, the likelihood of consistent utility increases with a reliable meeting calendar. As principals shape campus norms, they may initially lead PL meetings. The principal relinquishes managerial authority when teachers are confident in purpose, frameworks, roles, and expectations.

PLCs are not limited to one viable design. Waters describes three types of learning communities: teams that share similar goals, teams organized by topics, and subject department teams.[15] With the advent of stable video platforms, groups can conveniently expand to multiple campuses. Innovative ideas for teacher PLCs will multiply based on their merit. As a substantiated PL resource, teacher growth through collaboration with colleagues is essential. Kelchtermans et al. echo a consensus among contemporary educators: "The time of the isolated teacher educator belongs to the past, and 'communities of practice' reaching far beyond the local context are today both technically possible and expected."[16]

The four postulated proposals offer procedures to reduce the disjointed practices and disconnects between well-intentioned plans and the reported underwhelming PL experiences. They establish flexible and serviceable models. Meaningful implementation and improved end products (e.g., enhanced teacher skillsets, satisfaction with PL) are contingent on state and district partnerships, prudent use of resources, and listening to teachers' feedback.

CONCLUSION

Overburdened school districts can easily allow PL to become a pretense: "just one more thing" to cross off a long list. With state testing and accountability driving the school train and student safety in the first boxcar, PL may end up close to the caboose. Nevertheless, given the enormous annual investments in time and finances, school leaders are responsible for certifying authentic learning. Reiterating the BCG survey concerns cited earlier, constructing a plan should be prompted by two questions:

- Is the PL relevant to teachers as individuals?
- Is the delivery of the content efficacious?

Ascertaining legitimate answers to these questions should underpin decisions for collaboration and improvement.

Educators espouse multiple modes of delivery for PL as credible; for example, college courses, conferences, workshops, independent research, PLCs, online modules, and data analysis. However, the methods for personal growth are secondary to confidence in their effectiveness. In addition to the above questions on relevance and delivery are these:

- Is the training meeting the purpose of improving teaching with the requisite pedagogic skills?
- Is the approach cost-effective in building those skills?

School district administrators and teachers concur that effective PL contributes to the betterment of education. Despite endorsing PL's wisdom, teachers express dissatisfaction with the one-size-fits-all delivery of presentations. At the other end of the spectrum, individualizing appropriate training for every teacher is a logistical dilemma. States and districts should work together for pragmatic systems with a functional balance. A consequential PL structure for teachers is another pillar to uphold and raise the profession's status. As new PL findings from robust studies merge closer with practice, educators must focus on the present with mindful action.

Differentiated training is the "ideal" to align teachers' skillset development and connection with their singular classroom circumstances. In an increasingly globalized world, teachers have the additional challenge of preparing students in expanding multi-ethnic, multilingual, and multicultural classrooms. New knowledge doubles every year, and that pace can only accelerate. Simultaneously, the expectations for teachers, unlike technology, must be tenable in the classroom. Realistically, states cannot diagnose and prescribe for every teacher PL exigency. They can work with districts to standardize systems for developing practical applications.

At the macro level, expanded state guidance, particularly with research and vetting accessible choices, provides an umbrella for orchestrated progress. Local districts will take the lead in providing pathways, refining procedures, and supporting principals for campus implementation. The obligation of principals is astute PL leadership. Campus administrators collaborating honestly with teachers to promote earned autonomy and guide the complex dynamics toward individual agency should lead to productivity and improved satisfaction.

NOTES

1. Boston Consulting Group, 2014, 3.
2. Ibid.

3. Darling-Hammond, Hyler, & Gardner, 2017, 1.
4. King, 2019.
5. Netolicky, 2016, 1.
6. Jaquith et al., 2010, 9–10.
7. Ping, Schellings, & Beijaard, 2018, 1.
8. Ibid.
9. Serviss, 2021, 1–3.
10. Doğan & Adams, 2018, 634.
11. Ibid.
12. DuFour, DuFour, & Eaker, 2008.
13. DuFour et al., 2020.
14. Hadar & Brody, 2016.
15. Waters, 2021.
16. Kelchtermans, Vanderlinde, & Smith, 2017, 130.

Chapter 10

Critical-Need Educators

Substitute Teachers and Instructional Assistants

> Life is a series of steps. Things are done gradually. Once in a while there is a giant step, but most of the time we are taking small, seemingly insignificant steps on the stairway of life.
>
> —Ralph Ransom, American artist

Over the past two decades, school districts across the United States have endured a severe teacher shortage, and the coronavirus pandemic has only intensified a discouraging situation. Pessimistic projections for newly qualified teachers are troublesome, and the trend will further deteriorate classroom learning conditions. The National Center for Education Statistics reported that the number of bachelor's degrees awarded in education from 1970–1971 to 2017–2018 decreased from 176,307 to 83,621 nationally, a 52.6 percent decrease.[1]

During that same period, K-12 student enrollment in all schools has increased from 45 million in 1974 to 56.6 million today, a 25.7 percent increase. The shortage of master teachers, particularly in critical-need roles, is disproportionately more severe, with the most impoverished urban campuses struggling the most to fill vacancies. Addressing specific teacher certification areas and support roles (i.e., substitutes and instructional assistants) requires various strategies.

The Frontline Research and Learning Institute survey referenced in chapter 2 listed substitute teachers as the second most challenging vacancy area to fill after special education (SE).[2] The current approaches for enticing subs most often resemble a patchwork left to chance. Instructional assistants (IAs), perceived as extra help, are underutilized, and their potential is undervalued. Integrating these siloed positions into the educational pathway structure is an advantageous strategy.

A proactive teacher succession plan should move from the broad model (figure 6.1 in chapter 6) to the refined details appropriate for growing distinct roles. Attracting and retaining talent in those roles requires nuanced strategies within the model. This chapter isolates ideas for optimizing the recruitment and induction of two support positions as prospective teachers. As often overlooked educational paraprofessionals, substitute teachers and IAs have the untapped potential to enhance instruction while diminishing shortages.

SUBSTITUTE TEACHERS

Even prior to the pandemic, the escalating teacher shortage had increased the demand for substitutes. Responding to this situation, "some schools are lowering their standards for substitute teachers, which were already lower than those for full-time faculty."[3] In some cases, individuals leading a class have no college degree and only a two- or three-day training seminar. The other reaction to shortages has been to raise substitute pay, further hindering financially strapped districts. These ineffective responses are neither short- nor long-term solutions to a substantial staffing hardship detrimental to student progress.

As documented in multiple studies, teacher absences negatively affect student learning. One principal stated that "having a substitute teacher is just as impactful to a student's achievement as if they missed school that day."[4] As a principal, I have also experienced building safety concerns on days when a high percentage of subs replaced teachers. Another burden for districts is the financial strain from teacher absences. In 2017, teachers missed an average of 9.4 days per year. With a national average substitute compensation of $105 per full day,[5] "teacher absences cost districts an additional $1800 per teacher per year."[6]

Stereotyping substitute teachers as mere safety monitors perpetuates their self-perception of irrelevance. This narrow perspective is counterintuitive when considering the total instructional classroom time guided by substitutes. "Over the course of a kindergarten through 12th-grade education, the average student will spend an entire school year with a substitute teacher leading their education."[7] This significant amount of time is a lost opportunity never recovered. Imagine the systemic impact if that additional year constituted legitimate academic progression. The entire system warrants disruption, not only for its current ineffectiveness but considering its systemic potential as a pipeline for teachers.

Every state has express requirements for substitute teachers, which even differ from district to district. Guidelines sporadically change with the wavering supply and demand. Employment requirements range from as little as a high school diploma or General Educational Development (GED) test to possession of a bachelor's degree, while some states compel a substitute teaching licensure. Only seventeen states and the District of Columbia mandate that substitute applicants pass a criminal background check.[8] Poor urban and remote rural school districts experience the most severe hardships in finding qualified subs. Consequently, at-risk students suffer the most from inadequate or missing instruction.

In most cases, substitutes are compensated for actual days employed with an approved daily rate. Considering the state, school district, certification status, and college degree, "pay can vary dramatically, ranging anywhere from as low as $20 to as much as $190 per day."[9] The number of workdays available in many cases cannot be predicted from week to week. The job can be intimidating with frequent morning calls, little or no prep time, and the uncertainties involved in dealing with new students.

Retired teachers could contribute more time as substitutes, but state workday limitations impede their deployment. This experienced yet restricted pool of talent is hiding in plain sight. Addressing shortages could be bolstered by creating a cadre of priority retired teacher substitutes compensated at a higher daily rate. Given the various constraints for retirees, their expanded usage would, in most cases, require legislative changes. Applying a rigorous standard for reentry is essential for such a program to be effective. Criteria could consider local needs, previous teacher evaluations, and historical student performance data.

Retired teachers are increasingly being brought back to districts with high numbers of vacancies. Several states, including Illinois, have recently worked to relax some of the restrictions for retired teachers to mitigate severe situations. North Shore School District superintendent Michael Lubelfeld stated the following:

> I completely support the return, penalty-free, for retired teachers to return to the teaching force. Pulling retired teachers back into schools is one of several solutions states and districts are using to address teacher shortages, which hit high-need schools the most and are especially evident in the areas of math, science and special education.[10]

Opening the reentry door to *all* retirees does not work if the goal is heightened standards. Hiring retired teachers with exemplary records, especially those who can teach critical-need subjects, is educationally and economically sound. The allotment of positions could be based on district enrollment and would help limit the pool to high-quality retirees in specific areas. Bringing back proven veteran teachers without penalty to their pension is one aspect of a comprehensive substitute solution. The state investment is negligible and is educationally far superior to a scenario where student learning stops or regresses with rotating or less capable substitutes.

The typical substitute teacher has no benefits, no pension, and no future work guarantees, and consequently the role has little appeal as a lifetime career aspiration. Ownership of student progress is impossible if someone is subbing in several districts and frequently teaching different classes. Even getting to know students' names can be a formidable task, much less establishing trusting relationships. Moreover, the day's lessons with no prep time are frequently beyond a substitute's area of expertise. The system's utilitarian purpose is not student learning but classroom supervision and safety. A fresh, innovative structure is necessary. In analyzing the needs and issues, a strategic plan should respond to the following questions:

- How can substitute teaching become more appealing?
- How can substitute teachers better advance student learning?
- How can the position lead to job stability and advancement?

Designing career pathways for substitute teachers should be a judicious undertaking that advances educational goals. Principals quickly identify and appreciate reliable and competent substitutes. Many substitute teachers have post-secondary degrees, while others have significant college hours. Principals are in an optimal situation to recommend subs for sponsorship. Those exhibiting talent and strong instructional potential are ideal candidates for targeted pathway recruitment. Long-term substitutes would have student achievement data from benchmarks and state assessments for additional consideration.

Instituting a certification pathway for vetted substitute teachers offers benefits for multiple constituents. Partnering with local universities serves their education department, districts, enrolled substitutes, and students. Certain agreements would be necessary to assist an adept substitute toward teacher certification (e.g., MOUs with the university, post-certification commitment documents). Sponsoring certification and hiring acknowledged quality substitutes have a high probability of success. In my long-term experience, principals prefer to hire someone they have observed working effectively with children rather than an unknown, unproven first-year teacher. Substitutes have ample motivation to sign a multi-year pledge to remain with a district with an opportunity to double their income and begin receiving benefits.

SUBSTITUTE PATHWAYS

The proposed substitute pathway incorporates five distinct categories. The goal is to enhance applicant quantity and quality while adding another pipeline of future teachers. The prospect of an extended professional career with support systems builds commitment and motivation. A nascent career structure for substitutes can enhance work attitude, commitment, and professional purpose.

Preparatory Substitute. Not appreciably different than the current structures, a preparatory substitute fills the immediate need for absent teachers. Preparatory substitutes must have earned a minimum of ninety college hours, completed an application, undergone a criminal history background check, and attended a two-day training session. New substitutes would undergo a probationary period until sanctioned for continuance. After fifty official work days, human resource staff would call at least two principals and complete an appraisal survey. The candidate would be maintained or removed from the eligible district list based on a standard score.

As a preparatory substitute, the employees' daily pay would mirror the standard rates based on education: level 1 for no bachelor's degree, level 2 for a college bachelor's degree, and level 3 for a degree with a certified teacher license. Table 10.1 presents a hypothetical example of the pathway designations. One valuable feature of the appraisal requirement is terminating the circulation of ineffective or unreliable individuals.

Sanctioned Substitute. While the extreme shortage continues, districts will need to retain substitutes that may lack the skills to become effective teachers. Provided they keep students safe, follow procedures, and attempt to follow lesson plans, individuals will remain eligible as sanctioned substitutes. If the supply of individual applicants increases, standards should be raised correspondingly. Ideally, the sanctioned substitutes are the largest group, meeting the majority of short-term absences. Emerging candidates for pathway entry as a clinical substitute are selected from this category.

Clinical Substitute. The most innovative position in the proposed pathway is the clinical substitute. A cohort of the most talented prospects would be selected from the sanctioned list three times a year (fall, spring, and summer) to enroll in a local university's degree/certification or certification program. Expectations, timelines, and applications are available on the district website

Table 10.1 Sample Salary Scale for Substitute Teacher Pathway

Level	Pay Level	Salary	Benefits
Preparatory Substitute	1–3	$80, $100, $120	No
Sanctioned Substitute	2–3	$100, $120	No
Clinical Substitute	4	$150	No
Priority Substitute	4	$150	No
Endorsed Substitute	5	$175	Yes
*Long Term	5–6	$175, $200	Only if Endorsed Sub

* After ten consecutive days in the same role, the long-term-sub daily rate increases by one pay level for the last four categories.

and promoted at job fairs. Selection should prioritize critical-need teaching positions (e.g., SE and secondary math). Larger application pool certification areas such as elementary education would be limited to only the highest-rated candidates.

Qualifications for candidates include their designation as a sanctioned substitute, a nearly completed or earned bachelor's degree, and commendable recommendations from three principals. Those identified as emerging prospects in the talent management database would receive invitations to apply. The district pays tuition for necessary degree completion and certification through a university agreement. The program of study would be completed in no more than one year, and the candidates sign a pledge to continue employment for three years after completion. Cohort size each semester would vary contingent on the district's projected need and quality of candidates.

This category emphasizes a district's resolve for excellence and infusion of local talent. Instead of an escalating regional bidding war for unqualified and ineffective subs, teacher pathways signal a rational strategy. Now, becoming a substitute can stimulate intrinsic motivation and engagement for those who need support. While elevating substitute efficacy, the pathway simultaneously builds a vetted pool of teachers with a local connection.

Priority Substitute. Priority subs are employed from highly rated sanctioned substitutes, clinical subs, and select retired teachers. The designation represents high confidence that the sub will consistently advance student learning. Utilized for long- and short-term vacancies, this group may be designated as generalists or excel in a particular subject. Strategically aligning the placement of priority subs to academic needs strengthens the continuity of learning.

As discussed earlier, vetted retired teachers bring talent and experience. They also deserve higher compensation and the removal of penalties that would affect their annual pension. State legislative alterations for retaining a limited number of retired teachers offer multiple advantages. School districts may also be unaware of degreed-certified teachers living in the community. For personal reasons, they may not be interested in full-time teaching. Reaching out and offering conditional part-time work to someone designated as a higher-compensated priority sub may yield a productive relationship. Priority sub positions can be promoted by messaging select groups in the community via social media.

Some of the sanctioned substitutes may be exceptional even without certification. They may not be interested in the clinical program to progress as a full-time teacher. If the talent is apparent and the candidate meets the same application criteria as clinical substitutes, this group adds value to any campus because students continue to progress. As it avoids a bidding war for random prospects, the systemic investment in priority subs is sustainable and cost-effective.

Endorsed Substitute. An endorsed substitute has completed the degree and certification as a clinical substitute. These individuals are now recommended applicants in the teacher candidate pool. Endorsed substitutes remain in this category if a full-time teaching position with the district is unavailable. After application analysis, other experienced teachers can be approved at this level. A credentialed teacher may have moved into the area with solid evaluations, recommendations, and student data.

Priority and endorsed substitutes are scheduled first for long-term engagements. These employees are viable insurance to sustain learning while a teacher is on leave and are worth the augmented daily rate. Many districts, primarily urban and remote rural, struggle to fill positions following teacher resignations during the school year. A pre-screened applicant pool that campuses could access with confidence would be an indispensable resource.

The ubiquitous use of substitute teacher management software simplifies substitute placement and progression. Application features improve efficiency, including automated scheduling, absence and attendance tracking, analytics, reports, and real-time job notifications. Some programs match substitutes with specific classes and integrate them with other school management tools. Working with a company's programmers, tailoring a program to monitor and schedule with the new model is plausible and advisable.

INSTRUCTIONAL ASSISTANT

After examining staff data in 2016, I unexpectedly found that more than 100 IAs had bachelor's degrees in my district. Additional IAs were close to completing a degree, even though the Texas state IA requirements were only thirty credit hours. In follow-up conversations, principals expressed that many IAs were competent, dedicated, and could excel as classroom teachers. According to recent US Census Bureau statistics on teacher assistants (from a database of 30 million profiles), over half had earned at least a bachelor's degree (see figure 10.1).[11]

One significant advantage in targeting IAs is their familiarity with specific student groups. Assistants are employed in classrooms having critical-need teacher shortages. SE and early childhood classrooms are the primary work assignments for IAs. Many IAs have extensive experience along with an understanding of curriculum and pedagogy. They are already acclimated to the demands of the teaching environment and need little induction as they become teachers. IAs could double or triple their salary, while the district would be rewarded with enthusiastic teachers for high-need teaching positions.

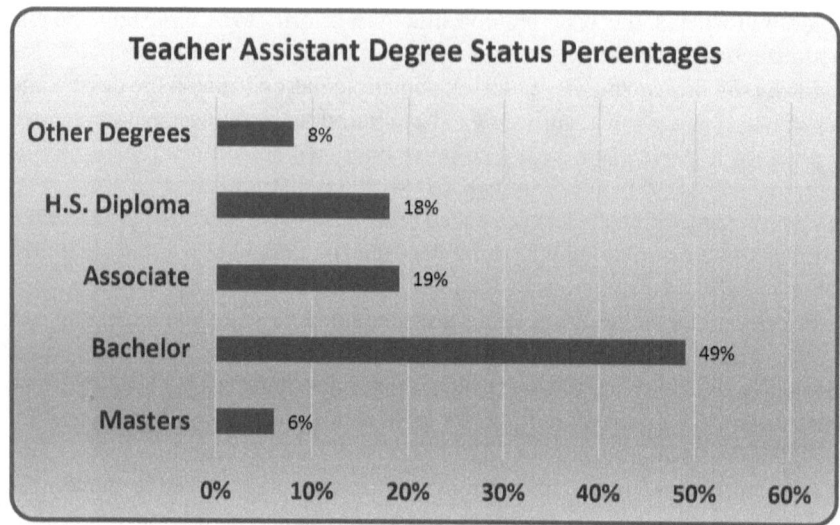

Figure 10.1 Distribution of Degrees for Instructional Assistants. *Source*: Zippia (2021). Teacher assistant statistics and facts in the US. Retrieved from https://www.zippia.com/teacher-assistant jobs/demographics/.

Experienced IAs enjoy another incentive: they have already invested eligible time in state retirement systems.

An IA pathway to becoming a successful teacher is as viable as a substitute teacher. Supporting a skilled IA toward teacher certification requires certain agreements (e.g., MOUs with the university, commitment documents). Like clinical substitutes, assisting with certification and hiring a known, quality IA is likely to succeed. With a minimum-size cohort, universities will work with districts to be flexible in scheduling for candidates and sometimes offer reduced tuition.

The cost-benefit differential for investment in IA certification is significant. Calculating using the Learning Policy Institute's estimate tool, the cost of replacing an urban teacher is about $21,000. The Learning Policy Institute reports that "beginning teachers with little preparation are 2½ times more likely to leave the classroom after 1 year, compared to their well-prepared peers."[12] Compare a new teacher's allegiance to a district to that of an IA who has been employed for five years. The IA has community roots and commits for three years after receiving certification. This option is definitively low-risk, high-reward, and cost-effective for the IA, school system, and the university.

The US Bureau of Labor Statistics estimated the accelerated growth for certified early childhood teachers. "Employment of preschool teachers is projected to grow 18 percent from 2020 to 2030, much faster than the average for all occupations."[13] This prediction preceded the mounting national endorsement for expanded early childhood opportunities. If "Build Back Better" or similar legislation does obtain approval, the need for early childhood teachers will move to the top of the vacancy list.

> We're going to need to exponentially increase the number of pre-K teachers in our country if Build Back Better becomes reality . . . preschool teachers will need to have a bachelor's degree in early childhood education within six years, and then there are some exceptions that people have been grandfathered in.[14]

In SE, IAs support teachers with both clerical and educational tasks. SE teachers depend on IAs because of the enormity of everyday tasks. Beyond the planning, lessons, and grading papers, responsibilities include scheduling and attending Individualized Education Program (IEP) meetings. Other administrative regulations occupying significant time involve preparing SE-IEP documents, sending parent notices, ongoing student evaluations, and coordinating students' transitions from school to adult life.[15]

Working with diagnosticians, physical therapists, psychologists, and counselors, the scope of experiences for IAs in SE is extensive. On-the-job training with certified SE teachers provides rich pedagogic learning not available in college classes. The SE teacher role is among the most demanding in education, and the turnover rate is nearly twice as high as general education teachers.[16] IAs with a practical understanding and appreciation of SE obligations have a higher probability of remaining in their teaching position and diminishing current attrition rates.

The pathway for IAs' certification parallels that for substitutes. Those IAs with two years of experience, excellent evaluations, and recommendations from their principal would be eligible to apply for the district program. The only caveat is continuance in the current employment area: early childhood or SE. Classes with both substitutes and IAs assist the university in improving professor-to-student ratios.

RECRUITING SUBSTITUTES AND INSTRUCTIONAL ASSISTANTS

The optimal recruiting strategy for substitutes and IAs is having a sustainable system for advancement in place. An arrangement that aligns with motivation theory becomes self-sustaining. Individuals intrinsically desire to work toward greater autonomy and expand personal agency. Substitutes and IAs naturally visualize themselves in teaching positions from their support roles. Eliminating barriers and timely encouragement may be the seminal formula for integrating latent talent.

Even with the financial support for certification, some employees may still have reservations about applying for advancement opportunities. Hesitation may stem from anxiety about college classes or concern with time away from family. Building confidence through cognitive coaching and assigning support mentors will help placate fears. I have found professors amenable to accommodating district cohorts in negotiating with university education departments. Scheduling classes immediately after school and at nearby locations assist candidates in finding work-life balance.

CONCLUSION

Students' lives are shaped by their experiences, both in and out of school. In response to others, they acquire components of self-concept spanning low self-esteem to confidence with a maturing agency. The safest place for interaction should be the school, with the primary years setting the trajectory for all future achievements. Some social contacts are more influential than others, but no role requiring connection with students is insignificant. From a helping hand from the bus driver to a kind word from the cafeteria worker, ideally, all the adults at school contribute constructively to the child's formative development.

In a high-functioning school culture, all staff members supporting students in various roles practice acceptance and impartial resolve. Not everyone is well-suited to nurturing students, and many leave the education profession after this realization. However, experienced substitutes and IAs enter the profession with "eyes wide open." The teacher shortage must be addressed holistically with burgeoning systems, and rethinking the progression of internal staff is part of the solution.

NOTES

1. National Center for Education Statistics, 2019.
2. Buttner, 2021.
3. Heyward, 2021, 1.
4. McGuire, 2018, 1.
5. National Substitute Teachers Alliance, 2021.
6. Saenz-Armstrong, 2020, 1.
7. Bowers, 2009, 6.
8. "Substitute Teachers," 2021.
9. "Substitute Teachers' Salary," 2021, 1.
10. Vercelletto, 2019, 1–2.

11. Zippia, 2022.
12. "What's the Cost of Teacher Turnover?" 2017, 3.
13. "Occupational Outlook Handbook: Preschool Teachers," 2022, 1.
14. Quilantan, 2021, 2.
15. Klein, 2004.
16. Buttner, 2021.

Chapter 11

Critical-Need Teachers
Early Childhood, Special Education, and Bilingual

> Disability need not be an obstacle to success . . . It is my hope that . . . this century will mark a turning point for inclusion of people with disabilities in the lives of their societies.
>
> —Stephen Hawking, theoretical physicist and cosmologist

The teacher shortages in early childhood education (ECE), special education (SE), and bilingual education disproportionately compromise learning for distinct student populations. Early childhood teachers nurture students during the most pivotal stage of child development in school. SE teachers instruct students requiring additional support for a broad spectrum of needs. Much of the responsibility confronts an undersupply of teachers. Bilingual teachers have a complex responsibility: to educate and integrate an expanding population of diverse students who speak multiple languages with a variety of linguistic proficiencies.

One reason for the undersupply of teachers in these roles is the instructional challenges that exceed those in a traditional classroom. Each teaching role identified above is unique, and recruiting strategies must interconnect the district's instructional goals with the market for candidates. The targeted talent search approaches differ for a secondary calculus teacher, ECE, or SE teacher. One group may be best acquired from select outside professions, while another may favor pragmatic internal talent expansion. In either case, waiting for applications to accumulate from human resource postings is untenable. Standard recruiting practices without resourceful incentives will fail to solve the predicament of escalating vacancies.

Chapter 11

EARLY CHILDHOOD TEACHERS

The most impoverished families are continually handicapped in preparing their children for early childhood programs. Participation in quality private ECE programs is financially prohibitive. Parents have less education to prepare their children before pre-K and often disregard available enrollment opportunities. Students participating in public programs are at a disadvantage in their early skills, behaviors, and health. Compounding inequity, deficits in early development, or misdiagnosis of English Language Learners (ELLs) lead to over-placement in SE.

The initial years in school are the most consequential for all subsequent learning and development. Every year, 40 percent of children enter kindergarten one to three years behind in acknowledged readiness skills.[1] The task of playing catch-up is monumental, even with tenacious intervention. Readiness for the ensuing grade levels involves more than mastering academic standards. Researchers are finding that self-regulation and executive function skills are "foundational for children's development of social, emotional and cognitive competence to achieve early school success and positive social relationship[s]."[2] A majority of the 40 percent will never recover to desired functional levels without consistent and quality whole-child instruction during their early successive years.

The salience of ECE is unequivocal. A growing commitment to universal pre-K for three- and four-year-olds is encouraging, along with possibilities such as "Build Back Better" federal funding. A factsheet from the House Committee on Education and Labor makes the following bold prediction: "Through this investment we will have free, universal, high-quality preschool for three- and four-year-olds."[3] Missing is a critical caveat: over time, with continued support. The enthusiasm for transformational classrooms is unrealistic without a cadre of prepared ECE teachers. The United States is far from being an ideal ECE ecosystem. Nationally, districts are starting from a significant deficit of teachers for the *current* ECE students.

The National Institute for Early Education Research at Rutgers University projected substantial numbers for this staffing dilemma. Enrolling only 70 percent of three- and four-year-olds requires 40,000 to 50,000 new classrooms with a teacher and instructional assistant (IA). Compounding the problem, half the current teachers "need some additional education to complete a BA degree with specialized training in early childhood, about 125,000 teachers."[4] The proposed "Build Back Better" program, financed for six years with federal funds, could mitigate the decrease in substantial staffing projections.

In addition to staffing concerns, plans for the anticipated "high-quality" program conspicuously neglect logistical forethought for such a significant national initiative. One issue is classroom space. The 40,000 to 50,000 additional specialized ECE classrooms do not exist. Another noteworthy legislative omission is a plan for valid assessment tools and systems to appraise the quality of pre-K programs. Educators remember the free-for-all of state testing for No Child Left Behind, with few tangible gains for students.

My cautionary apprehensions should not be misinterpreted: I entirely endorse the resolve of the "Build Back Better" initiative for ECE. The admonition is to safeguard the planning for lasting efficacy. Essential components include advanced strategies for the infusion of teachers, procurement of facilities, and consistent national assessments for comparative analysis. Millions of dollars may be wasted on "babysitting" ECE children with few developmental benefits without attending to these issues. For this book, explicit practices only address the integration of new teachers.

When unprepared to venture at scale, the prudent approach is establishing goals and incremental steps. The general language of the 4-billion-dollar package for universal pre-K touts a mixed delivery model:

> The proposal builds on existing state programs to provide federal dollars to support equitable, free, and inclusive access to high quality pre-K for every three- and four-year-old in child care programs, schools, Head Start centers, and family-based settings. It also includes support for raising wages for early educators.[5]

The initial priority should be enticing pathways for ECE teachers. For these teacher programs to approach realizing goals for students, they must include rigorous certification standards.

Raising wages for early educators is a pivotal enticement for prospective teachers. The US Bureau of Labor Statistics reported that in 2019, the median annual salary for pre-K teachers was $30,520, compared to $59,420 for kindergarten teachers.[6] This discrepancy prevails because the criteria for pre-K teachers are diverse and inconsistent. Nationally, twenty-seven states require a bachelor's degree and ten mandate only an associate's degree with a child development credential. Other state departments of education have varying degrees of preparation expectations. Montana does not license pre-K teachers and imposes *no* educational requirements.[7]

New funding should prioritize teacher salaries with the contingency of implementing professional standards over time. The Institute of Medicine and the National Research Council recommend that "all teachers in the nation's preschools should have a bachelor's degree in early childhood development or early education."[8] Studies have demonstrated that students completing high-quality ECE programs were more successful than peers who did not attend such programs in three ways: students were (1) less likely to be placed in SE, (2) less likely to be retained in a grade, and (3) more likely to graduate from high school. The researchers emphasized that social-emotional skill development plays an important role.[9] Pedagogy in an ECE classroom must be distinguishable from that in later elementary grades, and specialized teacher training is critical.

The baseline requirement for an ECE teacher should be a bachelor's degree and ECE certification. Allowing states five years to progressively meet this prototype is a reasonable expectation. My recommended standards for an effective model would stipulate the following:

- A degreed and certified ECE teacher for every three- and four-year-old classroom;
- ECE teacher salaries that are at least equivalent to those of all other district teachers;
- ECE classroom size that does not exceed twenty students; and
- An IA is added for each group of twelve to twenty preschoolers.

Setting benchmark goals for progressive implementation should be included in the state application process for federal funding. Multiple additional strategies are suggested for attaining the proposed reference model. The justification? Because ECE (1) is the most critical stage of child development and learning; (2) disproportionally excludes the most disadvantaged student populations, sustaining systemic inequity; (3) has the least funding, least cohesive curriculum, and most inconsistent assessment standards; and (4) projects a 40,000–50,000 teacher deficit. Practical approaches to meeting the five-year targeted goals include the following:

- Student teachers are hired as clinical interns and compensated at IA rates with a commitment to continue with the district as an ECE teacher upon completion of a degree and certification.
- Pathways are designed to move from IA to ECE teacher (discussed in chapter 10), with increased compensation at progressive steps and district tuition reimbursement.
- Recruitment of current first- through third-grade teachers or new certified elementary teachers with incentives and sponsorship for ECE certification.
- Placing the most at-risk students in mixed classes with the most accomplished ECE master teachers.

The largest, most stable, and sustainable pool of teacher applicants are those with general elementary education credentials. Certified elementary teachers, particularly those in first through third grades, are often ideal candidates for ECE grades. If capable, caring teachers are incentivized to earn an additional certificate; a staffing reorganization can benefit the entire school. To make a sports analogy, the Baltimore Orioles shifted "Iron Man" Cal Ripken Jr. from shortstop to third base toward the end of his career. In addition to balancing the team and playing outstanding defense, he was selected as a third baseman to the American League All-Star team in each of the next five years. Change must be purposeful, for example, because an individual has talent, never a reaction solely to fill a vacancy.

I believe the best teachers should work in the primary grades for students ages three to seven. Students are more resilient in surviving a weak teacher in the later grades if they have a solid foundation in ECE. All students deserve outstanding teachers, but learning gaps are increasingly difficult to close each passing year.

> Students who are placed with highly effective teachers for three years in a row significantly outperform average students . . . Unfortunately, the opposite is true as well—a student with even one ineffective teacher may not catch up to his peers for up to three years, and having one excellent teacher doesn't fully compensate for the effect of an ineffective one. Worse yet, students with three bad teachers in a row rarely catch up at all.[10]

The recruitment proposals discussed and a master teacher pathway for ECE teachers will help bridge the shortages and cultivate expert staff. Incentives for internal and external first- through third-grade teachers include sign-on bonuses and assistance with certification cost and preparation. A two-year promissory commitment to teaching ECE grades with an option to return to a higher grade will appeal to teachers. Substantiating a commitment of systemic support toward ECE teachers encourages loyalty and permanency. The generational opportunity of "Build Back Better" can revitalize campuses through ECE. The United States *can* get it right on the first iteration with a reasoned strategy.

The role of principals in shaping ECE campuses cannot be overestimated in relation to teacher development. Curricular materials, instructional activities, and assessment protocols are developmentally incompatible with those for later elementary grades. When a principal without adequate training is designated at an ECE campus, teachers may be channeled toward counterproductive practices. Anxiety over accountability metrics and a deficit of leaders knowledgeable in pre-K learning culture contribute to the recurrent digression from whole-child pedagogy. Although leadership models are beyond the scope of this book, the influence of principals on teachers' professional growth is crucial to success in the early years.

SPECIAL EDUCATION TEACHERS

The National Center for Education Statistics identifies fourteen distinct types of students with disabilities eligible for services under the Individuals with Disabilities Education Act of 1975.[11] In 2019–2020, the SE student population

Table 11.1 San Antonio ISD Special Education Teacher New Hires over Five Years

Special Education Turnover					
New Special Education Teacher Hires					
2013–2014	2014–2015	2015–2016	2016–2017	2017–2018	5-Year Average
75	46	70	59	41	58.2
Baseline average of 358 teachers = turnover rate of **16.2%**					
New Special Education Instructional Assistant Hires					
2013–2014	2014–2015	2015–2016	2016–2017	2017–2018	5-Year Average
62	71	83	97	74	77.4
Baseline average of 439 IAs = turnover rate of **17.6%**					

comprised 7.3 million or 14 percent of all public-school students ages three to twenty-one.[12] Students within that age group received services for various conditions, from autism and emotional disabilities to speech, vision, or hearing impairment. The individual differences and services required in one classroom can be overwhelming for teachers.

Like most inner-city districts, recruiting and retaining talented teachers for SE was particularly demanding for the San Antonio Independent School District. According to the data in table 11.1, over five years, the turnover rate for SE teachers (16.2 percent) and IAs (17.6 percent) was consistently high. Given the severely limited pool of candidates and the many obligations of the position, new talent procurement strategies were employed to meet ongoing classroom vacancies.

SPECIAL EDUCATION TURNOVER

Prior to my retirement in 2019 and the disruption of Covid-19, some creative actions were beginning to attract more SE teachers. One approach used by an increasing number of districts is early pre-hiring. Using the turnover data from table 11.1 as an example, pre-hiring forty-one SE teachers and sixty-two SE IAs poses a minimal risk of overstaffing. Job fairs for the following school year can be held as early as October and November. External candidates with solid data and evaluations are offered contracts and sign-on bonuses at those events. Contracts and reduced sign-on bonuses are used for highly rated clinical interns, student teachers, and IAs completing their degree and certification. The weakness of bonuses is that the experienced talent may only be transferred from one district to another.

A second proposition is a variation of the ECE recruitment of current first- through third-grade teachers, only expanded to include *all* certified teachers. A two-year *Promise Program* recruits and selects (1) current regular classroom teachers with SE certification, and (2) current teachers willing to become certified in SE. In the latter case, the district would offer preparation classes and pay for the certification exam. Requirements to participate in the *Promise Program* are the following:

- Two years of successful teaching experience
- Evaluations that are proficient or higher in all domains
- Evidence of student performance growth

Teachers commit to teaching SE with an option to return to their regular classroom position after two years. Those participating would receive a recognition bonus after completing the SE role. Early in the spring of year two, a "promise" teacher would communicate their intentions for the following year in writing. In the San Antonio example, if an average of twelve teachers entered the program annually, a significant percentage of vacancies would be filled with proven teachers over five years. Even with a 60 percent rate of returning to their previous positions after two years, at the end of five years, thirty-five SE teachers continue with students.

As noted in the previous chapter, leveraging funding for IAs allows student teachers to be hired as clinical teaching interns with a cohesive pathway. A concurrent action assists existing IAs in finishing degrees and attaining certification. As a productive long-term strategy, "growing your own" reduces attrition. In both scenarios, vetted candidates benefit from an intern salary at a slightly elevated rate and mentorship with an experienced master teacher. Students are rewarded with higher-quality instructional support and consistency. The district reduces turnover and saves on new teacher onboarding (more than $20,000 for each new hire).[13] Lastly, local universities enroll additional students and strengthen their ability to qualify for grants through collaboration with local districts.

Standards for quality control should be uncompromising. A thorough collaborative selection process with universities and principals requires objective evaluation tools, including joint observations. Memorandums of understanding and blueprints for administration include calendar timelines, website promotion, information meetings, and a process for data collection and analysis. Accentuated in the effort is the comprehensive pathway for those accomplished in SE to advance as master teachers.

BILINGUAL TEACHERS

The decisive advantages of being bilingual are both professional and social. The escalating number of ELL will enrich our culture if given the opportunity. In the expanding international job market, bilingualism is a growing component in vacancy requirements as corporations serve a more diverse and multilingual clientele, foreign and domestic. With globalization, translators and interpreters are increasingly in demand for both the public and private sectors. The Department of Labor lists occupations requiring bilingual candidates in the top fifteen fastest-growing careers. From 2010 to 2020, the United States experienced a 42 percent growth in these professions, rising to nearly 25,000.[14] Forecasters anticipate this tendency to continue into the next several decades.

The number of citizens in the United States speaking two or more languages continues to grow. With that expansion, traditional English-only classroom teachers are ill-equipped to educate students from more diverse backgrounds. Zeigler and Camarota provide data on the shifting demographics:

> In 2018, a record 67.3 million U.S. residents (native-born, legal immigrants, and illegal immigrants) spoke a language other than English at home. The number has more than doubled since 1990 and almost tripled since 1980. Since 1980, the number who speak a foreign language at home grew nearly seven times faster than the number who speak only English at home.[15]

Of the 350 different languages spoken in the United States, the Census Bureau (2015) reported that after English, the most prevalent languages were Spanish at 37.5 million, Chinese at 2.9 million, Tagalog at 1.6 million, and Vietnamese at 1.4 million.[16] In addressing the growing diverse influx of students, dual-language programs have become more prevalent; dual programs exist for several languages, but most campuses are English–Spanish.

Title VII of the Elementary and Secondary Education Act (ESEA) or the Bilingual Education Act was enacted in 1968. Federal supplemental funding for bilingual services supports (1) educational resources, (2) training for teachers and IAs, (3) development and distribution of materials, and (4) projects involving parents. The Equal Educational Opportunities Act of 1974 reinforced the ESEA, making it compulsory for school districts to overcome language barriers that hinder ELL. Individual states have resisted embracing bilingual education, but research identifies diverse academic advantages.[17]

Most states welcome the legislative execution of bilingual education, and parental interest is especially keen for dual-language programs. However, the considerable number of teacher vacancies and demand for bilingual teachers will likely accelerate without a deliberate response. One barrier to altering the status quo is the severe shortage of teachers proficient in two or more languages. Given the shortage of qualified teachers, districts must look to creative staffing solutions such as "growing your own," the J-1 Teacher Exchange Program, and the use of technology.

Imitating the human capital-building strategies with ECE and SE teachers, like cultivating substitutes, IAs, student teachers, and clinical interns, are operative practices. Particularly with Spanish, which represents the majority of students, identifying native speakers for teacher pathways is an obvious scheme. The other replication is identifying and recruiting certified elementary education teachers fluent in Spanish. In 2017, California took proactive steps

> by providing $5 million in grant funding to school districts, charter schools, and county offices of education to provide professional development for teachers who have a bilingual authorization but have not been teaching in bilingual settings and for bilingual instructional assistants who are interested in becoming teachers.[18]

These approaches are facilitated when talent management keeps extensive employee data for all instructional roles. Exploring possible staffing solutions is viable using analytic tools when identification data is comprehensive and accurate.

The J-1 Teacher Exchange Program is part of the Fulbright–Hays Act established in 1961. The program allows experienced foreign teachers to work in US classrooms for one to three years, possibly with a two-year extension. Students receive the added advantage of learning about another culture integrated with content skills. The qualifications to teach through the J-1 program, according to its website, are as follows:

- Be working as a teacher in the home country at the time of application, or, if not working as a teacher, otherwise meet the eligibility qualifications and (a) have recently (within twelve months of application) completed an advanced degree and (b) have two years of full-time teaching experience within the past eight years.
- Have a degree equivalent to a Bachelor's degree in either education or the academic subject field in which they intend to teach.
- Satisfy the standards of the US state in which they will teach.
- Be of good reputation and character.
- Be seeking to enter the United States for full-time teaching as a teacher of record at an accredited educational institution in the United States.
- Possess sufficient proficiency in the English language.[19]

San Antonio ISD used this option to employ ten dual-language teachers from Spain in the fall of 2019. The local investment was a cost-effective $400 per candidate, with most application processing done through a regional education service center. Interviews were conducted with district bilingual department staff sent to Spain. If considering this option, school districts should review the sponsoring organization's history, cost, and success rate. States and regional centers could serve as intermediary agents to enable districts by streamlining the cost and paperwork for the J-1 program. An untapped source for bilingual Spanish teachers is Central and South America. With competent talent amenable to working in the United States, establishing agreements with Latin American countries would help alleviate the severe shortage.

LANGUAGES OTHER THAN SPANISH

The overwhelming variety of native languages spoken in schools creates a monumental pedagogic dilemma. For example, the Los Angeles Unified School District identified ninety-two different student languages in 2021, yet offered instruction in only ten.[20] Districts without specialized teaching staff or resources must look for innovative ways to facilitate student learning. Small numbers of students speaking less-common languages are a particular hardship for schools. Assisted learning programs (e.g., Rosetta Stone) with non-speaking teacher support are not ideal but are the only option for many districts.

A superior option using technology is virtual learning. Small numbers of students with wide geographic distribution make this the most economical approach. A child with a native Vietnamese language in rural Arizona could receive same-language instruction from a teacher in Rhode Island. As educators realized during the pandemic, virtual learning is not as effective as face-to-face classroom instruction but superior to computer-software instruction alone. Leadership among state departments of education should collaborate by employing cooperative agreements. More extensive virtual networks increase the number of language-specific teachers to meet the unique needs of students, regardless of the learner's locale, language level, or socioeconomic status.

CONCLUSION

Federal and state supplemental financing is based on the philosophy that equal funding is *not* uniformly fair. Categorical resources for individuals with disabilities, ELLs, and the economically disadvantaged enable historically underserved students to have a chance for success in a competitive society. The purpose of the federal Head Start program is to "promote the school readiness of infants, toddlers, and preschool-aged children from low-income families."[21] With the momentum for universal pre-K, adjustments should be considered in using funds for class size, student screening, and integrated classrooms. Moreover, while multiple factors contribute to the optimal classroom, the initial priority is cultivating quality teachers.

Career pathways and master teacher opportunities alone are unlikely to entice the formidable numbers of applicants essential for the hard-to-fill positions in ECE, SE, and bilingual education. Although stipends and bonuses contribute to the recruiting effort, they are not a remedy. Districts must establish and sustain strategies for long-term succession rather than trying to outbid neighboring districts. A solution is best realized via internal systems, providing advantages for a broader range of candidates in addition to traditional university graduates.

Early childhood, SE, and bilingual teachers comprise three of the most time-intensive and demanding educational roles. The capabilities of these leaders in the classroom also have substantial long-term effects on achieving social and economic equity. All students deserve a world-class education, but a greater focus on early intervention and acceleration prepares a more significant number more effectively over an extended period. The expression "critical-need teachers" is not hyperbole when one considers the potential of those teachers to guide the trajectory of so many lives.

NOTES

1. "Conquering the Readiness Gap," 2019.
2. He et al., 2021, 2.
3. Scott, 2021, 2.
4. Barnett, 2021, 1.
5. Fortner, 2021, 2.
6. "Occupational Outlook Handbook' Preschool Teachers," 2022.
7. "Preschool Teacher Requirements," 2020.
8. Ibid., 4.
9. McCoy et al., 2017.
10. Friedman, 2018, 5–6.
11. "The NCES Fast Facts: Students with Disabilities," 2021.
12. "Students with Disabilities," 2021.
13. "What's the Cost of Teacher Turnover?" 2017.
14. Kurtz, 2013.
15. Zeigler & Camarota, 2019, 1.
16. "Census Bureau Reports at Least 350 Different Languages Spoken," 2015.
17. Sparks, 2015.
18. Garcia, 2020, 4.
19. "Exchange Visitor Program," 2020.
20. "Multilingual & Multicultural Education," 2021.
21. "Head Start Services," 2021, 1.

Chapter 12

Critical-Need Teachers
Math, Science, and Computer Science

> The important thing in science is not so much to obtain new facts as to discover new ways of thinking about them.
>
> —William Lawrence Bragg, physicist

Pedagogic skills and caring interpersonal relationships are requisite for any teacher's success. Teachers possessing empathy for students is sacrosanct. However, as grade levels advance, pedagogic structures change. The content becomes more specialized and the range of teacher certification requirements more extensive. Secondary teachers impart a narrower scope of knowledge and skills, distinguishing them from elementary generalists. For example, a third-grade teacher can review content and easily exceed the math understanding of his/her class, while the high school calculus teacher must thoroughly know their subject from day one. Ubiquitous student progression in schools begins with one teacher in self-contained classrooms until about fifth grade, when students transition to multiple single-subject classes in middle and high schools.

Teachers with expertise in math, science, and computer science (CS) (STEM subjects) are subject experts. And although they are vital in cultivating skills for humanitarian and economic progress, serious shortages prevail. Outstanding teachers in these disciplines help produce the next generation of innovators in multiple fields. Nevertheless, those with classroom potential avoid education as a profession. Changing career perceptions and employment interests is no easy task. Understanding the required skillsets, motivational factors, and appealing employment conditions precedes crafting distinctive strategies for recruiting and retaining these specialized teachers.

The competitive job market opportunities distinguish math, science, and CS teachers from other critical-need teachers (i.e., early childhood, special education, and bilingual). A competent university graduate in these disciplines will have more employment opportunities and a higher starting salary. On average, graduates with degrees in applied mathematics, CS, and physics receive a starting salary exceeding $60,000 in non-teaching positions.[1] In contrast, the mean starting teacher salary in the United States is $41,163.[2] Given this significant degree of compensation difference, teacher pathways alone are unlikely to persuade graduates in these robust academic disciplines to become teachers.

One root cause of the vacancy dilemma is the industrial model promoting teacher value equivalency, as discussed in chapter 8. This embedded narrative decidedly inhibits progress in securing high-need math, science, and CS teachers. When setting compensation, the competing market for specialized skills in the private sector must be considered. Educators must acknowledge that *the universal teacher salary scale is obsolete* for legitimate teacher professional transformation to occur. At a minimum, competitive subject-specific stipends should be integrated into the salary structures. If a social studies teacher is offended that the physics teacher has a higher salary, he/she can always work to pass the physics certification exam.

Overcoming barriers and enticing teachers into these three STEM subjects require creative thinking. In mapping a recruiting blueprint, forethought includes individual motivation factors, district incentives, and outside partnerships. Growing a pool of new prospects is a crucial priority. Once recruited and hired, all teachers must meet the same standards with performance expectations, evaluations, and pathway requirements. Innovation is necessary as districts struggle, inhibit progress, and neglect student needs.

SHORTAGES AND RECRUITING-RETENTION STRATEGIES

Unsurprisingly, the high number of STEM vacancies is even more acute in high-poverty cities and remote rural schools. This reality adds another layer of concern when confronting the situation. Salary, career advancement prospects, working conditions, and geographic location are compelling motivational factors in an applicant's decision process. Forecasting the reasoning behind the employment preferences of teacher prospects is essential in constructing strategic plans. While some recruiting tactics are germane to all three subject areas, some distinguishing differences require specific approaches.

Math. The troubling 2020 school survey discussed in chapter 2 reported that 46 percent of districts had unfilled vacancies in secondary math.[3] This shortfall is juxtaposed against an optimistic outlook for university math graduates' employment outside of teaching. The US Bureau of Labor Statistics has projected the growth in math jobs for the current decade:

> Employment in math occupations is projected to grow 28 percent from 2020 to 2030, much faster than the average for all occupations, and will add about 67,200 jobs. Growth is anticipated as businesses and government agencies continue to emphasize the use of big data, which math occupations analyze.[4]

Without aggressive recruitment measures, the conditions for securing math teachers will likely move from inadequate to unacceptable.

Resourceful steps begin by recognizing that *salary is a factor*. Although it is improbable to match most competing salaries, a comfortable living wage for newly graduating math teachers is fundamental. This action alone would place talent management departments in a healthier position. Promoting a $15,000 stipend could solicit college majors *and* math graduates employed in other sectors. If gregarious, non-teaching math employees work in relative isolation, salary alone may not drive their career decisions.

The hypothetical $15,000 may or may not be the optimum tipping point. Determining a stipend baseline is a fundamental decision in appealing to latent candidates. Hu and Hirsh's analysis of four valid studies summarized that financial concerns considerably influence behaviors toward job choice, albeit not exceedingly. They concluded the following: "Nonetheless, the current results indicate that people are willing to accept significantly lower salaries in exchange for more meaningful work."[5] The follow-up question is: How do we make the work meaningful?

For prospective math teachers, finding a work culture offering purpose, support, and the possibility of earned autonomy can compensate for a modestly reduced salary.[6] School districts offering pathways and programs have begun to address this vision. The guidance and mentoring connecting teachers with the campus learning community must be consistent and authentic. Campus leadership cultivating respect, appreciation, and shaping professional agency is the corresponding commitment beyond monetary remuneration.

Science. Astronomer Carl Sagan astutely stated, "Every kid starts out as a natural-born scientist, and then we beat it out of them. A few trickle through the system with their wonder and enthusiasm for science intact."[7] Sustaining students' innate curiosity in any subject is related to a teacher's ability to create a stimulating environment. Hands-on science classes are a prototypical venue for discovery and for sparking curiosity. Designing

146   *Chapter 12*

captivating lab experiences is the purview of the talented science teacher, whose two desired attributes are content mastery and a pedagogic adeptness to engage students.

A 2021 survey of science teachers by the National Academies of Sciences, Engineering, and Medicine (NASEM) was reported in *Call to Action for Science Education: Building Opportunity for the Future*. Relevant findings are presented below and in figure 12.1:

- less than one-half of teachers reported using recommended NASEM instructional practices at least once a week;
- only about 25 percent reported that they place heavy emphasis on increasing students' interest in science;
- students in high-poverty elementary and middle schools were less likely than students in more affluent schools to do "hands-on" work every week;

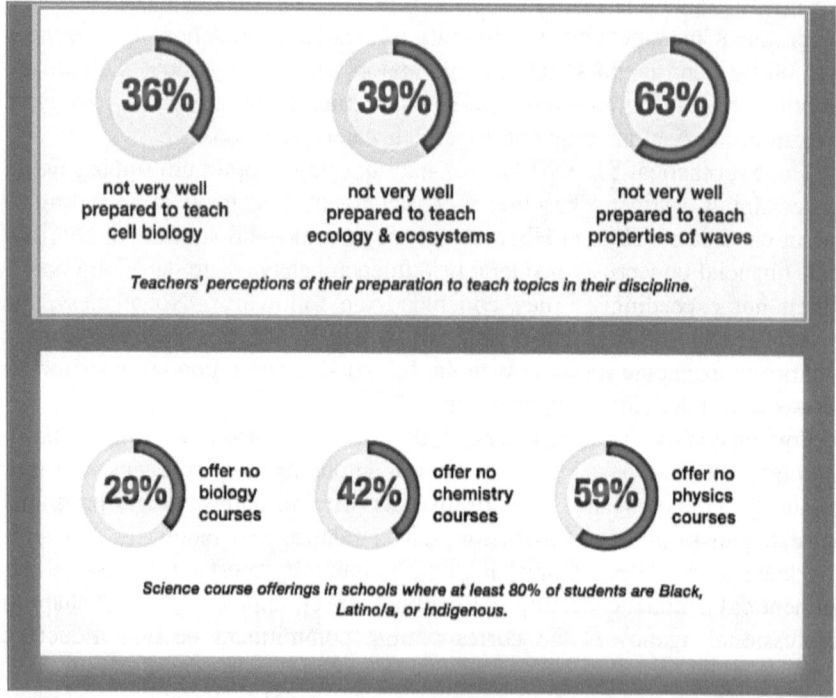

Figure 12.1 **Teachers Survey Results.** Reproduced with permission from the National Academy of Sciences, Courtesy of the National Academies Press, Washington, D.C. *Source*: National Academies of Sciences, Engineering, and Medicine, 2021. Call to Action for Science Education: Building Opportunity for the Future. Washington, DC: The National Academies Press. https://doi.org/10.17226/26152.

- a majority of elementary teachers (69 percent) reported they are not very well prepared to teach science;
- scores of secondary teachers say they are not very well prepared to teach many topics related to their disciplines;
- physics is not offered as a course in 59 percent of high-minority high schools and 31 percent of low-minority high schools; and
- no chemistry class is taught in 42 percent of high-minority high schools and 18 percent of those with primarily white students.[8]

The data indicate that a shortage of certified science teachers is not the only pertinent issue for school districts. Instructional time, student equity, specific course offerings, and teacher preparation are concerns in building solutions. Districts must create optimum conditions to attract new talent by expanding beyond conventional teacher procurement methods. Coalitions with state, district, university, and alternative certification establishments are necessary to address the initial undertaking: growing a pool of talented applicants.

While the projected growth for non-teaching life, physical, and social science positions is less than their math counterparts, the US Bureau of Labor Statistics forecasts a healthy 8 percent growth this decade. This trend will result in 113,800 new jobs, particularly in biomedical research, psychology, and environmental protection.[9] A 2020 American Association of Employment in Education survey reported that the need for physics teachers exceeds almost all other subject areas.[10] Like math majors, salary stipends must be part of the solution. In 2021, the median annual wage for life, physical, and social science jobs was $72,740, compared to the mean of $41,146 for teachers.[11]

A longer-term strategy would be to promote STEM subjects as early as elementary and middle school, emphasizing possibilities for females and students of color. While planting seeds for additional teachers, the effort confronts inequity in these professions and promotes diversity in the classroom. Females comprise almost half of the US workforce, yet they remain substantially underrepresented in STEM professions. Women have increased their participation from 8 percent of STEM employees in 1970 to 27 percent in 2019. However, men still dominate the majority of positions at 73 percent.[12] Federal data (2018) identified college STEM graduates representing only 7 percent of Black students and 12 percent of Hispanic students.[13] By influencing mindsets early, stereotypes are decreased, and the workforce can be enriched with heterogeneity.

Computer Science. Code.org is an advocacy coalition that promotes CS education. According to chief operating officer Cameron Wilson, "There is a need to get at least one [computer science] teacher in every school in this country, [but] right now there's usually only one in a district."[14] While shortages of math and science teachers are severe, with CS, districts are practically starting from scratch. Alternative certification partnerships with universities and other state-approved comprehensive educator preparation programs are a lifeline to building relevant programs.

CS is a more recent, developing, in-demand course within the secondary school curriculum. Minimal teacher prospects are preparing to meet the growing number of requests by parents and students. Unfortunately, curricular offerings are uncommon due to the vast disparity between family wishes and available staff. Shein reported the insufficient number of CS teachers graduating from US universities:

> Only 36 teachers graduated from universities with computer science degrees in 2017, compared with 11,157 math teachers and 11,905 science teachers, according to the nonprofit Code.org. In 2016, 75 teachers graduated from universities equipped to teach the subject, the organization reports.[15]

The code.org website illustrates the disparity between parents' wishes for their children's opportunities and the limited number of high school offerings (see figure 12.2).

The scant supply of CS teachers could increase using the strategy suggested for teachers of less common foreign languages (e.g., Vietnamese, Somali, Haitian). As discussed in the previous chapter, a transitional option is virtual learning. While using the same online tools, the structure would require distinctive guardrails. Foreign language and CS courses differ in

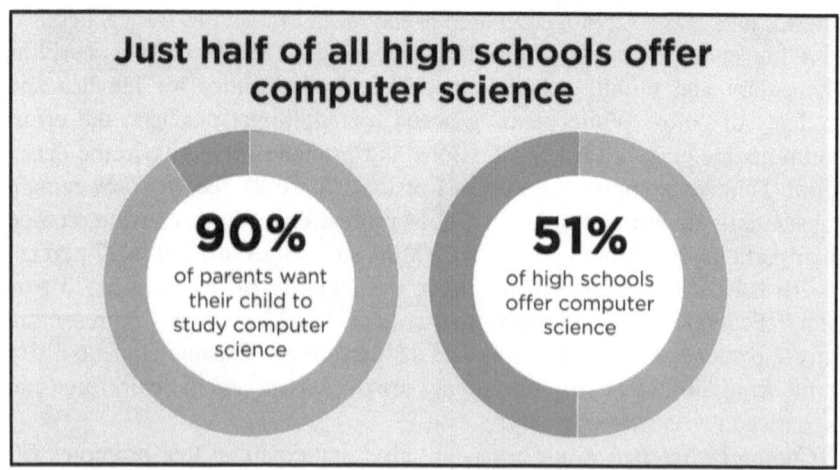

Figure 12.2 Interest and Offerings for High School Computer Science Courses. Reproduced from code.org with permission. *Source*: US Department of Education, 2022, 1. Code.org. (2022). Why Computer Science? Retrieved with permission from https://code.org/promote.

context and virtual class design. Expanded lab settings must incorporate substantial student assistance to meet the augmented demand for CS courses. In most cases, a bilingual or foreign language virtual class in Somali has a few students. An offering in computer coding, programming, or web development could easily attract multiple students at all secondary grade levels.

CS course essentials include operative lab facilities, reliable computers, and a full-time teacher mentor. Soliciting an "inclined" teacher (one with interest and technical aptitude) would serve three purposes:

1. The classroom teacher will develop skills, assist students, and keep them on track.
2. Classroom and online teachers will collaborate on pacing students.
3. The classroom teacher will master the content and potentially take the certification exam in the future.

Agreements with universities or commercial online course providers must modify courses for age-appropriate levels. Enhancing students' virtual learning motivation, a full-time teacher assigned to the CS class provides both structure and encouragement. Assuming fifteen to twenty students per class, online instructors can only present material with limited student interaction. The assigned teacher offers interpersonal stimulation and logistic guidance. "Learning by teaching" is an advantageous context to prepare teacher mentors for certification, thereby increasing staff for the future. State education departments should share a leadership role with policies, incentives, and cooperative agreements.

FEDERAL AND STATE INCENTIVES

The US Department of Education (DOE) offers grants for districts to invest in the teaching profession and address critical-need teacher shortages. The Supporting Effective Educator Development (SEED) grant program accepts applications from eligible institutions to increase the procurement of highly effective educators.[16] An institution of higher education and a national non-profit entity (e.g., a school district) can partner to establish a pipeline for STEM teachers. The funding is also eligible for teacher residency and for state "grow your own" (GYO) programs.

In 2022, the SEED program "will award $65 million to support the implementation of evidence-based practices that prepare, develop, or enhance the skills of educators."[17] SEED funding may support "reasonable" stipends that are "necessary to carry out the proposed project and meet the absolute priority" in the application.[18] Businesses are becoming more proactive with monetary and in-kind support of STEM programs, recognizing the anticipated future job growth. Companies promoting pathways include Google ($50 million in awards), Microsoft (renewable $5,000 scholarships), Facebook ($200 million in grants), General Motors, AT&T, and Intel.[19]

The DOE Federal Perkins Loan Program is earmarked for US college students. It is based on financial need and assists in funding their post-secondary education, with a ten-year repayment period allowed at a fixed interest rate of 5 percent. However, full-time teachers in shortage areas such as STEM courses qualify for the cancellation of up to 100 percent of their loan. A state educational agency designates those hard-to-fill teaching fields.[20] This is another way of assisting economically disadvantaged high school students to prosper as future STEM teachers.

In the past decade, state GYO programs have been utilized at an accelerated rate to target high-need teachers. State GYO grants advocate partnerships among school districts, universities, and community organizations to recruit and prepare residents for community schools. A report by Garcia found that all but three states (North Dakota, Vermont, and Wyoming) have some type of GYO program, although considerable variation exists in program design and strategy.[21] Some programs pursue students even before they enter college:

> Several states, such as Maryland, Nevada, and Oklahoma, have scholarship programs to support high school students who want to become teachers. While they are called scholarships, these programs come with some strings attached: recipients must agree to teach in the state for a specified number of years and in some cases risk having to pay the money back if they do not fulfill their service requirements. Scholarship programs are often closely linked to shortage areas.[22]

Federal, state, and local agencies should continue exploring and evaluating model partnerships, incentives, tuition assistance, and loan-forgiveness strategies. We can share findings and refine best practices for recruiting teachers.

THE UNIVERSITY OF TEXAS AT AUSTIN INITIATIVES

Models of STEM teacher development have distinguished the University of Texas at Austin in judiciously addressing issues of recruiting quality candidates in math, science, and CS. A collaborative effort with the university, the Dana Center, and Microsoft launched the UTeach and WeTeach_CT programs. Burgeoning partnerships with local school districts have begun to make promising inroads for recruiting teachers with authoritative content knowledge.[23]

UTeach is an insightful university-based teacher preparation program. The initiative's primary purpose is to expand the number of qualified STEM teachers in US secondary schools. Established at UT Austin in 1997, the engagement of nonprofits, school districts, and university students has propelled its expansion.[24] The UTeach Institute in Austin supports the advancement of UTeach programs at other national universities. Participation has grown to include forty-nine universities in twenty-three states and the District of Columbia. The UTeach programs have produced more than 7,000 teacher graduates. Another accomplishment is that 68 percent of those graduates teach in K-12 schools with a majority of economically disadvantaged students.[25] The goal is to prepare non-education college students in science and mathematics to embrace becoming secondary teachers.

Initially focused only on mathematics and science, the UTeach Institute recently augmented the initiative, offering engineering and CS licensure programs. WeTeach_CS is an outgrowth of UTeach, building on its success and widening STEM career options. The UT Austin collaborative recognized the consequential shortage of CS teachers in Texas and has achieved progress in reducing this shortfall:

> Since September 2015, WeTeach_CS has supported over 500 Texas educators to achieve certification in Grade 8–12 Computer Science, more than doubling the capacity of Texas schools to provide high-quality CS courses to their students.[26]

Most STEM majors initially enroll in a university without the intention of becoming a teacher. UTeach and WeTeach_CS present an additional option. Each program "allows them to earn both a STEM degree and teaching certification without requiring additional time or cost."[27] Graduating with a teaching certificate and having classroom field experience has inspired many college graduates to bring their talents to the classroom.

Zalaznick reinforced the proposed suggestions and reiterated that multiple strategies must be implemented by policymakers and district leaders. He delineates eight recommendations to help fill crucial positions such as STEM teachers:

- Candidate incentives: Offer tuition assistance and loan forgiveness to teacher candidates who will work in shortage areas, with the amount of the incentives based on the severity of shortages.
- Program incentives and accountability: Provide increased funding and higher ratings to preparation programs that produce more teachers in shortage areas.

- Program design: Preparation programs should offer field experiences in urban and rural settings emphasizing inclusive pedagogy.
- GYO programs/residencies: Promote train-in-place preparation programs offered by school districts and other organizations that offer apprenticeships. Build up certification pathways for paraprofessionals and other district employees.
- Alternate routes: Create streamlined, flexible certification pathways that appeal to non-traditional teaching candidates.
- Compensation: Provide higher pay for teaching high-need subjects in high-need settings, and offer signing bonuses to teachers in harder-to-fill areas.
- School leadership: Develop principal pipelines that produce school leaders skilled in recruiting and retaining teachers.
- Working conditions: Conduct climate surveys to identify teacher needs and address concerns that lead to turnover.[28]

Each STEM teaching role identified above is unique, and recruiting strategies must bridge the district's instructional goals and the market for candidates. Once candidates have committed to an intern role, the district must then ensure rewarding professional experiences. Critical to this objective is placement with an exemplary teacher and conscientious principal. For the campus, the execution of recruiting includes marketing and customer service.

AS SYSTEMS DEVELOP

Reiterating the proposal in chapter 6, creating a priority substitute pool of retired teachers at a higher daily compensation rate is a rational recourse to facilitate the transition. Hiring experienced math and science teachers should take precedence, requiring exceptions for retiree eligibility rules. A rigorous reentry standard (e.g., evaluations and student performance data) is necessary for such a program to be credible and effective. Hiring retired teachers for long-term assignments is increasingly being done in districts with high numbers of vacancies and with successful outcomes.[29]

CONCLUSION

After World War II, confidence in the technological superiority of the United States was widespread. The launch of the Russian satellite Sputnik in 1957 disturbed that self-assurance, raising concerns about public education systems, particularly science. Congress responded the following year with the National Defense Education Act. This legislation increased funding for K-12 through university education, instituted low-interest loans for college students, and emphasized science and technology education. One of the benefits of this investment was hands-on science laboratory experiences, a staple in today's schools.[30]

Rather than reacting to phantom fears, a rational and preemptive strategy should relate to established objectives. The humanitarian reasons alone for improving math, science, and technology education are significant: for example, equity, health, and climate change. Progress directly relates to a rigorous foundational curriculum and talented teachers. Like other hard-to-fill teaching positions, pathways and master teacher opportunities alone may not suffice to secure necessary teaching talent. Targeted pre-K-12 partnerships with universities and businesses work toward mutual advantages.

Union concerns about the impact of differentiated salaries on teacher morale are insufficient to outweigh societal responsibility to students. Yes, all proficient teachers may deserve increased compensation. However, the bottom line is that some certified subject areas have greater exigencies than others in providing comprehensive offerings to students. Cultivating a competent growth network of teachers in math, science, and CS require customized remuneration scales. Given the attrition rate of many teachers, applicant pool quantity may be as salient as striving for quality.

Stipends are an essential part of the solution. However, money alone will not mitigate recruiting the total number of teacher applicants required for quality universal STEM programs. Multiple strategies—such as participating in UTeach and WeTeach_CT, loan forgiveness, and flexible certification pathways—are requisite to entice talent into a new profession. Recruiting is only half the challenge; the other half is retaining prospects in a nurturing culture. Once STEM teachers are onboarded, campus administrators and STEM coordinators must shepherd building trust, agency, and satisfaction in their teaching careers.

NOTES

1. Das, 2022.
2. Seril, 2021.
3. Buttner, 2021.
4. "Math Occupations: Occupational Outlook Handbook," 2022, 1.
5. Hu & Hirsh, 2017, 8.
6. Pink, 2011.
7. "Carl Sagan," 1996, 3.
8. National Academies of Sciences, Engineering, and Medicine, 2021.
9. "Life, Physical, and Social Science Occupations: Occupational Outlook Handbook," 2022.
10. "2021–2022 Educator Supply & Demand Report," 2020.

11. "Life, Physical, and Social Science Occupations: Occupational Outlook Handbook," 2022.
12. Martinez & Christnacht, 2021.
13. Bushweller, 2021.
14. Ahmad, 2017, 1.
15. Shein, 2019, 17.
16. "Supporting Effective Educator Development Grant Program," 2022.
17. U.S. Department of Education, 2022, 1.
18. "Supporting Effective Educator Development (SEED) Program Fiscal Year 2020," 2020, 3.
19. Partida, 2021.
20. Department of Education, 2022.
21. Garcia, 2020.
22. Ibid., 12.
23. Dana Center Communications, 2020.
24. "Expanding and Strengthening the Stem Teacher Workforce through UTeach," 2022.
25. Ibid.
26. "UT Austin Collaborative Tackles Math and Computer Science Teaching Shortages," 2020, 4.
27. "Expanding and Strengthening the Stem Teacher Workforce through UTeach," 2022, 1.
28. Zalaznick, 2021, 4–5.
29. Vercelletto, 2019.
30. Powell, 2007.

Chapter 13

Executing the Teacher Plan

Our goals can only be reached through a vehicle of a plan, in which we must fervently believe, and upon which we must vigorously act. There is no other route to success.

—Pablo Picasso

A school district's talent management (TM) department assumes the core stewardship for the succession of quality personnel. Prioritizing their efforts, like any organization, is key to accomplishment. TM staff must *first and foremost* ensure they procure the primary practitioners and influencers with students: teachers and principals. External pressure, personal relationships, or funding deadlines should not interfere with the order of staffing emphasis. Students will excel if a campus has an exemplary leader and teaching staff. All other staff may add value and sustain operations, but they are peripheral and play indirect supporting roles in student learning. This chapter exclusively examines the planning for teachers by building systems to generate sustained transformation.

SUCCESSION HANDBOOK FOR TALENT MANAGEMENT

A comprehensive succession handbook is TM's map and compass, beginning with purpose, timelines, and precedence of actions. In accentuating the hiring of quality teachers, explicit systems with detailed protocols must be in place. Altering TM procedures with every new administrator leads to inconsistencies and staff frustration. A handbook updated and reviewed by TM staff annually safeguards coherent practices. The Equitable Access Support Network, established in 2014 by the US Department of Education, assists states with educator equity plans. Their *Talent Management Guide for School Districts* is an excellent template for building a customized district handbook.[1] The appendices include vetted resources for recruitment, hiring, and retention.

Standardizing handbooks, orientations, and periodic reviews contribute to the TM staff becoming organizationally aware. Consistent ethical practices protect the entire department from accusations of bias. When staff understand the grand scheme, team efficiency improves in several ways. Support divisions in a school system frequently lose perspective of how they contribute to student success. Cross-training and peer observation foster understanding and respect for the contributions of department colleagues. Talking about the "why" in individual roles should accompany the "how-to." All staff realizing the relationship between specific TM projects and the district's student achievement objectives underpin a highly functioning team.

When responding to a TM procedural question, the reply is too frequently, "That's not my area, let me transfer you to . . ." A limited grasp by individuals of the positions around them is a characteristic of people working in silos. Industry researcher Caroline Miller articulated the multiple rewards of departmental cross-training:

- Potentially reduced absenteeism and employee turnover;
- Ability to keep employees engaged through assignment rotation;
- Increased opportunities for employee advancement;
- More ability to promote from within, reducing recruiting costs;
- Increased flexibility for scheduling;
- Employees are better able to collaborate and identify ways to improve processes; and
- Increased efficiency.[2]

When staff assimilate and internalize the handbook and expand their training, versatility is molded for other roles. Continuous growth and advancement should also be associated with monetary rewards. Aspects of the TM organizational structure are a microcosm of teacher pathways for motivation and productivity.

PROPOSAL FOR PROCURING AND ELEVATING TEACHERS

Data collection and analytics are core functions in recruiting, hiring, and retaining teachers. Commercial businesses offer district software tools that advertise predictive analytics for choosing the best candidates. Unfortunately, even if these programs or practices are marginally beneficial, they do not address the main impediments to growing teacher talent. The preliminary requisite is creating desirable roles. Fine-tuning the final hiring decisions from a pool of weak applicants is a cosmetic investment without long-term impact.

Through each hiring phase, tracking the number of applicants by certification, time spent on each step, and the speed in extending offers is fundamental to efficiency. Developing a research mindset for all TM employees requires orientation to examine data files and objectively analyze trends. Every district has unique teacher staffing needs, and the information extracted from data drives planning. TM initiatives may take two to three years of data collection to yield valid conclusions. However, even using data to reduce time frames is more reliable than instinct alone. What is working, and what should be discontinued? What will continue with an adjustment? Building, evaluating, and streamlining teacher lifelines, namely new candidates, enrich campus talent. Using statistical formulas over time (i.e., regression, factor analysis), departments determine robust versus unreliable partnerships, optimal time use, and worthwhile resource expenditures.

Another constructive endeavor is data mining with *all* teachers by comparing records in different fields. Data mining is the analysis of large amounts of information to determine trends and patterns. Student performance data (e.g., academic, social-emotional, attendance, behavior), correlated with teachers, teacher leaders, master teachers, instructional coaches, and priority substitutes, maximizes optimal student assignments. Incorporating algorithmic formulas to identify outstanding performance, underachievement, or any concerning anomalies helps leaders respond appropriately.

The *Optimizing Quality Cycle* in figure 13.1 illustrates a system to build sustainable teacher pools and the evolving refinement of processes. The quality cycle's objective is to progressively improve the predictive validity for hiring and retaining successful teachers and enhancing the campus learning culture. Its seven components include (1) promoting the teacher model, (2) evaluating recruiting tools and costs, (3) operative teacher profiles, (4) making staffing decisions based on performance, (5) retaining high-performing teachers, (6) refining quality and diversity, and (7) making future forecasts. A comprehensive plan is fundamental to advancing the goal of elevating the teaching profession.

Promoting the Teacher Model. When forming an exemplary teaching staff, recruitment and retention are initiated by championing the district's "brand." That brand, teacher pathways, represents the prominent public association with the district. If the messaging resonates, area teachers and university education majors become aware and tell others. Shared conversations relay the narrative. "They have the pathway model with steps for career development and increased salary. Some of their staff are master teachers

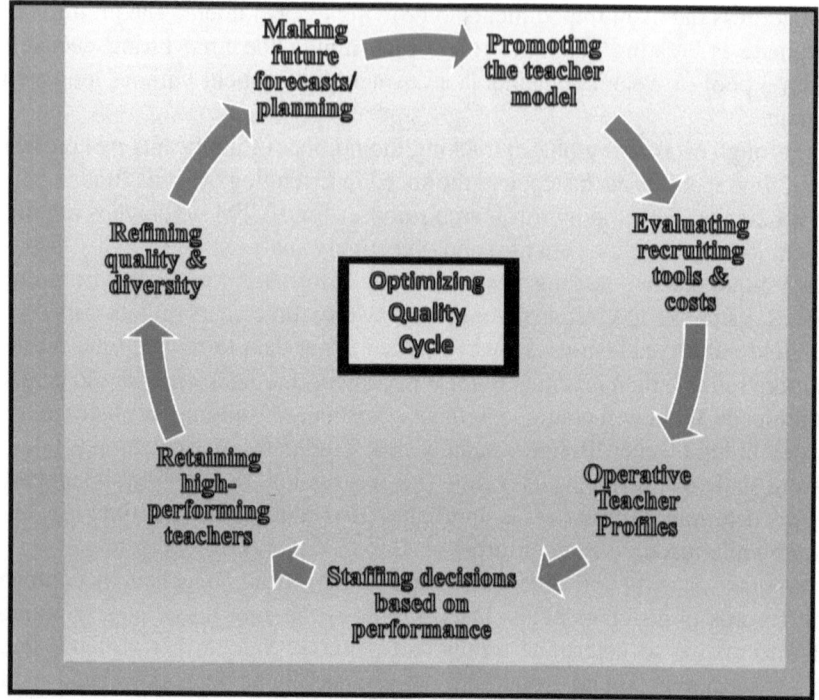

Figure 13.1 Optimizing Quality Cycle for Teacher Talent. Weber, 2022. *Source*: Self-created.

making $$." Generating regional interest will attract a growing aggregate of capable applicants central to sustained transformation.

Wallace et al. studied the value of branding in industry practices and concluded that branding and industry image are vital in attracting human capital and contribute to strategic aims. Branding provides a framework to simplify and focus priorities and increase productivity. It is also essential for improving employee recruitment, retention, and commitment.[3] The branded teacher model stimulates curiosity and interest by contrasting with traditional roles without internal pathway opportunities.

Communicating the innovative model utilizes websites, relevant social media, local news articles, and job postings. Early applicants will be attracted to the novel opportunity. Conversely, skeptics will view it as a fad. Teachers are suspicious of "expert gurus" and reluctant to acknowledge passing fads in education. Nonetheless, endorsements will grow with persistent messaging and fidelity to the plan. The teacher pathway's self-determination features, such as earned autonomy and self-actualization, will entice talent.[4]

The assignment of teacher recruitment has become more competitive, with the severe shortages worsening due to the pandemic. Options for advertising teacher positions have expanded with social media tools to connect with specific groups. Newspaper advertisements or isolated posters in human resource departments are antiquated protocols. District and professional organization websites are the most-viewed announcements of teacher openings. Recording website hits and application questions such as "How did you learn about this opening?" is part of the feedback loop.

In-person job fairs are still popular with new and veteran teachers alike. Applicants appreciate a venue where they can interview multiple campus principals and make comparisons. Detailed logistical preparations ensure smooth processes and impress candidates. A congenial space and compelling recruitment materials complement the event's ambience. Presentations and conversations at job fairs underscore the district brand, allowing applicants to visualize their connection with a progressive team.

If local elections disrupt the board makeup or if a new superintendent is hired, teachers often experience anxiety. They want to know if resolute support for district initiatives will be sustained. An underlying commitment by the board of trustees and the administration's steadfastness over several years will also quell doubts. Updating the board annually on the advancement of teacher pathways with transparent reports will reinforce their guardianship. Momentum is initiated through district promotion but ultimately achieved through consistency, word-of-mouth teacher endorsement, and student success.

Explicit performance criteria for securing and maintaining leadership roles only incentivize conscientious individuals.[5] Understanding that stipends are not a property right will not deter competent teachers from applying. However, applicants want assurances of job security with reasonable expectations and sustained program investment. The district should strategically build community trust. Posting expansion charts of master teachers, teacher leaders, and master's cohorts on the TM webpage elicits credibility for prospective applicants. As more teachers accept the pathway model brand, they solidify the endorsement of the redesigned professional culture.

Evaluating Recruiting Tools and Costs. The logistics of timelines, locations, protocols, and media tools are all subject to scrutiny for refinement. Periodic reviews contribute to systemic progression, including examining data on advertising websites, auditing expenditures, staff debriefing, and survey feedback from applicants and partners. From diagnosis and district-wide feedback, technical improvements are ongoing in coding, formatting reports, and integrating with other district information systems.

Evaluating tools and cycle phases range from technical upgrades to student achievement. System assessments are considered in the context of answering recurring questions about efficacy. How long does it take for someone to complete an application? What do university professors hear from their student teachers? Is performance different with teachers hired in February versus those hired in May? Objectively soliciting and reflecting on divergent questions drives system evaluation. Improvement is then contingent on making appropriate adjustments.

TM departments sometimes falsely assume that accepted standard practices are in place. For example, "wait time" for applicants in the pool or after being interviewed is a potent indicator. If districts fail to make an offer within thirty days or less from when the teacher applies, "the odds of a teacher rejecting your offer increase by 60 percent."[6] System algorithms with timed alerts built into the programs help eliminate inadvertent oversights. Automated electronic reminders increase productivity when programmed with project planners, timelines, and other routine practices.

Collecting accurate data on applicants is necessary to authenticate the quality cycle. Most applicants will submit resumes, but some may be missing academic or contact information. Having TM staff register individuals at job fairs and input data ensures that all necessary information is included. Online applications must only accept submissions when essential documentation is complete. A section for suggestions on the application assists the department in molding the form to be user-friendly and concise.

The primary goal of cycle evaluation is the relative annual progress in hiring and retaining talent. All cycle phases link to the invigoration of quality teachers and student attainment. Factors considered include total applicants by certification, education, institution, and demographics. From extractions on teacher performance and student data, meaningful relationships drive decisions. Talent assessment of teachers is categorized for specific groups of students. Process validity is secured over time by following annual employee performance and retention.

The evaluation phase of the *Optimizing Quality Cycle* objectively assesses the system's outcomes, from detailed elements to broad district goals. Discussions and recommendations are part of regular staff meetings, reviews with research specialists, and progress reports to the superintendent. Annual updates to the school board combine evaluation findings with forecasting projected district staffing needs.

Operative Teacher Profiles. Teacher profiles are individual records of performance history within the classroom. With accurate data fields, TM staff can extract components for correlation studies and identify patterns or tendencies vis-à-vis mean standards. By identifying statistically robust factors, districts can raise the efficacy of recruiting, professional learning, retention, and other elements. Of primary interest is the relationship between teacher characteristics and student growth. Integrated with other district data systems (e.g., student profiles, student performance data), explicit assignments and creative strategies promote student engagement and learning. Analysis of teacher profiles precipitates sound decisions on pathways and class assignment selection.

Table 13.1 presents an annual profile example for an elementary classroom teacher. Studying significant trends becomes tenable by collecting multiple metrics for teachers and their students. For longitudinal analysis, chronicled data are archived at the end of each school year.

Distinct profiles by level and role include current and prospective teachers. Table 13.2 delineates the types of positions with unique profiles. Queried fields can be selected, sorted, and extracted for analysis and reports. Over time, holistic analysis of multiple metrics on teachers and their students contributes impartial data to evaluate, select, and place in leadership roles. Teachers can access their profiles and request corrections to errors or misleading metrics. For example, if a low composite test score only included five students, the entry should be N/A. Evaluations and accountability are more readily accepted when teachers perceive fairness and transparency.

Robust analytics directly relate to sample size and metric quality. The reliability of inferences about student performance improves when examining larger populations. Replication of analysis methods over several years enhances predictive validity. With a high confidence level that Mr. Spencer connects with students and closes achievement gaps with sixth-grade math students, a deliberate placement decision is rational. As a master teacher, his contributions are worth the recognition and additional compensation. The ability to accelerate progress and boost the academic trajectory for a targeted group of at-risk students has a significant likelihood of success when assigned the right teacher.

Staffing Decisions Based on Performance. Teacher performance over time is the most complex and sensitive dataset to interpret and utilize for staffing decisions. Performance encompasses two main components: evaluations and student performance. Student performance should include aggregate measures (e.g., academic growth, social-emotional adjustment, engagement, attendance) and never solely the scores on an isolated test. As discussed in chapter 5, evaluations can be converted into numeric scores using weights for ratings on each appraisal domain.

Any district with a research department is fortunate. Leveraging specialists with statistical analysis experience is advantageous for the TM department throughout the quality cycle. Research specialists providing training, guidance, and oversight acclimates staff to the scientific method. Independent companies such as Hanover Research will contract with educators on an as-needed basis for smaller districts on special projects. Department interaction with administrators in special education, bilingual, and other content coordinators also yields constructive viewpoints in understanding data trends.

Table 13.1 Example of Annual Elementary Teacher Profile

Teacher Name	Identification Number	Assignment	Evaluation Index 0–5	Undergraduate Degree/Institution
Amanda Williams	78215	Grade 3	3.87	BS Elementary Ed., University of Texas
Gender F	Ethnicity AA	Class Size 23	Campus Riverside El	Campus ED % 74%
Graduate Degrees/Institution	Certifications	Class State Math Mean	Class State Reading Mean	Class ED %
MA in Reading, Rice University	- K-5 Elementary - Bilingual	Passing—88 Growth—67	Passing—93 Growth—83	78%
Teacher Absences—personal and illness	Class Attendance Rate 96.2%	Discipline Referrals	Years of Experience	Years of Experience in Current Grade
4	Reading	1	8	5
Math MAP BOY—EOY	Class ELL % 18%	ESS	SES	Special Education %
183.7–193.3 185.3–194		82	85	8%
Awards N/A		Training - PBL Level 2 - Restorative Behavior	Path Program Masters in Reading	Pathway Assignment Teacher Leader—Grade-level Chair

Notes: AA = African American; ESS = Engagement Student Survey; MAP = Measures of Academic Progress; SES = Social-Emotional Student Self-Report; BOY = Beginning of Year; EOY = End of Year; ED = Economically Disadvantaged.

Table 13.2 Sample Teacher Profile Database for 2021–2022

Pool	Category	Current number
Prospective Teachers	Preparatory Substitute	734
	Sanctioned Substitute	433
	Clinical Substitute	16
	Priority Substitute	54
	Endorsed Substitute	65
	Instructional Assistant ECE	71
	Instructional Assistant SPED	86
	Instructional Assistant Bilingual	11
	Student Teachers	Fall = 87 / Spring = 73
	Clinical Teaching Interns	Fall = 25 / Spring = 23
Current Teachers	Total Teachers	2,344
	Teacher Leaders	845
	Master Teachers	600
Pathway Programs	Eligible to Retire (all groups)	338
	Certification Assistance	33
	Master of Reading	34
	Masters in Early Childhood	17
	Masters in Early Special Education	20
	Masters in Bilingual	31
	Masters in Secondary Core	Math = 16 / Science = 12

In collaboration with campus principals, staffing decisions are made for the *ultimate long-term benefit of students*. Intentional placement of master teachers or those with exceptional talent in one subject, such as reading, is paired with higher-need student groups. Some teachers may have an exceptional capacity for captivating disengaged students. Others may excel in leading grade-level meetings with creative planning. Master teachers with the interest and aptitude for research influence campus learning culture. TM and principals' examination of teacher performance encourages leadership-ready teachers to expand their campus impact.

Data from teacher profiles guide informed decisions while tempered by examining individual behavior. No system is definitive in predicting the optimal pairing with a group of students. Nevertheless, decisions made with data have a higher probability of guiding teachers into pathways and programs, prompting a stimulus for upgrading district performance. Fortunately, principals can adjust placements based on classroom observations if assignments are not meeting objectives.

Improving Quality and Diversity. District teacher quality is estimated based on evaluations and student growth across numerous indicators and grade levels. Early childhood screening tools assess motor development, social-emotional skills, executive function, language, and cognition.

Achievement is studied across these domains, determining a composite readiness status for kindergarten. Elementary through middle school has a plethora of formative and summative assessments and grades for review. As students advance chronologically, teachers often pay less attention to social-emotional learning (SEL) data. Educators recognize that teacher quality also correlates to indicators such as SEL surveys, student attendance, behavioral referrals, and grade retention.

High school students' data, procured via different assessment tools (e.g., SAT, ACT, GPA, exit exams), is evaluated in the context of college and career readiness. Graduation and dropout rates are prominent indicators in comparing districts. These metrics are significant but limited in reaching an overarching perspective. Many students become lost and disconnected in the expansive high school setting, and a Gallup survey reported the engagement of only four in ten students.[7] Individual graduation plans for *all* students should be monitored throughout high school and the associated teacher impact, not only those bound for college. Increasing numbers of districts are collecting data on their students' post-graduation progression. Although time-intensive, tracking graduates provides a realistic understanding of the educational system's longitudinal success.

Student passing rates, dual credit attainment, advanced placement scores, extra-curricular achievements, and career certifications all relate to high school teacher quality. Student surveys provide information about the extent of engagement in their classes. The contributions of teachers outside core subjects are sometimes overlooked. Talented teachers in the arts, athletics, and elective courses connect students with school. Research demonstrates that students participating in these offerings are significantly less likely to drop out of high school.[8] Master teachers add systemic value across all grade levels and subjects.

Permissible demographic data included in the teacher profiles (i.e., gender, ethnicity) are vital in maintaining teacher diversity. Studies indicate that minority students perform better in school and later in life when taught by teachers of the same race or ethnicity. The underrepresentation of minority teachers "could be having the effect of limiting minority students' educational success."[9] In 2015, the teacher-to-student ratio for Hispanics was 24 percent students to 9 percent teachers, and for African Americans, 13 percent students to 8 percent teachers.[10] The "role model effect" of having a black teacher increases a black student's likelihood of enrolling in college and decreases that of dropping out of high school.[11] Proactively establishing post-secondary partnerships to balance this disproportion is relevant in advancing student achievement on all campuses.

Hiring minority teachers representing student demographics is enhanced by pursuing reciprocal relationships with select universities. A district's starting point is identifying institutions with the highest representation of Hispanic[12] and African American students.[13] An example for Texas districts is presented in table 13.3. Working with universities and alternative certification programs to enroll and support quality instructional assistants and substitute teachers is another path toward propagating diversity. This strategy has distinct advantages in securing multilingual candidates for high-need bilingual and special education roles.

Retaining High-Performing Teachers. Appreciating teachers' aspirations, validating their opinions, and consulting for career options improve teacher retention. Recognizing and intervening before a teacher decides to transfer or leave the profession is a pivotal part of the process. The caveat with retention at the district level is that strategies are purposely limited to those achieving or progressing. Teachers earn the privilege of being included on a priority retention list through documented performance. This replicated corporate business model supports sustaining the most high-performing talent working with students.

Identification occurs through principal input, evaluations, and student data analysis. Most principals can readily name their top instructional leaders and those progressing in that direction. Confidential principal surveys request they identify those teachers considered impossible to replace. TM staff can verify performance data for any recommendations needing follow-up. A consistent data standard is recommended because selection can be questioned through open records requests. Union representatives in the San Antonio Independent School District were critical of this retention initiative. Their perception was that the process diminished those teachers not identified for retention.

Table 13.3 Texas Universities with the Most Hispanic or Black Students

Identifying Universities for Diversity	
Texas Universities with Highest Percentage of Hispanic Students	
University	Percentage
Texas A&M International University	95
University of Texas-Rio Grande Valley	91
University of Texas-El Paso	84
Our Lady of the Lake University	76
Texas A&M University-Kingsville	72
St. Mary's University of San Antonio	67
Texas Universities with Largest Enrollment of Black Students	
University	Number
Prairie View A&M University (Prairie View, TX)	7,199
University of North Texas (Denton, TX)	4,263
University of Houston (Houston, TX)	3,800
Texas State University (San Marcos, TX)	3,374

The industrial union mindset that all teachers are equally deserving is unfounded. The acknowledgment of a teacher's performance should be celebrated by all and stimulate imitation by coworkers. Reiterating the TNTP study cited earlier, the daunting reality is that it takes up to eleven hires to replace an outstanding teacher.[14] The retention of high-performing teachers advocates for students, and adult jealousy is misplaced. Progressive standards aligned with leadership pathways contribute to a culture elevating the teaching profession.

Encouraging recognized talent to remain as teachers is legal and ethical when administered with discretion and integrity. The underlying purpose is to enrich service for students. My conversations with a district retention specialist and targeted teachers were encouraging in their perceptions. Teachers' feedback expressed sincere appreciation that the district valued their contributions. In one case, a transfer closer to home, and in another, a change in teaching subject prevented two outstanding teachers from leaving for a wealthier suburban district. Perpetuating the tenure of talented teachers is a stabilizing endeavor, with increasing numbers of districts now employing retention specialists.

Making Future Forecasts. Forecasting is forming data-driven estimates that predict coming trends. The cycle's metacognitive component involves reflecting on the entire system, making adjustments, and ultimately staffing *decisions*. Calculating applicant pools, teacher attrition rates (i.e., promotions, retirement, resignations), and student membership projections is a routine part of the TM department's responsibility. Staffing determinations are more complex. Interpreting positive or negative trends and altering strategies often entails mining down to individual campus-level analyses. Causation of teacher resignations should not be assumed only through composite data correlations. Some anomalies require a more discerning investigation.

A sizeable teacher turnover rate at one or two campuses may skew district metrics, with the underlying reasons being campus climate and leadership. Student teachers accepting more positions in a neighboring district may stem from a university professor's partiality. An inflated daily pay rate in other districts could entice dependable substitutes. Unforeseen circumstances, such as the pandemic, influence teachers' actions separately from district systems. Personnel trends must be viewed in a broad personal, social, and economic context.

Forecasting includes establishing teacher-student ratios for efficiency and modifying them based on the performance of identified groups. Community demographic and teacher retention estimates are only a baseline for planning. As cohorts of teachers progress through levels of leadership, subsequent steps in the cycle bring about refinements. Comparing goals with actual metrics and qualified with introspection, subsequent year assignments should consider *all* potential outcomes. Speaking with pathway teachers and incorporating their feedback is part of a successful equation. Another recognized practice for expanding an understanding of staff attrition is face-to-face exit interviews with those separating from employment.

Nuanced decisions hypothesize the accurate placement of teachers to maximize student learning. Queried analysis can identify the most influential teachers in closing learning gaps with specific students or subjects. While decisions should be supported objectively, another consideration involves closely reviewing teacher/classroom circumstances. An outstanding teacher may have extenuating circumstances (e.g., illness, family trauma) that affect students' progress in any particular year. A given class may have had an 80 percent mobility rate throughout the school year. While objective metrics are essential, so are ongoing conversations with principals. Accurately forecasting teaching assignments is a layered process, and the collaborative undertaking has latent rewards for students.

CONCLUSION

Education leaders debate which pillars of educational systems contribute most to student achievement. They acknowledge that planning and execution are profoundly consequential, emphasizing curricula, professional learning, TM, or technology. My bias favors the accentuation of *talent* and is based on evidence that teachers' selection and placement have the most lasting implications for students.[15] Operating with a severe shortage of qualified prospects makes the planning strategy both compelling and daunting. Attention to all elements of a talent plan for teachers contributes to the culminating efficacy.

TM team members must understand a district system's purpose and embrace performing multiple duties. Given the complexity of sequences for managing teacher talent, collaboration requires a degree of competence in analysis. Cross-training, coaching staff, and encouraging constructive feedback are integral to continuous growth. Ideas and suggestions from *all* during debriefing sessions should be welcomed and contribute to TM staff development and personal agency.

Incorporating motivational theory and a cycle of analytics, the plan for teachers is a paragon of a district succession strategy. Teachers play *one* role in the TM succession handbook, yet they comprise more than half of the employees and over 80 percent of the professional staff.[16] As stated earlier, procuring and retaining teacher and principal talent is the department's most salient responsibility. A well-trained TM staff, collaborating with principals, can implement teacher pathways and programs with a clear process and tenacity. Staff expand their expertise in diverse roles by fostering a deductive mindset with an awareness of the vision. Sharing responsibility and cohesive work makes "the whole greater than the sum of its parts." Once a superlative plan is in place, the TM commences deployment. They can either fail for lack of team execution or succeed through collective synergy.

NOTES

1. "Increasing Equitable Access to Excellent Educators," 2017.
2. Miller, 2020, 3.
3. Wallace et al., 2014.
4. Ryan & Deci, 2000.
5. Baer, 2014.
6. Montgomery, 2017, 2.
7. Busteed, 2013.
8. Crispin, 2017.
9. Figlio, 2017, 5.
10. Lindsay et al., 2017.
11. Rosen, 2018.
12. Smith-Barrow & Moody, 2020.
13. "Colleges with the Largest Enrollment of Black, Non-Hispanic Students," 2021.
14. The New Teacher Project, 2013.
15. Opper, 2019.
16. "Staff, Teachers, and Teachers as a Percentage of Staff in Public Elementary and Secondary School Systems," 2017.

Chapter 14

Financing for Stability

What we see today is an American economy that has boomed because of policies and developments of the 1950s and '60s: the interstate-highway system, massive funding for science and technology, a public-education system that was the envy of the world and generous immigration policies.[1]

—Fareed Zakaria

The argument throughout this book is that the "elixir" for educational excellence is empowered teachers working in a tiered system for progressive leadership. Teachers elevate their professional agency by being grounded in a supportive structure to earn increasing autonomy. Pathways to a master teacher role include a commitment to research and accountability through multiple student growth measures. This endeavor will require additional financing but dynamically create advantages for students and society. Preceding adaptation are three conditions for funding: (1) it must be fair, (2) it must be based on sound educational premises, and (3) it must include valid accountability measures.

Financing structures for teachers and education, in general, are difficult to separate. In approaching this chapter, I propose more comprehensive solutions rather than solely addressing funding a teacher initiative. The entire budgetary system balances federal, state, and local bases and is inconsistent and unfair. All educators and students would prosper from adequate and dependable resources. Each new generation's education deserves the same opportunities for excellence. Students' narrow educational time frame should be protected from recurring budgetary crises or partisan political impulses.

LEARNING FROM THE PAST

The George W. Bush administration touted a "Texas Education Miracle," which was later reconstituted as the blueprint for No Child Left Behind (NCLB). In 2001–2002, that miracle came to pass when the high-poverty Houston Independent School District reported fast-rising test scores and a 1.5 percent dropout rate. Houston's remarkable purported results were audaciously fraudulent, as brought to light on *60 Minutes* and in other credible reports. After more than a decade of NCLB implementation, significant achievement gaps remain, and most high school graduates feel unprepared for twenty-first-century learning.[2] Unsurprisingly, as it was structured around false premises, NCLB was a house of cards, as students made only marginal gains in math and no progress in reading.

The deadline for every campus and district to have 100 percent of their students "proficient" in reading and math was 2014. In retrospect, NCLB was an overall failure. Even the libertarian Cato Institute reported, "there is little evidence that the No Child Left Behind Act has spurred significant, lasting improvements in academic outcomes."[3] Stanford professor Linda Darling-Hammond gives NCLB some credit for spotlighting long-standing race and class inequalities and insisting that all students be entitled to qualified teachers. However, she admonished the law's negative impact on schools. The statute's fundamental weakness was its failure to address the root causes of disparate student performance.

> Students will not learn at higher levels without the benefit of good teaching, a strong curriculum and adequate resources. Merely adopting tests and punishments will not create genuine accountability. In fact, adopting punitive sanctions without investments increases the likelihood that the most vulnerable students will be more severely victimized by a system not organized to support their learning.[4]

The year following NCLB's implementation, federal education funding increased more than threefold to $9.5 billion. Think about this: what if that financial infusion had supported universal pre-K? If we choose that path, the lessons learned can translate into investments for meaningful future innovation.

EXTENDED COMMITMENT

Patience for delayed fulfillment is a challenge for many, particularly in a rapidly paced society. Financial investors like to reap dividends quickly in bull markets. Elected officials want to initiate legislation that delivers fast, tangible results to their constituents. Innovative initiatives consider risk versus reward, and a precise timeline is usually part of venture agreements. However, the schedule for expected performance outcomes differs when providing funds for children's learning. Students develop at their own independent pace.

Academic studies on early childhood learning, such as those from the Chicago Child-Parent Centers[5] and the Perry Preschool Program,[6] are significant but require thirty-plus years to see results. English Language Learners (ELLs) can take four to seven years to acquire academic proficiency.[7] Multiple types of autism and dyslexia require observation and individual planning throughout the student's school years. Almost half the nation's children have experienced one or more types of severe childhood trauma,[8] and counseling can take months or years to reduce fear and restore trust. The developmental progression for students is as varied as each individual's DNA.

An astute society can postpone gratification for future rewards. The cases identified above are only some examples of learning requiring extended time and patience. With persistence, pragmatic goals, and meaningful accountability, progress is possible. The President's Council of Economic Advisers analyzed the monetary returns for childhood development investment and early education.[9] Evidence is compelling for both short- and long-term economic rewards identified for parents, children, and society.

The study estimated that the remuneration to society is roughly $8.60 for every dollar spent on expanding early learning initiatives. About half of the recovered funds are projected to come from increased earnings when the children become adults.[10] These projections are based on sound economic simulation models. Even with understated calculated predictions of financial advantages, many political authorities remain skeptical. The general public endorsement will expand following corroborating evidence from additional longitudinal studies. While waiting for this to happen, students should not be penalized until the Catch-22 is resolved.

Communities have the right to expect teacher accountability with students meeting tangible growth objectives. What is less understood by the public is the scope of teacher responsibility for student development. High-stakes state testing is only one independent growth indicator. Teachers monitor short-term (i.e., semester, yearly) gains with formative and summative assessments in several domains. Development with academic skills, socializing, engagement, and ownership of learning collectively contribute to future-ready graduates. A baseline of year-to-year cohort advancement is distinct from an individual student's extended progression pre-K through graduation. Learning can cease or regress at any point in the education process. Data on an entire class is valuable, but too many individuals are lost in grade transitions. This reality reinforces the need for long-term systemic investment in documenting and analyzing student learning from "big data" and through case studies.

Robust accountability systems must accompany the substantive expansion of budgets for pre-K-to-12 education. The unsound premises of NCLB included a flawed evaluation system. Data for the analysis was based solely on isolated scores, reading, and mathematics in grades 3 through 8 and 10. Legitimate geographic comparisons were impossible because every state had different assessments and standards. The statute was then punctuated with punitive measures for any campus or district not meeting these inconsistent criteria. Prerequisites for legitimately upgrading teaching and learning include time, forbearance, and valid education studies. The welfare and education of children warrant protection from partisan politics with simplistic "sticks and carrots" governance. It is feasible to invest in instructional innovation with credible accountability. The stewardship of trustworthy investments lies with those responsible for reforms and objective oversight.

Zakaria insightfully observes that "American politics is now hyperresponsive to constituents' interests" and "those interests are dedicated to preserving the past rather than investing for the future."[11] His examples, Eisenhower's highway systems, and Johnson's "Great Society" initiatives stimulated the US economy for decades with constructive disruption and growth. Reminiscing on the nostalgic classroom norms of previous generations is regressive and detrimental. A boom in education efficacy requires investments in innovative systems and research. Management must be guided by autonomous education leaders whose only concern is the learning environment for students. A blueprint of reasoned expectations and controlled settings should include a requisite commitment from all stakeholders. This understanding precedes investments and protects sustained funding.

FUNDING FORMULAS

As one of the last legislative accomplishments of Roosevelt's New Deal, the Fair Labor Standards Act of 1938 (FLSA) established a minimum wage, "time-and-a-half" for overtime pay for exceeding forty hours a week, and prohibited "oppressive child labor." This historic statute and subsequent amendments dramatically improved conditions for US workers. Hourly paid employees were less susceptible to unfair or arbitrary salary decisions. Children deserve the same protection underwritten with per-pupil spending for education.

In 2018, schools in the United States spent an average of $12,624 on each student, the fifth-highest among the thirty-seven other developed nations in the Organisation for Economic Co-operation and Development. Moreover, across the nation, states have minimal consistency for allocations. The internal US disparity is substantial, ranging from $23,321 per-pupil spending (PPS) in New York to $7,610 in Idaho.[12] Cost of living is also a factor to consider, but this is still a 67 percent disparity between the highest and lowest states!

A Baseline for States. A national minimum per-pupil expenditure would help to reduce that vast disparity between states. With twelve states budgeting less than $10,000 PPS, students cannot obtain the resources or opportunities afforded to others who receive more than double that amount. In enacting new legislation, Congress should support an equity mandate for states to allocate an established minimum bar. Approaching parity for poor school districts would extend subsidiary state compensatory and Federal Title funds. States would require a transition timeline, with the Department of Education providing seed money with national subsidies.

The National Bureau of Economic Research authors Jackson and Mackevicius conducted a meta-analysis of studies on school spending. Thirty-one credible causal studies met their inclusion criteria. Of those, 90 percent found an overall positive effect from increased school spending on student performance. Their findings reinforce the need for reformed funding formulas because allocations correlate highly with student achievement and equity.

> On average, a $1000 increase in school spending (sustained over four years) increases test scores by 0.0352σ, high-school graduation by 1.9 percentage points, and college-going by 2.65 percentage points. In relative terms, this is a 2.3 percent increase in high school graduation and a 6.5 percent increase in college-going.[13]

A minimum PPS phased in over three to five years is expected to significantly elevate academic performance and the number of college-ready graduates. Beyond following the research, there is an ethical and legal responsibility stemming from our constitution.

Equitable funding is fundamental in promoting the general welfare and aligns with the Fourteenth Amendment clause stating that "no state shall . . . deny to any person within its jurisdiction the equal protection of the laws."[14] Protection for students was further delineated in the Equal Educational Opportunities Act of 1974, which declared "it to be the policy of the United States that all children enrolled in public schools are entitled to equal educational opportunity without regard to race, color, sex, or national origin."[15] The courts have been inconsistent and even oppositional to education being a guaranteed federal right (e.g., *San Antonio Independent School District v. Rodriguez*, 1972). The indolent progress of judicial verdicts should not hinder students. Enlightened legislation is necessary to move the needle. Society cannot plead ignorance to funding's direct influence on a student's likelihood of prosperity.

A minimum state PPS is controversial because it involves the extensive redistribution of funding sources. Education is the responsibility of the states, yet it has increasingly been delegated to local support. According to a 2017 US census report, 44.6 percent of funding for public education came from local sources, mostly from property taxes.[16] Over-reliance on local funding contributes to generational inequity. Communities raise vastly different totals of revenue based on their local property values. Reviewing NCES data, local community financing for public education ranges from 67.4 percent in Illinois to 1.9 percent in Hawaii (see table 14.1).[17] Push-back would be expected against state ownership of school funding. However, the net advantages outweigh resistance to change and better serve most students.

By relying mainly on local taxes for funding schools, states perpetuate the wide variance between wealthy and poor districts. The first constituents to

Table 14.1 Percentage of Funding Sources for Public Education by Individual State

Percentage Share of Revenues for Public Elementary and Secondary Education by Source of Funds and State, 2015–2016 School Year

State	State (%)	Local (%)	Federal (%)	State	State (%)	Local (%)	Federal (%)
Hawaii	89.4	1.9	8.6	Tennessee	46.2	42.3	11.5
Vermont	89.3	4.0	6.6	Arizona	45.9	41.4	12.6
N. Mexico	70.0	16.2	13.7	Georgia	45.8	44.6	9.5
Minnesota	66.8	27.5	5.6	Wisconsin	45.5	47.3	7.1
Idaho	65.3	24.1	10.6	Ohio	44.9	47.4	7.7
Alaska	64.6	23.0	12.4	Maryland	43.9	50.2	5.8
Kansas	63.1	28.4	8.4	Colorado	43.7	49.2	7.1
Washington	62.2	30.4	7.4	Louisiana	43.5	43.8	12.7
N. Carolina	62.1	26.3	11.6	New Jersey	42.7	53.1	4.2
Michigan	60.2	30.9	8.9	New York	41.7	53.2	5.0
California	59.4	32.1	8.5	Rhode Island	41.4	50.9	7.7
N. Dakota	57.8	33.1	9.1	Texas	40.9	48.6	10.6
Wyoming	57.6	36.4	6.0	Connecticut	40.3	55.3	4.3
Delaware	57.4	34.3	8.3	Virginia	39.5	53.8	6.6
Indiana	55.6	36.4	8.0	Maine	39.4	53.6	7.0
W. Virginia	55.5	34.1	10.4	Florida	39.3	49.2	11.6
Kentucky	54.7	33.6	11.6	Mass.	37.8	57.2	5.0
Alabama	54.7	34.2	11.2	Pennsylvania	37.6	55.6	6.8
Utah	54.6	37.0	8.3	Nevada	35.6	55.5	8.9
Iowa	53.8	38.9	7.3	Nebraska	33.0	58.6	8.3
Oregon	52.3	40.0	7.6	Missouri	33.0	58.4	8.6
Mississippi	51.2	34.1	14.7	New Hamp.	32.9	61.4	5.7
Arkansas	51.1	37.3	11.6	S. Dakota	30.4	55.8	13.8
Oklahoma	48.3	40.2	11.5	Illinois	24.1	67.4	8.4
Montana	47.7	39.6	12.6	D. C.	0.0	90.1	9.9
S. Carolina	47.7	42.8	9.5	Overall	47.0	44.8	8.3

Source: US Department of Education, National Center for Education Statistics, School Year 2015–2016 (Fiscal Year 2016), December 2018, https://nces.ed.gov/pubs2019/2019301.pdf

resist state control of funding would be affluent parents and school boards from property-wealthy neighborhoods. In some cases, their PPS may even be reduced through redistribution. However, prosperous districts have advantages beyond the allocated PPS. Parents with moderate-to-high incomes provide fundraisers, booster clubs, personal resources, and external field experiences unavailable to economically disadvantaged students. School boards would lose control of setting local tax rates for elections but maintain control of most other responsibilities (e.g., bond elections, legal issues, fiscal management, and personnel issues).

Revisiting Equity. The Education Law Center (ELC) published a report analyzing state school finance systems emphasizing the fair distribution of resources to the most disadvantaged students. The authors make four assumptions about how school funding systems should be designed:

1. A fair funding system should provide levels based on student needs.
2. Student poverty is the most critical variable affecting funding levels and can serve as a proxy for other measures of disadvantage, such as racial segregation, limited English proficiency, and student mobility.
3. Fair funding systems are designed "progressively" so that funding increases relative to student poverty.
4. A sufficient overall level of funding is a crucial starting point for any funding formula to be successful.[18]

ELC defines "fair" state school funding as "a financial system that ensures equal educational opportunity." Distribution of funding to districts must provide a sufficient level "to account for additional needs generated by student poverty."[19] This requires exceeding the baseline funding described above for identified at-risk students.

State finance systems are ranked on continuums of progressive to regressive based on the degree of support they provide districts serving higher-needs students. A state is considered progressive if at least 5 percent of supplemental funding above the per-pupil allotment is distributed to high-poverty communities. When high-poverty districts receive 5 percent less than low-poverty districts, the allocation is regressive. For a progressive finance approach to be effective, ELC's fourth assumption is a caveat: a sufficient PPS foundation must be in place.[20] Alaska and New Jersey are two of the most progressively funded states.

Whether or not 5 percent is the ideal metric, progressive funding is educationally and economically constructive. States would annually certify the implementation of their baseline and progressive funding system. Also designated as "weighted" funding, additional funds are based on student needs from a set of criteria. Federal funds use weighted funding formulas to supplement identified students. Examples include Title I, Part A for low-income schools, Title III, Part A for English-language acquisition, the Individuals with Disabilities Education Act, Part B for special education, and Head Start for pre-K. While federal sources are stringent in resource usage, state and local funding enjoy latitude in progressive versus regressive spending.

High-poverty communities warrant enhanced support with well-compensated master teachers, reduced classroom size, and added resources. The same funding for all poor schools does not necessarily translate to fairness for students' needs. A school with a mean community income of $45,000 may be drastically dissimilar from another with a mean community income of $18,000, yet both qualify for the same Title I distribution. Federal supplemental funds for high-need students are a staple of school finance but leave much room for refinement and reclassification. An American University article reiterated this point:

> Title I needs substantial reform. In addition to making more money available for the program, the Federal government can revise the funding formula to better target high-need districts. It can also redesign the oversight system so it doesn't unnecessarily burden states or lead to ineffective use of money simply to comply with Title I regulations.[21]

Significant spending differentials remain both between states and within their local districts. Closing gaps is crucial but should not be done without some circumstantial flexibility. In phasing out inequities, legislators should consider regional logistics and the cost of living. Student achievement will accelerate when funding reflects adequate baseline PPS allocations and progressive formula weights are revamped for at-risk populations.

SOURCES OF FUNDING

Federal. The federal government would benefit from defining its limited purpose while maintaining an influential posture in upgrading education. Compelling federal leverage includes a national vision, normalizing financing, protecting equity, and providing incentives for promising innovative designs. Infusing additional funds into states will enable budget offices to transition to more equitable apportionment systems. Congress has many options for the general procurement of additional funds for education; the challenge is finding consensus.

The philosophical and ethical platform of a nation is reflected in its budget. Constitutions codify the frameworks for principles, beliefs, and statutes. Does the financial distribution best promote the national welfare in executing the US Constitution? Historically, it has been open to a wide range of perspectives and interpretations. Democratic nations with similar constitutions demonstrate contrasting investment patterns. In 2021, the United States spent "more on defense than the next 9 countries combined."[22] This pretentious funding appropriation is misaligned with every other country globally. Inspecting the military by budget categories also raises questions of values. Of the 725-billion-dollar budget, only 27 percent is for personnel, while *73 percent is expended on contractors for products and services.* Perhaps we are secure enough to reduce the rate of purchases for new weapons.

One available budgeting option is internal reappropriations by Congress. The $725 billion spent on defense in fiscal year (FY) 2020 amounted to 11 percent of all federal spending. Former President Trump's Department of Education budget request for the same FY was $64 billion, a 10 percent reduction from 2019. Combining both budgets equates to a federal military-to-education spending ratio of about 92 percent to 8 percent. Total education spending from federal, state, and local resources was $640 billion in 2020. Altering the military-to-education ratio partially—79 percent to 21 percent—would increase the federal spending on pre-K-12 education by 100 billion dollars. This shift would boost state and local budgets, accounting for about 92 percent of district education funding by almost 16 percent.

Like the example above, reappropriation would help facilitate state funding formula transitions. Reducing the record of $447 billion spent on defense contractors in 2020 would also incite political backlash from these formidable industries. Leadership decisions indicate the conscience of a nation. Reminiscent of the tobacco industry's attempts to erode, obscure, and denounce the science behind lung cancer and emphysema, lawmakers must have the courage to be truthful and fight for the greater public welfare. Righteousness means empathizing with those bearing a minimal political voice.

Additional funding should begin with a commitment and vision from the federal government. Incentives for innovative grants to establish research lab schools and professional teacher pathways assist states with constructive models. Chapter 3 delineated the generous benefits reserved for armed service members. These resourceful incentives for recruitment and stability resulted in a global model for a volunteer military. Comparable structures for progressive teacher levels of leadership tied to skill, experience, and performance could have a transformational impact.

States. Constitutionally, states have the primary authority to administer public education. The responsibilities empowered to state education departments include maintenance, operation, curriculum, educator certification, testing, accountability, and instructional materials. While controlling the primary educational functions, states' delegation of funding to local districts leaves insufficient equity assurance. States relinquish their obligation to fairness in education by designating a substantial percentage of financing schools to local districts. They "have largely failed to keep up with the growing wealth disparities across their communities."[23] Politicians universally embrace the critical role of education in employment and economic health. Espousing the value of education is welcome, but without ensuring its well-being, the rhetoric is hollow, and the performance data illuminates the implicit bias.

State constitutions articulate an obligation to fund and organize an effectual public education system, and their elected representatives pass laws governing school practices. While governments may delegate considerable power to local districts, they can take back the specific authority for funding. Rather than waiting for court interventions to mandate compensation for regressive budgeting, preemptive state control could ensure a nondiscriminatory system to distribute resources.

How a state procures funds for education also has implications for egalitarianism. Education is the most significant single expenditure for any state with personal financial consequences on its citizens. The taxation systems in the United States are categorized under three broad designations: regressive, proportional, and progressive. Horton provides a summary:

- A regressive tax system levies the same percentage on products or goods purchased regardless of the buyer's income and is thought to be disproportionately burdensome on low earners.
- A proportional tax applies the same tax rate to all individuals regardless of income.
- A progressive tax imposes a greater percentage of taxation on higher income levels, operating on the theory that high-income earners can afford to pay more.[24]

Property tax affords the largest share of local revenue for schools nationally. Unfortunately, it is also the most regressive. Shifting to a proportional (flat) tax (e.g., sales tax, some state income taxes) or a progressive tax (e.g., federal income tax brackets) is a rational approach to achieving equity. Alternatively, the effect becomes proportional if a state collects all the property tax and redistributes it from the general fund.

Independent organizations have unique formulas for rating the states with the "best" school systems. Indeed, districts and schools show significant variance in quality, but there are too many social and economic variables to give these rankings authoritative credence. Particular states may have fewer economically disadvantaged students, more funding, or a more stable teaching population. In identifying exemplars for innovation, the criteria must be narrow. Specifically, Hawaii and Vermont provide examples that warrant further study and possible replication for equitable and progressive funding.

In Hawaii, allocations for the operation of public schools are distributed from a general fund. No property tax funds are levied for education support, and 93 percent of the budget goes directly to schools. Hawaii is the only single, unified, statewide school district with direct oversight of schools and ninth overall in PPS. This structure allows for flexible responsiveness in adapting to the imperatives of education funding. Weighted funding for special needs (WSF) accounts for 50 percent of education appropriations. About 17 percent of Hawaii's schoolchildren attend costly private schools, the highest percentage in the nation. Of those in the public system, about 47 percent are eligible for free and reduced lunch. Another educational challenge is that 18 percent of students are ELLs, comprising seventy different spoken languages. Hawaii has confronted its issues and now ranks among the top states in the country for education funding equity.

In 2003, Vermont passed Act 68, which eliminated the education portion of local property taxes. It transitioned to a statewide property tax that is centrally distributed for school funding. A surtax was imposed on communities spending above a set percentage of the previous year's per-pupil average. This discouraged property-wealthy towns from approving appreciably more spending than their less prosperous neighbors. With the second-highest per-pupil funding in the nation, detachment from local property wealth, and progressive formulas, low-income students have exemplary value-added conditions to close learning gaps. "Policymakers seeking to implement meaningful reforms . . . should look to Vermont's pursuit of funding equity and see that true progress can be made."[25]

Local. Local control of public education has a substantial and mixed history. Boards of education have been a hallmark of public education in the United States for over a century. They are considered a bastion of democratic representation and community decision-making. Beginning with the Massachusetts Bay Colony in 1647, there are more than 14,000 public school districts today. Reiterating from chapter 8, examples of leadership from local officials range from dynamic to ineffective and, at times, even corrupt. Fortunately, state oversight systems are in place to intervene in unwarranted decisions or remove school boards if necessary.

Recommendations to diminish the political nature of local boards are beyond the scope of this book. Notwithstanding general authority, removing their tax levying power may be one constructive step in an improved funding structure. Eliminating this single facet from local jurisdiction, that of administrating tax ratification elections, does not diminish the board's prominent role in governance. Trustees working closely with the superintendent must still make countless consequential decisions impacting student prosperity in their community.

CONCLUSION

The volition to recalibrate a nation's traditional budgeting practices may seem like an unrealistically heavy rock to push uphill. Nevertheless, the rationale behind competently educating our children through equitably increased budgets is more credible vis-à-vis support for any defense contractor or corporate tax cut. Because vulnerable students' voices are mute, the call for action must be constantly repeated.

> Repetition can affect beliefs about truth. People tend to perceive claims as truer if they have been exposed to them before. This is known as the illusory truth effect, and it helps explain why advertisements and propaganda work, and also why people believe fake news to be true.[26]

The argument ideally includes research on student learning and economic prosperity. For those citizens not impassioned by reason or repetition, the campaign should include anecdotal stories about children. The adverse consequences of reduced direct teacher-student interaction were evident during the pandemic starting in 2020. Those scenarios of learning regression are newsworthy reminders.

In funding education, US government entities invariably place students, particularly the poorest, at the mercy of politics. School finance reform must emphasize baseline excellence for every campus, starting with teacher quality. Stable and progressive funding necessitates rethinking taxation and distribution of school funding. Progress for reform warrants budget consistency for long-term innovation. A synergetic balance with federal equity legislation, state management of funding and curriculum, and local guidance establish more pragmatic divisions of governance. For US public education to reclaim its previous "envy of the world" status, fundamental system disruption must incorporate finance restructuring.

NOTES

1. Zakaria, 2011, 1.
2. Davis, 2021.
3. McCluskey, 2015, 6.
4. Darling-Hammond, 2007, 11.

5. Reynolds et al., 2002.
6. Belfield et al., 2021.
7. Hakuta et al., 2000.
8. Stevens, 2013.
9. Council of Economic Advisors, 2015.
10. Ibid.
11. Zakaria, 2011, 3.
12. Hanson, 2021.
13. Jackson & Mackevicius, 2021, 3.
14. Fourteenth Amendment, Section 1, 1868.
15. Equal Educational Opportunities Act, 1974.
16. "More than Half of School Expenditures Spent on Classroom Instruction," 2017.
17. Cornman et al., 2018.
18. Baker, Farrie & Sciarra, 2018, iii.
19. Ibid., 2.
20. Ibid.
21. "Inequality in Public School Funding: Key Issues & Solutions," 2020, 5.
22. "The United States Spends More on Defense than the Next 9 Countries Combined," 2022, 1.
23. "Nonwhite School Districts Get $23 Billion Less than White Districts," 2021.
24. Horton, 2021.
25. Marar, 2020.
26. Hassan & Barber, 2021, 1.

Postlude
One Viewpoint in an Idea World

It's the job that's never started as takes longest to finish.
—J. R. R. Tolkien, *The Lord of the Rings*

The thought came to me to conclude this narrative with a tale of two teachers. The scenario involves one idealistic young woman becoming frustrated with mediocrity, losing enthusiasm, and leaving her once-cherished students, and one insecure young man, uncertain of his calling, finding fulfillment in a reinvigorated, teacher-centric school district. Simulating "what if" storylines may arouse the imagination but convey unrealistic expectations for educators. The decisions impacting schools are rarely collaborative or predictive in the long term. My hope is to move in a better direction pragmatically.

Education in the United States has never been coherent in purpose or linear in direction. Teachers are portrayed as deities or demons, depending on the political moment. Student progress moves two steps forward, one backward, and a few to the side. Perspectives from educators, parents, and political pundits have historically been and remain divisive over public education priorities. Excessive time spent arguing about vaccines, Critical Race Theory, or book bans could be spent working together on substantive issues. History suggests continued inconsistency and reacting to a crisis, but reasoned ideas may be accepted as an educational epiphany at the opportune moment.

The optimist in me believes that society will embrace the idea that educational change based on research can, in time, promote the common good. What if the education conversation centered on equity and economic advancement for impending generations? Can we step away from single-issue rhetoric, seek more universal goals, and impartially consider children? What if education were more akin to science and medical practices? Perhaps these questions can move from the rhetorical realm and be confronted pragmatically.

Researchers know not to presume an outcome. It is unscientific to profess that isolated actions will have a "butterfly effect" on the teaching profession. Hence, I spare readers the hopeful story of the "once upon a time" insecure young man. However, without safeguarded, calculated risks, progress is thwarted. Venturing forward with innovative actions is an obligation when the baseline education system is struggling. Teacher shortages have long surpassed the tipping point, impeding our children's learning and requiring action. Execution is conscientious and auspicious if the pioneering "approach" is based on controlled methods and existing studies.

Educators espouse the desire for students to think critically, question, and verify as indispensable for lifelong learning. When teachers practice those same aspirations through integrating actual research, they shape students' vantage points in practice. The "approach" expands promising pilot studies and research findings across disciplines. Of equal salience, the investigative mindset of teachers can merge the delivery of information with the discovery of new knowledge. A teacher's growth pathway with progressive steps parallels the inquiry-based learning desired for their students. Advancing from the mentored practitioner to the researching master teacher is this author's prognosis for the future of education.

Recently, I heard a teacher speak at a school board meeting. She began her remarks with a self-deprecating introduction: "I am just a teacher." Her statement conveys a perceptual sentiment all too pervasive in US society. Suggesting insignificance leads to confirmation bias. Self-worth derives from imagining how others view you. Her statement made me wonder if this teacher began her career feeling undervalued or if this feeling manifested over time. In either case, the system and culture must prevent its replication.

From Dewey's laboratory school in the 1890s to the present, educators have encouraged organizing schools as communities of inquiry with ongoing research. Psychologists espouse constructivist learning theory where students build knowledge in a social setting. The best teachers guide students to sustain their natural passion, leading to ownership of learning and creative ideas. Sir Ken Robinson, an advocate for creativity in education, outlined the principles regarding the circumstances for schools to thrive. One of my favorite quotations of his relates to creating the conditions for learning:

> Human resources are like natural resources; they're often buried deep. You have to go looking for them, they're not just lying around on the surface. You have to create the circumstances where they show themselves. Education is a personal process.[1]

Although Robinson was talking about students, the mission of edifying personal agency is more encompassing. If archaic structures repress teachers' growth, they will struggle to instill agency in their students. As prisms shaping children's radiance, teachers must flourish to revamp societal perceptions of their prominence. When teachers become the archetype of competence, with its corresponding self-esteem, they become professionals *in practice*, and students will seek to join the community.

A child's curiosity is quickly extinguished, and a teacher's passion can suffer the same fate. Positive innovation can be suppressed with the words "That's not how we do it here." Orthodox thinking and accepting complacency are misguided when a system is deteriorating. When will the United States react responsibly to the teacher crisis? Will we learn from the education setbacks during the pandemic? My suggestion is to *start with teachers*, construct an ecosystem and culture that emanates professionalism, designs progressive levels of expertise, compensates generously for results, and allows earned autonomy to elevate teachers. As an author, I am grateful for the freedom to express my opinions, built upon experience and the ideas of many others.

NOTE

1. Robinson, 2010.

Appendix

Acronyms

ACP	Alternative Certification Program
ACT	American College Testing
AFT	American Federation of Teachers
AIR	American Institutes for Research
AP	Advanced Placement
BCG	Boston Consulting Group
BE	Bilingual Education
CARES	Coronavirus Aid, Relief, and Economic Security Act
CBA	Collective Bargaining Agreement
CS	Computer Science
DC	Dual Credit
DDI	Data-Driven Instruction
DOE	Department of Education
ECE	Early Childhood Education
ELC	Education Law Center
ELL	English Language Learner
EPI	Economic Policy Institute
ESEA	Elementary and Secondary Education Act
ESL	English as a Second Language
ESSA	Every Student Succeeds Act
FLSA	Fair Labor Standards Act
GDP	Gross Domestic Product
GPA	Grade Point Average
GYO	Grow Your Own
IA	Instructional Assistant
IALS	International Association of Laboratory and University Affiliated Schools

IB	International Baccalaureate
IC	Instructional Coach
IEP	Individualized Education Program
MOU	Memorandum of understanding
MT	Master Teacher
MTR	Master Teacher Researcher
MTSS	Multi-Tiered System of Support
NAEP	National Assessment of Education Progress
NASEM	National Academies of Sciences, Engineering, and Medicine
NBC	National Board Certification
NCES	National Center for Education Statistics
NCLB	No Child Left Behind
NCTQ	National Council on Teacher Quality
NEA	National Education Association
NLRA	National Labor Relations Act
OCI	Opportunity Culture Initiative
OECD	Organisation for Economic Cooperation and Development
PDK	Phi Delta Kappa International
PISA	Programme for International Student Assessment
PL	Professional Learning
PLC	Professional Learning Communities
PPS	Per-Pupil Spending
RIF	Reduction in Force
RTT	Race to the Top
SAISD	San Antonio Independent School District
SDE	State Department of Education
SE	Special education
SEED	Supporting Effective Educator Development
SEL	Social-Emotional Learning
STEM	Science, Technology, Engineering, and Math
T-TESS	Texas Teacher Evaluation and Support System
TFA	Teach for America
TIA	Teacher Incentive Allotment
TIF	Teacher Incentive Fund
TTI	Talent Transfer Initiative
TM	Talent Management
VR	Virtual Reality
WSF	Weighted Funding for Special Needs

Bibliography

"2021–2022 Educator Supply & Demand Report (Digital Access): American Association for Employment in Education." Glue Up, 2020. https://aaee.glueup.com/event/2021-2022-educator-supply-demand-report-digital-access-53997/.

Abbott, Andre. *The System of Professions: An Essay on the Division of Expert Labor.* Chicago, IL: University of Chicago Press, 2014.

Adelman, Clem. "Kurt Lewin and the Origins of Action Research." *Educational Action Research* 1, no. 1 (1993): 7–24. https://doi.org/10.1080/0965079930010102.

Adler v. Bd. of Educ., 342 U.S. 485, 493 (1952). That school authorities have the right and the duty to screen the officials, teachers, and employees as to their fitness to maintain the integrity of schools as a part of ordered society cannot be doubted.

Ahmad, Zahra. "Filling the Pipeline for Computer Science Teachers." *Science.* American Association for the Advancement of Science, 2017. https://www.science.org/content/article/filling-pipeline-computer-science-teachers.

Al-Bahrani, Muna Abdullah, Suad Mohammed Allawati, Yousef Abdelqader Abu Shindi, and Bakkar Suliman Bakkar. "Career Aspiration and Related Contextual Variables." *International Journal of Adolescence and Youth* 25, no. 1 (2020): 703–11. https://doi.org/10.1080/02673843.2020.1730201.

Alexander, Don, David Chant, and Bernard Cox. "What Motivates People to Become Teachers." *Australian Journal of Teacher Education* 19, no. 2 (1994). https://doi.org/10.14221/ajte.1994v19n2.4.

Allegretto, Sylvia, and Lawrence Mishel. "Teacher Pay Penalty Dips but Persists in 2019: Public School Teachers Earn about 20% Less in Weekly Wages than Nonteacher College Graduates." Economic Policy Institute, 2020. https://www.epi.org/publication/teacher-pay-penalty-dips-but-persists-in-2019-public-school-teachers-earn-about-20-less-in-weekly-wages-than-nonteacher-college-graduates/.

Allensworth, Elaine M., and Holly M. Hart. *How Do Principals Influence Student Achievement? Leadership.* Chicago, IL: University of Chicago, 2018. https://consortium.uchicago.edu/sites/default/files/2018-10/Leadership%20Snapshot-Mar2018-Consortium.pdf.

"Arizona Teachers Academy." College of Education, University of Arizona, July 15, 2021. https://coe.arizona.edu/arizona-teachers-academy.

"Autonomy Improves Our Performance." The Peak Performance Center, 2021. https://thepeakperformancecenter.com/business/performance-management/autonomy-improves-performance/.

Baer, Drake. "Science Says this Personality Trait Predicts Job Performance." *Business Insider*, December 19, 2014. https://www.businessinsider.com/conscientiousness-predicts-job-performance-2014-12.

Baker, Bruce D., Danielle Farrie, and David Sciarra. "Is School Funding Fair? A National Report Card." Education Law Center, Rutgers University, February 2018. https://edlawcenter.org/assets/files/pdfs/publications/Is_School_Funding_Fair_7th_Editi.pdf.

Balthazard, Claude. "What Does It Mean to Be a Professional?" Human Resources Professionals Association, August 2015. https://hrpa.s3.amazonaws.com/uploads/2020/10/What-it-means-to-be-a-professional.pdf.

Barnett, W. Steven. "Universal Pre-K: 5 FAQs." National Institute for Early Education Research, July 2021. https://nieer.org/wp-content/uploads/2021/07/UPK_Fact_Sheet_2.3.pdf.

Barrett, Sharon Kebschull. "Opportunity Culture Overview." Opportunity Culture. Brookings Institute, January 11, 2018. https://www.opportunityculture.org/2018/01/11/brookings-air-study-finds-large-academic-gains-in-opportunity-culture/.

Beckham, Joseph, Barbara Klaymeier Wills, and Kent M. Weeks. "School Boards: Responsibilities, Duties, Decision-Making and Legal Basis for Local School Board Powers." State University, 2020. https://education.stateuniversity.com/pages/2391/School-Boards.html.

Belfield, Clive R, Milagros Nores, Steve Barnett, and Schweinhart Lawrence. "The High/Scope Perry Preschool Program: Cost Benefit Analysis Using Data from the Age-40 Followup." *Journal of Human Resources*, July 2021. https://doi.org/10.3368/jhr.XLI.1.162.

Belluz, Julia, Brad Plumer, and Brian Resnick. "The 7 Biggest Problems Facing Science, According to 270 Scientists." *Vox*, July 14, 2016. https://www.vox.com/2016/7/14/12016710/science-challeges-research-funding-peer-review-process.

Bernazzani, Sophia. "What Millennials Want from Work: Flexibility, Not Salary." *The Predictive Index*, July 22, 2021. https://www.predictiveindex.com/blog/why-flexibility-is-a-better-perk-than-salary/.

Biden, Joe. "President Biden Addresses NEA Representative Assembly." https://Educationvotes.nea.org/2020/07/03/Joe-Biden-to-Educators-You-Are-the-Most-Important-Profession-in-the-United-States/. Speech, July 2, 2020.

Boston Consulting Group. "Teachers Know Best: Teachers' Views on Professional Development." GFO - Bill & Melinda Gates Foundation, 2014. https://usprogram.gatesfoundation.org/-/media/dataimport/resources/pdf/2016/11/gates-pdmarket-research-dec5.pdf.

Bowers, Trent. "From Survive to THRIVE: What Great Substitute Teachers Do Differently." Worthington Schools, 2009. https://www.worthington.k12.oh.us/.

Bradley, Steve, and Colin Green. *The Economics of Education: A Comprehensive Overview*. New York: Academic Press, 2020.

Bridle, Helen, Anton Vrieling, Monica Cardillo, Yoseph Araya, and Leonith Hinojosa. "Preparing for an Interdisciplinary Future: A Perspective from Early-Career Researchers." *Futures* 53 (2013): 22–32. https://doi.org/10.1016/j.futures.2013.09.003.

"Burn-out an 'Occupational Phenomenon': International Classification of Diseases." World Health Organization, 2019. https://www.who.int/news/item/28-05-2019-burn-out-an-occupational-phenomenon-international-classification-of-diseases.

Bushweller, Kevin. "How to Get More Students of Color into STEM: Tackle Bias, Expand Resources." *Education Week*, June 29, 2021. https://www.edweek.org/technology/how-to-get-more-students-of-color-into-stem-tackle-bias-expand-resources/2021/03.

Busteed, Brandon. "The School Cliff: Student Engagement Drops with Each School Year." Gallup.com, March 13, 2020. https://news.gallup.com/opinion/gallup/170525/school-cliff-student-engagement-drops-school-year.aspx.

Buttner, Annie. "The Teacher Shortage, 2021 Edition." Frontline Education, 2021. https://www.frontlineeducation.com/blog/teacher-shortage-2021/.

Bybee, Eric Ruiz, Kathryn I. Henderson, and Roel V. Henderson. "An Overview of U.S. Bilingual Education: Historical Roots, Legal Battles, and Recent Trends." Brigham Young University, 2014. https://scholarsarchive.byu.edu/cgi/viewcontent.cgi?article=2627&context=facpub.

"Carl Sagan." *Psychology Today*. Sussex Publishers, January 1996. http://www.psychologytoday.com/articles/199601/carl-sagan?page=3.

Caron, Christina. "Spanking Is Ineffective and Harmful to Children, Pediatricians' Group Says." *New York Times*, November 5, 2018. https://www.nytimes.com/2018/11/05/health/spanking-harmful-study-pediatricians.html.

Carroll, Thomas G. "Policy Brief the High Cost of Teacher Turnover." National Commission on Teaching and America's Future, 2018. https://nieer.org/wp-content/uploads/2015/06/NCTAFCostofTeacherTurnoverpolicybrief.pdf.

Caruso, Karen N. "A Practical Guide to Performance Calibration: A Step-by-Step Guide to Increasing the Fairness and Accuracy of Performance Appraisal." viaPeople, Inc., October 2013. https://cdn2.hubspot.net/hub/91252/file-338193964-pdf/Practical_Guide_to_Performance_Calibration_October_2013.pdf.

Carver-Thomas, Desiree, and Linda Darling-Hammond. "Teacher Turnover: Why It Matters and What We Can Do about It - FCIS." Learning Policy Institute, August 2017. https://www.fcis.org/uploaded/Data_Reports/Teacher_Turnover_REPORT.pdf.

"Census Bureau Reports at Least 350 Languages Spoken in U.S. Homes." U.S. Census Bureau. Department of Commerce, November 3, 2015. https://content.govdelivery.com/accounts/USCENSUS/bulletins/122dd88.

"Characteristics of Public School Teachers." National Center for Education Statistics. U.S. Department of Education, Institute of Education Sciences, 2021. https://nces.ed.gov/programs/coe/indicator/clr.

Chen, Grace. "New Poll Shows What Parents Think of Current State of Public Schools." *Public School Review*, January 28, 2020. https://www.publicschoolreview.com/blog/new-poll-shows-what-parents-think-of-current-state-of-public-schools.

Chen, Sandy. *Illustrations on Classroom Equity*. 2022. Two illustrations of Equity versus Equality. Taipei, Taiwan .

Chetty, Raj, John N. Friedman, and Jonah E. Rockoff. "The Long-Term Impacts of Teachers: Teacher Value-Added and Student Outcomes in Adulthood." *NBER*, December 22, 2011. https://www.nber.org/papers/w17699.

"College Graduates by Major." Digest of Education Statistics. National Center for Education Statistics, 2019. https://nces.ed.gov/programs/digest/d19/tables/dt19_322.10.asp.

"Colleges with the Largest Enrollment of Black, Non-Hispanic Students." *CollegeXpress*, 2021. https://www.collegexpress.com/lists/list/colleges-with-the-largest-enrollment-of-black-non-hispanic-students/376/.

"Conquering the Readiness Gap." readingfoundation.org. Children's Reading Foundation, 2019. https://readingfoundation.org/download/x9fl1z.

Cornman, Stephen Q., Lei Zhou, Malia R. Howell, and Jumaane Young. "Revenues and Expenditures for Public Elementary and Secondary Education: School Year 2015–16." National Center for Education Statistics, December 2018. https://nces.ed.gov/pubs2019/2019301.pdf.

Council of Economic Advisors. (2015). The economics of early childhood investments. Retrieved from https://obamawhitehouse.archives.gov/sites/default/files/docs/early_childhood_report_update_final_non-embargo.pdf.

Covey, Stephen R., James C. Collins, and Sean Covey. *The 7 Habits of Highly Effective People: Powerful Lessons in Personal Change*. New York: Simon & Schuster, 2020.

Cowen, Joshua M., and Katharine O. Strunk. "The Impact of Teachers' Unions on Educational Outcomes: What We Know and What We Need to Learn." *Economics of Education Review* 48 (October 2015): 208–23. https://doi.org/10.1016/j.econedurev.2015.02.006.

Crispin, Laura M. "Extracurricular Participation, 'At-Risk' Status, and the High School Dropout Decision." Association for Education Finance and Policy, 2017. https://watermark.silverchair.com/edfp.

"Criteria for Accreditation (CRRT.B.10.010): Policies." Higher Learning Commission, 2022. https://www.hlcommission.org/Policies/criteria-and-core-components.html.

Croft, Michelle, Gretchen Guffy, and Dan Vitale. "Encouraging More High School Students to Consider Teaching." ACT, 2018. https://www.act.org/content/dam/act/unsecured/documents/pdfs/Encouraging-More-HS-Students-to-Consider-Teaching.pdf.

Department of Education. (2022). Participating in the Perkins Loan Program. 2021–2022 Federal Student Aid Handbook. Retrieved from https://fsapartners.ed.gov/knowledge-center/fsa-handbook/2021-2022/vol6/ch3-participating-perkins-loan-program.

Danielson, Charlotte F. "Implementing the Framework for Teaching in Enhancing Professional Practice." Association for Supervision and Curriculum Development, 2009. https://eric.ed.gov/?id=ED531509.

Darling-Hammond, Linda, Audrey Amrein-Beardsley, Edward Haertel, and Jesse Rothstein. "Evaluating Teacher Evaluation." kappanonline.org. *Phi*

Delta Kappan, August 11, 2012. https://journals.sagepub.com/doi/abs/10.1177/003172171209300603.

Darling-Hammond, Linda. "Evaluating 'No Child Left Behind'." *The Nation*, May 2007. https://search.proquest.com/docview/2262996653.

Darling-Hammond, Linda, Carol Campbell, A. Lin Goodwin, Karen Hammerness, Ann McIntyre, Mistilina Sato, Ee-Ling Low, Ken Zeichner, and Dion Burns. *Empowered Educators How High-Performing Systems Shape Teaching Quality around the World*. San Francisco, CA: Jossey-Bass, 2017.

Darling-Hammond, Linda, Maria E. Hyler, and Madelyn Gardner. "Effective Teacher Professional Development." Learning Policy Institute, 2017. https://learningpolicyinstitute.org/product/effective-teacher-professional-development-report.

Das, Bidisha. "These 17 College Degrees Have the Highest Starting Salaries." *The College Post*, March 7, 2022. https://thecollegepost.com/highest-starting-salary-college-degrees/.

Davis, Ben. "Do High School Students Feel Prepared for the Real World?" MV-organizing.com, May 31, 2021. https://www.mvorganizing.org/do-high-school-students-feel-prepared-for-the-real-world/.

DeMitchell, Todd A. *Teachers and Their Unions: Labor Relations in Uncertain Times*. Lanham, MD: Rowman & Littlefield, 2020.

DeMitchell, Todd A., and Joseph J. Onosko. "Vergara v. State of California: The End of Teacher Tenure or a Flawed Ruling?" 2016. https://gould.usc.edu/why/students/orgs/ilj/assets/docs/25-3-DeMitchell-Onosko.pdf.

DeMonte, Jenny. "A Million New Teachers Are Coming." AIR, May 2015. https://www.air.org/sites/default/files/downloads/report/Million-New-Teachers-Brief-deMonte-May-2015.pdf.

Department of Education. (2022). Participating in the Perkins Loan Program. 2021-2022 Federal Student Aid Handbook. Retrieved from https://fsapartners.ed.gov/knowledge-center/fsa-handbook/2021-2022/vol6/ch3-participating-perkins-loan-program

Doğan, Selcuk, and Alyson Adams. "Effect of Professional Learning Communities on Teachers and Students: Reporting Updated Results and Raising Questions about Research Design." *School Effectiveness and School Improvement* 29, no. 4 (2018): 634–59. https://doi.org/10.1080/09243453.2018.1500921.

Dorn, Emma, Bryan Hancock, Jimmy Sarakatsannis, and Ellen Viruleg. "Covid-19 and Learning Loss: Disparities Grow and Students Need Help." McKinsey & Company, June 23, 2021. https://www.mckinsey.com/industries/public-and-social-sector/our-insights/covid-19-and-learning-loss-disparities-grow-and-students-need-help.

Downey, Maureen. "New Poll: Majority of Parents Don't Want Their Kids to Become Teachers." *Boston 25 News*, August 29, 2018. https://www.boston25news.com/news/education/new-poll-majority-of-parents-dont-want-their-kids-to-become-teachers/822751945/.

"Driven by Data: Using Licensure Tests to Build a Strong, Diverse Teacher Workforce." National Council on Teacher Quality (NCTQ), 2021. https://www.nctq.org

/publications/Driven-by-Data:-Using-Licensure-Tests-to-Build-a-Strong,-Diverse-Teacher-Workforce/.

DuFour, Richard, Rebecca Burnette DuFour, and Robert E. Eaker. *Revisiting Professional Learning Communities at Work: New Insights for Improving Schools*. Bloomington, IN: Solution Tree, 2008.

DuFour, Richard, Rebecca Burnette DuFour, Robert E. Eaker, Thomas W. Many, and Mike Mattos. *Learning by Doing: A Handbook for Professional Learning Communities at Work*. Bloomington, IN: Solution Tree Press, 2020.

Elmore, Richard F. *Instructional Rounds in Education: A Network Approach to Improving Teaching and Learning*. Cambridge, MA: Harvard Education Press, 2009.

Engzell, Per, Arun Frey, and Mark D. Verhagen. "Learning Loss Due to School Closures during the COVID-19 Pandemic." *Proceedings of the National Academy of Sciences* 118, no. 17 (2021). https://doi.org/10.1073/pnas.2022376118.

"Exchange Visitor Program." Bureau of Educational and Cultural Affairs, US Department of State, 2020. https://j1visa.state.gov/programs/teacher/.

"Expanding and Strengthening the Stem Teacher Workforce through Uteach." UTeach Institute, April 6, 2022. https://institute.uteach.utexas.edu/seed.

Feldman, Sarah, and Felix Richter. "Infographic: Steady Rise for Women in STEM but Gender Gap Remains." *Statista Infographics*, February 11, 2019. https://www.statista.com/chart/16970/women-stem/.

Figlio, David. "The Importance of a Diverse Teaching Force." Brookings Institute, 2017. https://www.brookings.edu/research/the-importance-of-a-diverse-teaching-force/.

Fink, John, Takeshi Yanagiura, and David Jenkins. "What Happens to Students Who Take Community College 'Dual Enrollment' Courses in High School?" Academic Commons. Columbia University, September, 2017. https://doi.org/10.7916/d8vd7b15.

Flaherty, Colleen. "Teacher Education Programs Continue to Suffer 'Death by a Thousand Cuts.'" *Inside Higher Ed*, October 28, 2020. https://www.insidehighered.com/news/2020/10/28/teacher-education-programs-continue-suffer-death-thousand-cuts.

Fortner, Alyssa. "7 Things to Know about Child Care and Universal Pre-K in the Build Back Better Act." Center for Law and Social Policy (CLASP), November 1, 2021. https://www.clasp.org/blog/7-things-know-about-child-care-and-universal-pre-k-build-back-better-act.

Friedman, Alex. "The Long-Term Effects of Ineffective Teachers." *Brooklyn Math Tutors*, October 4, 2018. https://www.brooklynmathtutors.com/the-long-term-effects-of-ineffective-teachers.

"Frustration in the Schools: Teachers Speak Out on Pay, Funding, and Feeling Valued — The 51st Annual PDK Poll of The Public's Attitudes toward the Public Schools." *Phi Delta Kappan*, 101, no. 1 (2019): K1–K24. https://pdkpoll.org/.

Garcia, Amaya. "A New Era for Bilingual Education in California." kappanonline.org. Phi Delta Kappa International, January 25, 2020. https://kappanonline.org/a-new-era-for-bilingual-education-in-california/.

Garcia, Amaya. "Grow Your Own Teachers: A 50-State Scan of Policies and Programs." *New America*. Accessed July 25, 2020. https://d1y8sb8igg2f8e.cloudfront.net/documents/Grow_Your_Own_Teachers_.pdf.

García, Emma, and Eunice Han. "The Impact of Changes in Public-Sector Bargaining Laws on Districts' Spending on Teacher Compensation." Economic Policy Institute, April 2021. https://www.epi.org/publication/the-impact-of-changes-in-public-sector-bargaining-laws-on-districts-spending-on-teacher-compensation/.

García , Emma, and Elaine Weiss. "Low Relative Pay and High Incidence of Moonlighting Play a Role in the Teacher Shortage, Particularly in High-Poverty Schools: The Third Report in 'The Perfect Storm in the Teacher Labor Market' Series." Economic Policy Institute, 2019. https://www.epi.org/publication/low-relative-pay-and-high-incidence-of-moonlighting-play-a-role-in-the-teacher-shortage-particularly-in-high-poverty-schools-the-third-report-in-the-perfect-storm-in-the-teacher-labor-marke/.

Glazerman, Steven, Ali Protik, Bingru Teh, Julie Bruch, and Jeffrey Max. "Transfer Incentives for High-Performing Teachers: Final Results from a Multisite Randomized Experiment." IES, November 2013. https://ies.ed.gov/ncee/pubs/20144003/pdf/20144003.pdf.

Goldhaber, Dan, John Krieg, Natsumi Naito, and Roddy Theobald. "Making the Most of Student Teaching: The Importance of Mentors and Scope for Change." *MIT Press*, June 1, 2020. https://doi.org/10.1162/edfp_a_00305.

Haag, Pascale. "Laboratory Schools: A New Educational Phenomenon." *The Conversation*, June 12, 2017. https://theconversation.com/laboratory-schools-a-new-educational-phenomenon-79071.

Hadar, Linor, and David Brody. *Teacher Educators' Professional Learning in Communities*. London: Routledge, 2016. https://doi.org/10.4324/9781315645605.

Hakuta, Kenji, Daria Witt, and Yuko Goto Butler. "How Long Does It Take English Learners to Attain Proficiency?" University of California Linguistic Minority Research Institute, January 2000. https://web.stanford.edu/~hakuta/Publications/.

Hanson, Melanie. "College Enrollment Statistics [2022]: Total + by Demographic." *Education Data Initiative*, July 26, 2022. https://educationdata.org/high-school-graduates-who-go-to-college/.

Hanson, Melanie. "U.S. Public Education Spending Statistics." *Education Data Initiative*, August 2, 2021. https://educationdata.org/public-education-spending-statistics.

Hargreaves, Andy, and Michael Fullan. *Professional Capital: Transforming Teaching in Every School*. Routledge, 2012.

Harrington, Elizabeth. "Education Spending up 64% under No Child Left Behind but Test Scores Improve Little." *CNS News*, September 6, 2011. https://www.cnsnews.com/news/article/education-spending-64-under-no-child-left-behind-test-scores-improve-little.

Hassan, Aumyo, and Sarah J. Barber. "The Effects of Repetition Frequency on the Illusory Truth Effect." *Cognitive Research: Principles and Implications* 6, no. 1 (2021). https://doi.org/10.1186/s41235-021-00301-5.

Hawley, Willis, D., and Donna Redmond Jones. "Teacher Unions - Overview, Influence on Instruction and Other Educational Practices." StateUniversity.com, 2021. https://education.stateuniversity.com/pages/2486/Teacher-Unions.html.

He, Vincent Yaofeng, Georgie Nutton, Amy Graham, Lisa Hirschausen, and Jiunn-Yih Su. "Pathways to School Success: Self-Regulation and Executive Function, Preschool Attendance and Early Academic Achievement of Aboriginal and Non-Aboriginal Children in Australia's Northern Territory." *PloS One*, November 11, 2021. https://www.ncbi.nlm.nih.gov/pmc/articles/PMC8584680/.

"Head Start Services." Administration for Children and Families, 2021. https://www.acf.hhs.gov/ohs/head-start-services.

Heckman, James. "Invest in Early Childhood Development: Reduce Deficits, Strengthen the Economy." *Heckman Equation*, 2012. https://heckmanequation.org/www/assets/2013/07/F_HeckmanDeficitPieceCUSTOM-Generic_052714-3-1.pdf.

Hendrikse, Nicolaas. "The Future of Work: Changing Values in a Multi-Generational Workforce." *GetSmarter Blog*, September 29, 2020. https://www.getsmarter.com/blog/market-trends/the-future-of-work-changing-values-in-a-multi-generational-workforce/.

Heyward, Giulia. "Substitute Teachers Never Got Much Respect, but Now They Are in Demand." *New York Times*, November 11, 2021. https://www.nytimes.com/2021/11/11/us/substitute-teachers-demand.html.

"Higher Education." United Nations - Academic Impact Search the United Nations A-Z Site Index, 2021. https://www.un.org/en/academic-impact/higher-education.

Hill, Andrew J., and Daniel B. Jones. "A Teacher Who Knows Me: The Academic Benefits of Repeat Student-Teacher Matches." *Economics of Education Review* 64 (2018): 1–12. https://www.sciencedirect.com/science/article/abs/pii/S0272775717306635.

"Hire Expectations: Big-District Superintendents Stay in Their Jobs Longer than We Think." *The Broad Center*, May 2018. https://fdocuments.in/document/hire-expectations-the-broad-hire-expectations-big-district-superintendents.html?page=1.

Horowitz, Juliana Menasce, Ruth Igielnik, and Rakesh Kochhar. "Trends in Income and Wealth Inequality." Social & Demographic Trends Project, Pew Research Center, August 17, 2020. https://www.pewresearch.org/social-trends/2020/01/09/trends-in-income-and-wealth-inequality/.

Horton, Melissa. "Regressive, Proportional, and Progressive Taxes: What's the Difference?" *Investopedia*, July 8, 2022. https://www.investopedia.com/ask/answers/042415/what-are-differences-between-regressive-proportional-and-progressive-taxes.asp.

Hu, Jing, and Jacob B. Hirsh. "Accepting Lower Salaries for Meaningful Work." *Frontiers in Psychology* 8 (2017). https://doi.org/10.3389/fpsyg.2017.01649.

Hume, Heidi. "The Great Resignation: An Analysis of Job Tenure over the Years." *CapRelo*, February 22, 2022. https://www.caprelo.com/insights-resources/industry-trends/the-great-resignation-an-analysis-of-job-tenure-over-the-years/.

"Increasing Equitable Access to Excellent Educators: A Talent Management Guide for School Districts." Equitable Access Support Network, June 2017. https://

www2.ed.gov/about/offices/list/oese/oss/technicalassistance/easntalentmgtguides chldistricts.pdf.

"Inequality in Public School Funding: Key Issues & Solutions for Closing the Gap." American University, 2020. https://soeonline.american.edu/blog/inequality-in-public-school-funding.

Ingersoll, Richard M, Elizabeth Merrill, Daniel Stuckey, and Gregory Collins. "Seven Trends: The Transformation of the Teaching Force." Scholarly Commons. CPRE Research Reports, October 2018. https://repository.upenn.edu/cpre_researchreports/108.

"International Lab Schools: Who We Are." International Association of Laboratory and University Affiliated Schools, 2021. https://www.ialslaboratoryschools.org/.

Jackson, C. Kirabo, and Claire Mackevicius. "The Distribution of School Spending Impacts." National Bureau of Economic Research, July 2021. https://www.nber.org/system/files/working_papers/w28517/w28517.pdf.

Jang, Sung Tae, and Aaron S. Horn. "The Relative Effectiveness of Traditional and Alternative Teacher Preparation Programs: A Review of Recent Research. MHEC Research Brief." *Midwestern Higher Education Compact*, February 28, 2017. https://eric.ed.gov/?id=ED587431.

Jaquith, Ann, Dan Mindich, Ruth Chung Wei, and Linda Darling-Hammond. "Teacher Professional Learning in the United States: Case Studies of State Policies and Strategies." Stanford University, 2010. https://edpolicy.stanford.edu/sites/default/files/publications/teacher-professional-learning-united-states-case-studies-state-policies-and-strategies_2.pdf.

Johnson, Lyndon B. Speech. Howard University Commencement Speech. Presented at Howard University, Washington, DC, 1965.

Kelchtermans, Geert, Kari Smith, and Ruben Vanderlinde. "Towards an 'International Forum for Teacher Educator Development: An Agenda for Research and Action." *European Journal of Teacher Education* 41, no. 1 (2017): 120–34. https://doi.org/10.1080/02619768.2017.1372743.

Kemp, Luke. "Are We on the Road to Civilisation Collapse?" *BBC*, February 18, 2019. https://www.bbc.com/future/article/20190218-are-we-on-the-road-to-civilisation-collapse.

Kettering Foundation, 2021. https://www.kettering.org/.

"Kindergarten and Elementary School Teachers: Occupational Outlook Handbook." U.S. Bureau of Labor Statistics, 2019. https://www.bls.gov/OOH/education-training-and-library/kindergarten-and-elementary-school-teachers.htm.

King, Fiona. "Professional Learning: Empowering Teachers?" *Professional Development in Education* 45, no. 2 (2019): 169–72. https://doi.org/10.1080/19415257.2019.1580849.

Klein, Sheri. "Reducing Special Education Paperwork." *Principal*. National Association of Elementary School Principals, September 2004. https://www.naesp.org/sites/default/files/resources/2/Principal/2004/S-Op58.pdf.

Kraft, Matthew A., and Allison F. Gilmour. "Revisiting the Widget Effect: Teacher Evaluation Reforms and the Distribution of Teacher Effectiveness."

Educational Researcher 46 (2017): 234–49. https://journals.sagepub.com/doi/10.3102/0013189X17718797.

Kurtz, Annalyn. "College Grads with Foreign Language Skills Will Have Better Job Prospects." *Cable News Network*, October 30, 2013. https://money.cnn.com/2013/10/30/news/economy/job-skills-foreign-language/.

Larson, Magali S. *Rise of Professionalism: A Sociological Analysis*. Berkley, CA: University of California Press, 1978.

Lazarev, Valeriy, Denis Newman, Li Lin, and Jenna Zacamy. "The Texas Teacher Evaluation and Support System Rubric, Properties and Association with School Characteristics." Empirical Education Inc., 2017. https://files.eric.ed.gov/fulltext/ED576984.pdf.

Lieberman, Myron. *The Teacher Unions: How They Sabotage Educational Reform and Why*. San Francisco, CA: Distributed by ERIC Clearinghouse, 2000.

"Life, Physical, and Social Science Occupations: Occupational Outlook Handbook." U.S. Bureau of Labor Statistics, Department of Education, April 18, 2022. https://www.bls.gov/ooh/life-physical-and-social-science/home.htm.

Lindsay, Constance A., Erica Blom, and Alexandra Tilsley. "Diversifying the Classroom: Examining the Teacher Pipeline." Urban Institute, October 5, 2017. https://www.urban.org/features/diversifying-classroom-examining-teacher-pipeline.

Litchfield, Paul, Cary Cooper, Christine Hancock, and Patrick Watt. "Work and Well-being in the 21st Century." *International Journal of Environmental Research and Public Health*, 13, no. 11 (2016): 1065. https://doi.org/10.3390/ijerph13111065.

Littlejohn, Stephen W., and Karen A. Foss. *Encyclopedia of Communication Theory*. Thousand Oaks, CA: Sage, 2009.

Loewus, Liana. "Principals Are Loath to Give Teachers Bad Ratings." *Education Week*, July 1, 2017. https://www.edweek.org/leadership/principals-are-loath-to-give-teachers-bad-ratings/2017/07.

Loewus, Liana. "Why Teachers Leave—or Don't: A Look at the Numbers." *Education Week*, January 10, 2021. https://www.edweek.org/teaching-learning/why-teachers-leave-or-dont-a-look-at-the-numbers/2021/05.

Mandela, Nelson. "It Always Seems Impossible until It's Done." Speech (attributed to Mandela), 2001.

Marar, Satya. "Vermont's School Funding Model Promotes Equity across School Districts." Reason Foundation, June 24, 2020. https://reason.org/commentary/vermonts-school-funding-model-promotes-equity-across-school-districts/.

Martinez, Anthony, and Cheridan Christnacht. "Women Are Nearly Half of U.S. Workforce but Only 27% of STEM Workers." US Census Bureau, October 8, 2021. https://www.census.gov/library/stories/2021/01/women-making-gains-in-stem-occupations-but-still-underrepresented.html.

Marzano, Robert J. "The Marzano Teacher Evaluation Model: Marzano Focused Teacher." Marzano Center, 2017. https://www.marzanocenter.com/wp-content/uploads/sites/4/2019/04/FTEM_Updated_Michigan_08312017.pdf.

"Math Occupations: Occupational Outlook Handbook." U.S. Bureau of Labor Statistics, April 18, 2022. https://www.bls.gov/ooh/math/home.htm.

McCluskey, Neal. "Has No Child Left Behind Worked?" Cato Institute, 2015. https://www.cato.org/testimony/has-no-child-left-behind-worked#.

McCoy, Dana Charles, Hirokazu Yoshikawa, Kathleen M. Ziol-Guest, Greg J. Duncan, Holly S. Schindler, Katherine Magnuson, Rui Yang, Andrew Koepp, and Jack P. Shonkoff. "Impacts of Early Childhood Education on Medium- and Long-Term Educational Outcomes." *Educational Researcher* 46, no. 8 (2017): 474–87. https://doi.org/10.3102/0013189x17737739.

McGrath, Kevin F., Deevia Bhana, Penny Van Bergen, and Shaaista Moosa. "Do We Really Need Male Teachers? Forget Those Old Reasons, Here's New Research." *EduResearch Matters*. Australia Association for Research in Education, November 24, 2019. https://www.aare.edu.au/blog/?p=4726.

McGuire, David. "Why Teacher Attendance Matters." *Indy K12*, December 23, 2018. https://indy.education/2018/12/21/why-teacher-attendance-matters/.

McKenzie, William, and Sandy Kress. "The Big Idea of School Accountability." Bush Institute at the George W. Bush Presidential Center, 2015. https://www.bushcenter.org/essays/bigidea/.

Mcleod, Saul. "Maslow's Hierarchy of Needs." *Simply Psychology*, December 29, 2020. https://www.simplypsychology.org/maslow.html.

Meador, Derrick. "Be a Difference Maker by Becoming a School Board Member." *ThoughtCo*, July 5, 2019. https://www.thoughtco.com/how-to-become-school-board-member-3194408.

Miller, Caroline. "Cross-Training Employees: Be Prepared for the Unexpected." BizLibrary, October 22, 2020. https://www.bizlibrary.com/blog/training-programs/cross-training-employees/.

Moe, Terry M. *Special Interest: Teachers Unions and America's Public Schools*. Washington, DC: Brookings Institution Press, 2012.

Montgomery, Nick. "Fascinating: Can Analytics Help Schools Hire the Best Teachers?" *eSchool News*, November 27, 2017. https://www.eschoolnews.com/2017/11/16/data-help-hire-best-teachers/.

"More than Half of School Expenditures Spent on Classroom Instruction." US Census Bureau, 2017. https://www.census.gov/newsroom/press-releases/2017/cb17-97-public-education-finance.html.

"Most Educated Countries 2021." World Population Review, 2021. https://worldpopulationreview.com/country-rankings/most-educated-countries.

"Multilingual & Multicultural Education." MMED Update Home Page, Los Angeles Unified School District, 2021. https://achieve.lausd.net/domain/22.

Mulvihill, Thalia M., and Linda E. Martin. "Are Alternative Certification Programs Necessary?" *The Teacher Educator* 54, no. 1 (2019): 1–3. https://doi.org/10.1080/08878730.2018.1546759.

National Academies of Sciences. "Call to Action for Science Education: Building Opportunity for the Future." *National Academies Press*, July 13, 2021. https://doi.org/10.17226/26152.

National Association for Bilingual Education, 2021. https://nabe.org/.

"National Board for Professional Teaching Standards." NBPTS. National Board Certification, March 24, 2022. https://www.nbpts.org/.

National Board Resource Center. Stanford University, 2022. https://nbrc.stanford.edu/.

National Center for Education Statistics. "Characteristics of Public School Teachers." National Center for Education Statistics, U.S. Department of Education, Institute of Education Sciences, 2021. https://nces.ed.gov/programs/coe/indicator/clr.

"NCTQ Databurst: State Oversight of Alternate Routes into Teaching." National Council on Teacher Quality, December 2020. https://www.nctq.org/dmsView/NCTQ_Databurst_State_Oversight_of_Alternate_Routes_into_Teaching_Dec2020.

National School Board Association. "Frequently Asked Questions." 2018. https://www.nsba.org/about-us/frequently-asked-questions.

National Substitute Teachers Alliance. 2021. "Frequently Asked Questions." https://www.nstasubs.org/?page_id=34.

Netolicky, Deborah M. "Rethinking Professional Learning for Teachers and School Leaders." *Journal of Professional Capital and Community* 1, no. 4 (2016): 270–85. https://doi.org/10.1108/jpcc-04-2016-0012.

"Nonwhite School Districts Get $23 Billion Less than White Districts despite Serving the Same Number of Students." *EdBuild*, 2021. https://edbuild.org/content/23-billion.

Notman, Nina, and Chris Woolston. "Fifteen to One: How Many Applications It Can Take to Land a Single Academic Job Offer." *Nature News*, July 24, 2020. https://www.nature.com/articles/d41586-020-02224-5.

"Occupational Outlook Handbook: Preschool Teachers." U.S. Bureau of Labor Statistics, July 1, 2022. https://www.bls.gov/ooh/education-training-and-library/preschool-teachers.htm.

Oparah, Ann. "Recognize Teachers as Professionals like Doctors, Lawyers, Others." *Other*, March 29, 2019. https://www.vanguardngr.com/2019/04/recognise-teachers-as-professionals-like-doctors-lawyers-others-educationist-tells-fg/.

Opper, Isaac M. "Teachers Matter: Understanding Teachers' Impact on Student Achievement." RAND Corporation, December 4, 2019. https://www.rand.org/pubs/research_reports/RR4312.html.

"Opportunity Culture Overview." Opportunity Culture, 2019. https://www.opportunityculture.org/our-initiative/participating-sites/.

"Opportunity Culture Student Outcomes." Opportunity Culture, 2019. https://www.opportunityculture.org/dashboard/growth/.

"OSDE Using $12.75 Million in Relief Funds for Paid Student Teaching." Oklahoma State Department of Education, 2021. https://sde.ok.gov/newsblog/2021-08-09/osde-using-1275-million-relief-funds-paid-student-teaching.

Paige, Rod. Comment Made in a Private Meeting with Governors at the White House. Washington, DC: Secretary of Education, 2004.

Partida, Devin. "6 Major Companies Supporting STEM Learning Programs." Schools Robot, RobotLAB, July 19, 2021. https://www.robotlab.com/blog/6-major-companies-supporting-stem-learning-programs.

Pethokoukis, James. "US Federal Research Spending Is at a 60-Year Low. Should We Be Concerned?" American Enterprise Institute, May 11, 2020. https://www.aei.org/economics/us-federal-research-spending-is-at-a-60-year-low-should-we-be-concerned/.

Phillips, D. C. *Encyclopedia of Educational Theory and Philosophy*, Vol. 2. Thousand Oaks, CA: SAGE Publications, Inc., 2014.

Pickett, Kate E., and Richard G. Wilkinson. "Income Inequality and Health: A Causal Review." *Social Science & Medicine* 128 (2015): 316–26. https://pubmed.ncbi.nlm.nih.gov/25577953/.

Ping, Cui, Gonny Schellings, and Douwe Beijaard. "Teacher Educators' Professional Learning: A Literature Review." *Teaching and Teacher Education* 75 (2018): 93–104. https://www.sciencedirect.com/science/article/abs/pii/S0742051X17320115.

Pink, Daniel H. *Drive: The Surprising Truth about What Motivates US*. East Rutherford, NJ: Penguin, 2011.

"Position Statement on Student Grade Retention and Social Promotion." www.nasponline.org/. National Association of School Psychologists, 2011. https://www.adlit.org/topics/social-emotional-issues/position-statement-student-grade-retention-and-social-promotion.

Powell, Alvin. "How Sputnik Changed U.S. Education." *Harvard Gazette*, October 11, 2007. https://news.harvard.edu/gazette/story/2007/10/how-sputnik-changed-u-s-education/.

"Preschool Teacher Requirements: Early Childhood Pre-K Teacher Requirements." How to Become a Preschool Teacher, Early Childhood Education Degrees. *Preschool Teacher*, February 2020. https://www.preschoolteacher.org/requirements/.

"Professional: Definition & Meaning." Merriam-Webster, 2022. https://www.merriam-webster.com/dictionary/professional.

"ProQuest Social Science Premium Collection database." ProQuest. Figure 4.1 reproduced with permission, 2021. www.proquest.com.

"Pulse of the American Worker Survey: A Third Year Begins: Life and Work in the Pandemic Era." Prudential Financial, February 2022. file:///Users/Downloads/AWS - A Third Year Begins - Fact Sheet - FINAL.pdf.

Quilantan, Bianca. "How Many Teachers Are Needed to Make Universal Pre-K Possible?" *POLITICO*, November 22, 2021. https://www.politico.com/newsletters/weekly-education/2021/11/22/how-many-teachers-are-needed-to-make-universal-pre-k-possible-799021.

"Ranking of the 20 Companies with the Highest Spending on Research and Development in 2018." Statista, 2021. https://www.statista.com/statistics/265645/ranking-of-the-20-companies-with-the-highest-spending-on-research-and-development/.

Ravitch, Diane. "A Brief History of Teacher Professionalism." White House Conference on Preparing Tomorrow's Teachers, March 7, 2002. https://www1.udel.edu/educ/whitson/897s05/files/ravitch_Teacher_Professionalism.htm.

"Relationship between Job Satisfaction and Self-Esteem." *UK Essays*, November 2018. https://www.ukessays.com/essays/employment/relationship-between-job-satisfaction-and-self-esteem.php.

"Research and Development Expenditure (% of GDP)." UNESCO Institute for Statistics, 2021. https://data.worldbank.org/indicator/GB.XPD.RSDV.GD.ZS.

Reyes, Pedro, and Celeste Alexander. "A Summary of Texas Teacher Attrition." texaserc.utexas.edu/, 2017. https://texaserc.utexas.edu/wp-content/uploads/2017/12/14-Brief-Teacher-Quality.pdf.

Reynolds, Arthur J., Judy A. Temple, Dylan L. Robertson, and Emily A. Mann. "Age 21 Cost-Benefit Analysis of the Title I Chicago Child-Parent Centers." *Educational*

Evaluation and Policy Analysis, December 1, 2002. https://journals.sagepub.com/doi/10.3102/01623737024004267.

Robinson, Sir Ken. "Bring on the Learning Revolution!" *TED Talk*, February 2010. https://www.ted.com/talks/sir_ken_robinson_bring_on_the_learning_revolution?language=n.

Robson, Kelly, Kaitlin Pennington, and Juliet Squire. "Overview of the History and Status of Teacher Unions." Bellwether Education, 2018. https://bellwethereducation.org/sites/default/files/Janus_BELLWETHER.pdf.

Roosevelt, Franklin D., Letter to Mr. Steward: National Federation of Federal Employees. "Letter on the Resolution of Federation of Federal Employees against Strikes in Federal Service." August 16, 1937.

Rosen, Jill. "Black Students Who Have One Black Teacher Are More Likely to Go to College." *The Hub*, November 12, 2018. https://hub.jhu.edu/2018/11/12/black-students-black-teachers-college-gap/.

Ross, Elizabeth, and Kate Walsh. "NCTQ State of the States 2019: Teacher and Principal Evaluation Policy." National Council on Teacher Quality (NCTQ), 2019. https://www.nctq.org/pages/State-of-the-States-2019:-Teacher-and-Principal-Evaluation-Policy.

"Rules for Teachers in 1872 & 1915: No Drinking, Smoking, or Trips to Barber Shops and Ice Cream Parlors." *Open Culture*, September 16, 2013. https://www.openculture.com/2013/09/rules-for-teachers-in-1872-1915-no-drinking-smoking-or-trips-to-barber-shops-and-ice-cream-parlors.html.

Ryan, Richard M., and Edward L. Deci. "Self-Determination Theory and the Facilitation of Intrinsic Motivation, Social Development, and Well-Being." *American Psychologist* 55, no. 1 (2000): 68–78. https://doi.org/10.1037/0003-066x.55.1.68.

Saenz-Armstrong, Patricia. "Roll Call 2020: A New Look at Teacher Attendance in the Nation's Largest School Districts." National Council on Teacher Quality (NCTQ), December 2020. https://www.nctq.org/publications/Roll-Call-2020.

"Schools and Staffing Survey, Public and Private Teachers, 2011–12." Datalab, National Center for Education Statistics, 2013. https://nces.ed.gov/datalab/QuickStats/Workspace/Index/64.

Scott, Robert C. "Build Back Better Act: House." House Committee on Education and Labor, November 2021. https://edlabor.house.gov/imo/media/doc/2021-11-18%20Ed%20&%20Labor%20BBB%20Fact%20Sheet.pdf.

Seril, Lindsey. "Teacher Salary by State." Study.com, December 8, 2021. https://study.com/academy/popular/teacher-salary-by-state.html.

Serviss, Jennifer. "4 Benefits of an Active Professional Learning Community." International Society for Technology in Education (ISTE), May 13, 2021. https://www.iste.org/explore/professional-development/4-benefits-active-professional-learning-community.

Shein, Esther. "The CS Teacher Shortage." Association for Computing Machinery (ACM), October 1, 2019. https://cacm.acm.org/magazines/2019/10/239667-the-cs-teacher-shortage/fulltext.

Smith-Barrow, Delece, and Josh Moody. "20 Colleges with the Most Hispanic Students." *US News & World Report*, 2020. https://www.usnews.com/education/best-colleges/slideshows/colleges-with-the-most-hispanic-students.

Snyder, Thomas D. *120 Years of American Education: A Statistical Portrait.* Office of Educational Research and Improvement, National Center for Education Statistics, 1993.

Solovey, Mark. "The Impossible Dream: Scientism as Strategy against Distrust of Social Science at the U.S. National Science Foundation, 1945–1980." *International Journal for History, Culture, and Modernity* 1(2019): 209–38. https://doi.org/10.18352/hcm.554.

Sparks, Sarah D. "Study of Dual-Language Immersion in the Portland Public Schools: Year 4." Rand Education November 2015. https://www.pps.net/cms/lib8/OR01913224/Centricity/Domain/85/DLI_Year_4_Summary_Nov2015v7.pdf.

Spiel, Christiane, Simon Schwartzman, Marius Busemeyer, Nico Cloete, Gili Drori, Lorenz Lassnigg, and Barbara Schober. "The Contribution of Education to Social Progress." *Rethinking Society for the 21st Century: Report of the International Panel on Social Progress*, June 2017, 753–78. https://doi.org/10.1017/9781108399661.006.

"Staff, Teachers, and Teachers as a Percentage of Staff in Public Elementary and Secondary School Systems, by State or Jurisdiction." National Center for Education Statistics, Digest of Education Statistics, 2017. U.S. Department of Education, 2017. https://nces.ed.gov/programs/digest/d17/tables/dt17_213.40.asp.

"State Requirements for Teacher Evaluation Policies Promoted by Race to the Top." Institute of Education Sciences. National Center for Education Evaluation, April 2014. https://ies.ed.gov/ncee/pubs/20144016/pdf/20144016.pdf.

"Status and Trends in the Education of Racial and Ethnic Groups 2018." National Center for Education Statistics, 2019. https://nces.ed.gov/pubs2019/2019038.pdf.

Stevens, Jane Ellen. "Nearly 35 Million U.S. Children Have Experienced One or More Types of Childhood Trauma." *ACEs Too High*, May 13, 2013. https://acestoohigh.com/2013/05/13/nearly-35-million-u-s-children-have-experienced-one-or-more-types-of-childhood-trauma/.

Stosny, Steven. "Desire vs. Emotional Need." *Psychology Today*, Sussex Publishers, 2013. https://www.psychologytoday.com/us/blog/anger-in-the-age-entitlement/201310/desire-vs-emotional-need.

Strikwerda, Liz. "Developing a Career Path Framework in 7 Steps for Your Employees." *WorkforceHub*, May 23, 2022. https://www.workforcehub.com/blog/create-career-paths-in-7-steps-or-lose-your-best-employees/.

"Students with Disabilities." National Center for Education Statistics, Condition of Education, 2021. https://nces.ed.gov/programs/coe/indicator/cgg.

"Student Teaching Scholarship for High-Need Fields." Indiana Commission for Higher Education (CHE), 2021. https://www.in.gov/che/state-financial-aid/state-financial-aid-by-program/student-teaching-stipend-for-high-need-fields/.

"Substitute Teacher Salary." Bestaccreditedcolleges.org, 2021. https://bestaccreditedcolleges.org/resources/substitute-teacher-salary.

"Substitute Teachers." National Education Association (NEA), 2021. https://www.nea.org/substitute-teachers.

"Summary of Appropriation for the 2022-23 Biennium: Texas." State of Texas, 2021. https://www.lbb.texas.gov/Documents/Appropriations_Bills/87/Final/6999_Special_Summary_Appropriations.pdf.

"Supporting Effective Educator Development (SEED) Program Fiscal Year (FY) 2020 Competition: Frequently Asked Questions (FAQs)." Office of Elementary and Secondary Education, April 12, 2022. https://oese.ed.gov/.

"Supporting Effective Educator Development Grant Program." Office of Elementary and Secondary Education, 2022. https://oese.ed.gov/offices/office-of-discretionary-grants-support-services/effective-educator-development-programs/supporting-effective-educator-development-grant-program/.

Sutcher, Leib, Linda Darling-Hammond, and Desiree Carver-Thomas. "A Coming Crisis in Teaching? Teacher Supply, Demand, and Shortages in the U.S." Learning Policy Institute, 2015. https://learningpolicyinstitute.org/product/coming-crisis-teaching.

"Teacher Incentive Allotment." tiatexas.org. Texas Education Agency, July 1, 2022. https://tiatexas.org/allotments/.

"Teacher Shortage Areas." US Department of Education (ED), December 9, 2020. https://www2.ed.gov/about/offices/list/ope/pol/tsa.html.

"Teacher Turnover: Stayers, Movers, and Leavers." National Center for Education Statistics, Condition of Education, 2015. https://nces.ed.gov/programs/coe/indicator/slc.

"Teacher Turnover: What You Need to Know." Association of California School Administrators, 2020. https://content.acsa.org/articles/teacher-turnover-what-you-need-to-know.

Texas Education Agency. "Texas Teacher Evaluation and Support System (T-TESS) Rubric." teachfortexas.org, 2016. https://teachfortexas.org/Resource_Files/Guides/T-TESS_Rubric.pdf.

TheBestSchools Staff. "Seven Ways You Can Earn College Credits While Still in High School." *Best Schools*, 2020. https://thebestschools.org/magazine/seven-ways-can-earn-college-credits-still-high-school/.

"The NCES Fast Facts: Students with Disabilities." U.S. Department of Education. National Center for Education Statistics, 2021. https://nces.ed.gov/fastfacts/display.asp?id=64.

"The New Americans Education and Employment Assistance Act: Hearing before the Subcommittee on Equal Opportunities of the Committee on Education and Labor," House of Representatives, Ninety-Third congress, second session on H.R. 9895, a bill to provide federal programs of educational, employment, and other assistance to areas with heavy concentrations of foreign born persons: Hearing held in Washington, DC, November 19, 1974. Bill (1974).

The New Teacher Project. *The Irreplaceables: Understanding the Real Retention Crisis in America's Urban Schools*. Brooklyn, NY: The New Teachers Project (TNTP), 2012.

"The United States Spends More on Defense than the Next 9 Countries Combined." Peter G. Peterson Foundation, 2022. https://www.pgpf.org/blog/2022/06/the-united-states-spends-more-on-defense-than-the-next-9-countries-combined.

Thompson, Gail L. "The Importance of a Growth Mindset in Turnaround Teachers." Illuminate Education, April 10, 2016. https://www.illuminateed.com/blog/2016/04/importance-growth-mindset-turnaround-teachers/.

Toch, Thomas, Robin M. Bennefield, Dana Hawkins and Penny Loeb. "Why Teachers Don't Teach." *U.S. News & World Report*, February 26, 1996, 62–71.

U.S. Constitution. Amend. XIV, Sec. 1, 1868.

"UT Austin Collaborative Tackles Math and Computer Science Teaching Shortages in Texas." UTeach Institute. University of Texas, June 2020. https://institute.uteach.utexas.edu/ut-austin-collaborative-tackles-math-and-computer-science-teaching-shortages-texas.

"UTeach Implementation." UTeach Institute. University of Texas at Austin, December 10, 2019. https://institute.uteach.utexas.edu/uteach-implementation.

Vercelletto, Christina. "Bringing Back Retired Teachers Offers Benefits, Challenges." K-12 Dive, July 16, 2019. https://www.k12dive.com/news/bringing-back-retired-teachers-offers-benefits-challenges/558687/.

Villaraigosa, Antonio. "Antonio Villaraigosa - There Are Teachers' Uni..." Quotesia, November 2021. https://quotesia.com/antonio-villaraigosa-quote/51024.

Vinelli, Andres, and Christian E. Weller. "The Path to Higher, More Inclusive Economic Growth and Good Jobs." Center for American Progress, April 27, 2021. https://www.americanprogress.org/issues/economy/reports/2021/04/27/498794/path-higher-inclusive-economic-growth-good-jobs/.

Visit Houston. "Facts and Figures." Houston Visitors Bureau, 2021. https://www.visithoustontexas.com/about-houston/facts-and-figures/.

Walker, Tim. "Almost One-Third of New Teachers Take on Second Jobs." National Education Association, 2019. https://www.nea.org/advocating-for-change/new-from-nea/almost-one-third-new-teachers-take-second-jobs.

Wallace, M., I. Lings, Roslyn Cameron, and N. Sheldon. "Attracting and Retaining Staff: The Role of Branding and Industry Image." *Workforce Development: Perspectives and Issues*. Springer, 2014. http://hdl.handle.net/20.500.11937/13075.

Warhol, Andy. *From A to B & Back Again: The Philosophy of Andy Warhol*. London: Picador, 1976.

Waters, Shonna. "The Power of Professional Learning Communities." *BetterUp*, September 13, 2021. https://www.betterup.com/blog/professional-learning-communities.

Weber, Matthew. *Confronting the Education Complex: Catalysts for Advancing Pre-k–12 Systems*. Kansas City, MO: Miraclaire Publishing, 2021.

Weisberg, Daniel, Susan Sexton, Jennifer Mulher, and David Keeling. *The Widget Effect: Our National Failure to Acknowledge and Act on Differences in Teacher Effectiveness*. Brooklyn, NY: The New Teacher Project, 2009.

"What's the Cost of Teacher Turnover?" Learning Policy Institute, September 2017. https://learningpolicyinstitute.org/product/the-cost-of-teacher-turnover.

"Why Computer Science?" Code.org, 2022. https://code.org/promote.

"Why Do Parents Choose Schools for Their Children?" National Center for Education Statistics, Institute of Education Sciences, July 30, 2020. https://nces.ed.gov/blogs/nces/post/why-do-parents-choose-schools-for-their-children.

"Why Do Teachers Leave?" Learning Policy Institute, 2016. https://learningpolicyinstitute.org/sites/default/files/Teacher_Exodus_Infographic.pdf.

Will, Madeline. "When Good Teachers Oversee Multiple Classrooms, Does Learning Improve?" *Education Week*, January 12, 2018. https://www.edweek.org/teaching-learning/when-good-teachers-oversee-multiple-classrooms-does-learning-improve/2018/01.

Will, Madeline. "You're More Likely to Pass the Bar than an Elementary Teacher Licensing Exam." *Education Week*, November 19, 2020. https://www.edweek.org/leadership/youre-more-likely-to-pass-the-bar-than-an-elementary-teacher-licensing-exam/2019/02.

Yin, Jessica, and Lisette Partelow. "An Overview of the Teacher Alternative Certification Sector Outside of Higher Education." Center for American Progress, December 5, 2020. https://www.americanprogress.org/article/overview-teacher-alternative-certification-sector-outside-higher-education/.

Youngs, Amy. "Why Cross-Disciplinary Research Matters." Global Arts and Humanities, Ohio State University, 2021. https://globalartsandhumanities.osu.edu/about/cross-disciplinary-research.

"Your Best Employees Are Leaving. But Is It Personal or Practical?" Randstad USA, August 28, 2018. https://rlc.randstadusa.com/press-room/press-releases/your-best-employees-are-leaving-but-is-it-personal-or-practical.

Zakaria, Fareed. "Are America''s Best Days Behind Us?" *Time*, 177, no. 10, March 14, 2011.

Zalaznick, Matt. "Is There Really a Teacher Shortage? Yes, but It's Hitting Some Areas Harder." District Administration, October 27, 2021. https://districtadministration.com/is-there-really-a-teacher-shortage-yes-but-its-hitting-some-areas-harder/.

Zeigler, Karen, and Steven A. Camarota. "67.3 Million in the United States Spoke a Foreign Language at Home in 2018." Center for Immigration Studies, October 2019. https://cis.org/sites/default/files/2019-10/camarota-language-19_0.pdf.

Zippia. "Teacher Assistant Demographics and Statistics [2022]: Number of Teacher Assistants in the US." Zippia, April 18, 2022. https://www.zippia.com/teacher-assistant-jobs/demographics/.

Index

Abood v. Detroit Board of Education, 98
accountability, 7–10, 25, 30, 50, 53–54, 58–59, 61, 64–65, 90, 103, 106, 115, 135, 151, 161, 169–72, 177
action research, 53
Adler v. Board of Education of the City of New York, 99
Advanced Placement, 73, 164
agency, 12
agency fees, 97–98
alternative certification program (ACP), 21, 26–27, 74–77, 78, 147–48, 165
Amazon, 45, 54
American Association of Employment in Education, 147
American College Testing (ACT), 22–23
American Federation of Teachers, 30, 96
American Institutes for Research, 76, 90
American Rescue Plan, ix
artificial intelligence, 45
AT&T, 150

bilingual education, 9, 15, 20, 72–74, 77, 79, 84, 131, 138–41, 144, 149, 161–63, 165
Bilingual Education Act, 9, 138
Bill and Melinda Gates Foundation, 109

Boston Consulting Group, 109
Brown v. Board of Education, 10
Build Back Better, 127, 132–33, 135

calibration, 59, 62–65
career ladder, 89
CARES Act, ix
Center for American Progress, 4
Chicago Child-Parent Centers, 171
clinical substitute, 123–26, 163
clinical teaching intern, 78–79, 84, 92, 137, 139, 163
Code.org, 147–48
collaborative walk-throughs, 59, 63, 65
collective bargaining agreement, 96
computer science, 15, 143, 147–48, 151
continuing contract(s), 100
corporal punishment, 9–10
Covid Relief Package, ix
cycle for valid teacher evaluations, 59–60, 67

Dana Center, 150
Danielson's Framework, 61
data-driven instruction, 53
data mining, 157, 166
diversity, 8–9, 36, 40, 71, 147, 157, 163–65
dual credit, 15, 72–73, 164

due process, 30, 96–97, 99–100, 103

early childhood, 1–2, 14–15, 73, 77–78, 91, 125–27, 131–33, 141, 144, 163, 171; education, 2, 14, 91, 127, 131, 145
earned autonomy, 37, 70, 72, 116, 145, 158, 185
Economic Policy Institute, 24, 34, 97
Education Law Center, 175
Elementary and Secondary Education Act, viii, 8, 138
endorsed substitute, 123, 125, 163
English as a second language, 9
English language learner(s), 132, 171
Equal Educational Opportunities Act, 138, 173
evaluation(s), 7, 26, 37, 57–68, 72, 74–75, 80, 89, 92, 99–101, 105, 112, 121, 125, 127, 136–37, 144, 152, 160–63, 165, 172
Every Student Succeeds Act, 61

Facebook, 150
Fair Labor Standards Act, 104, 172
Federal Department of Education, 52, 71, 173, 177; US Department of Education, 149, 174
Federal Perkins Loan Program, 150
forecasting, x, 144, 160, 166
Frontline Research, 20, 119
Fulbright-Hays Act, 139

General Motors, 150
Generation Z, 26, 33–34
Google, 45, 150
grade point average, 164
gross domestic product, 45
grow(ing) your own, 72, 137–38, 149

Head Start, 133, 140, 176
Higher Learning Commission, 73

Individualized Education Program, 127, 137
industrial union, 96, 104, 106, 166

Institute of Medicine, 133
instructional assistant(s), x, 73–74, 77–78, 119, 125–27, 132, 136, 139, 163, 175
instructional coach(s), 59, 74, 80, 158
Instructional Rounds, 66
Intel, 150
International Association of Laboratory and University Affiliated Schools, 48
International Baccalaureate, 73
Irreplaceable, 69

Janus v. American Federation of State, County, and Municipal Employees Council, 98
J-1 Teacher Exchange Program, 138–40

Kettering Foundation, 43

laboratory school, 47–49, 51, 91, 184
Learning Policy Institute, 76, 110, 126
literacy, 5–6
local school board, 101–3, 179

Marzano Causal Teacher Evaluation Model, 61
master's degree(s), 35, 39, 70, 72–74, 114
master teacher(s), ix, 1, 14, 48–49, 54, 59, 70, 74, 78–79, 83–85, 89, 91, 101, 112, 119, 134–35, 137, 141, 153, 157, 159, 161, 163–64, 169, 176, 184
master teacher-researcher, 54, 91–92
Microsoft, 150
Millennials, 33–34
MT pedagogues, 84, 91
multiple measures, 59, 60, 66, 105
multi-tiered system of support, 79

National Academies of Sciences, Engineering, and Medicine, 146
National Academy of Sciences, 146
National Assessment of Education Progress, 8
National Board Certification, 86

National Board for Professional
    Teaching Standards, 86
National Board Resource Center,
    86
National Bureau of Economic Research,
    173
National Center for Education
    Evaluation, 60–61
National Center for Education Statistics
    (NCES), x, xi, 6, 8–9, 20, 28, 35,
    119, 135, 174
National Council on Teacher Quality,
    21, 75
National Defense Education Act, 152
National Education Association (NEA),
    4, 30, 95–98, 103
National Labor Relations Act, 96
National Labor Relations Board, 96
National Research Council, 133
The New Teacher Project (TNTP), 57,
    69, 166
No Child Left Behind (NCLB), 4–5, 8,
    53, 59, 133, 170, 172

Opportunity Culture Initiative, 90
optimizing quality cycle, 57–58, 60
Organisation for Economic
    Co-operation and Development, 172

per-pupil spending, 172–73, 179
Perry Preschool Program, 171
Pew Research Center, 3
Phi Delta Kappa International, 24
Praxis, 21
preparatory substitute, 123, 163
President's Council of Economic
    Advisers, 171
priority substitute, 80, 123–25, 152,
    157, 166
probationary contract, 100–101
professional learning, 45, 48, 51, 79,
    109–14, 160, 167
professional learning communities,
    114–15
Programme for International Student
    Assessment, 21

progressive tax, 178–79
promise program, 136–37
proportional tax, 178

Race to the Top, 59
reduction in force, 99, 101
regressive tax, 178
Relay Graduate School of Education,
    74
retired teacher(s), 80, 121, 124, 152

San Antonio Independent School
    District v. Rodriguez, 173
sanctioned substitute, 123–24, 163
scientific method, 43, 46, 54, 161
Self-Determination Theory, 37, 89
social-emotional learning, 53, 164
special education, 11, 15, 20, 71–73,
    76–78, 84, 119, 121, 131, 135–36,
    144, 161–63, 165, 176
state department of education, 50–51
STEM, 35, 143–44, 147, 149–53
student agency, x, 12, 72, 185
student retention, 9–10, 164
student teacher, 70, 74, 76–78, 134,
    136–37, 139, 160, 163, 166
substitute teacher, 20, 73, 75, 77, 119–
    26, 165
succession, 69, 120, 167
succession handbook, 155, 167
superintendent(s), vii, 50, 80, 90–91,
    102, 121, 159–60, 179
Supporting Effective Educator
    Development, 144

talent management (TM), 19–20, 71,
    124, 139, 145, 155–57, 159–61, 163,
    165–68
Talent Management Guide for School
    Districts, 156
Talent Transfer Initiative, 89
teacher agency, 33, 37, 40, 116, 145,
    153, 169, 185
Teacher Incentive Fund, 85
teacher leader, 54, 70, 72–74, 76–79,
    81, 84, 86, 90, 157, 159, 162

teacher pathway, 14, 16, 37–38, 40, 59, 67, 69–72, 74, 79, 81, 114, 135, 139, 144, 156–59, 167, 177
teacher profile, 12, 157, 160–64
teacher profile database, 163
teacher retention, 13–14, 37, 74, 79, 86–87, 89–90, 156–58, 160, 165–66
teacher tenure, 98–101
Teach for America, 74
term contract, 100
Texas Education Agency, 62, 78, 86, 88
Texas Teacher Evaluation and Support System (T-TESS), 61–64
Texas Teacher Incentive Allotment, 85–88
Title I, vii, 87, 176

turnaround teachers, 83–84

Urban Teachers, 74
US Bureau of Labor Statistics, 14, 126, 133, 145, 147
US Census Bureau, 125, 138
Uteach, 150–51, 153

virtual learning, ix, 140, 148–49
virtual reality, 54

wealth gap, 3, 179
weighted funding for special needs, 11, 175, 179
WeTeach_CT, 150, 153
The Widget Effect, 57
World Health Organization, 25

About the Author

Dr. Matthew Weber retired in 2019 after serving the San Antonio Independent School District (SAISD) for five years as deputy superintendent. SAISD progressed from an F- to a B-rated district under the Texas Education Agency accountability system during his tenure. Some of Dr. Weber's accomplishments included implementing the district's Master Teacher Initiative, partnerships for innovative lab schools, university partnerships for teacher master's degrees, partnerships for clinical teaching interns, and establishing an early college high school.

His education career included multiple roles. After serving sixteen years teaching at ten different grade levels, he worked in leadership as a principal, department director, district program evaluator, and associate superintendent before his position with San Antonio. Dr. Weber's unconventional career has given him an educational perspective from distinctive viewpoints. After forty-one years as a public school educator, he retired as an idealist and a pragmatist. His second book, *Elevating the Teaching Profession*, envisions integrating practical experience with ongoing research.

Dr. Weber is currently serving as an adjunct faculty member at Texas A&M University–San Antonio. He is married to Joan, a retired elementary teacher, and they are the proud parents of Joshua, a physical therapist, and Zachary, a middle school teacher.

www.ingramcontent.com/pod-product-compliance
Lightning Source LLC
Chambersburg PA
CBHW032041300426
44117CB00009B/1149